ENCYCLOPEDIA
of NORTH AMERICAN
SPORTING DOGS

Published by Willow Creek Press
P.O. Box 147, Minocqua, WI 54548

For information on other Willow Creek titles, call 1-800-850-9453

Library of Congress Cataloging-in-Publication Data

The encyclopedia of North American sporting dogs / written by sportsmen for sportsmen ; edited by Steve Smith.
   p. cm.
  ISBN 1-57223-501-2 (hardcover : alk. paper)
  1. Hunting dogs--United States. 2. Hunting dogs--Canada. I. Smith, Steve, 1947-
  SF428.5+
  636.75'097--dc21
                      2002003121

Printed and Bound in China

Photo Credits

(listed by source alphabetically)

AKC/Close Encounters Photography: 179

AKC/Mary Bloom: 178, 210, 211

Denver Bryan/DenverBryan.com: 37, 44-45, 48, 60-61, 62, 67, 68-69, 73, 74, 75, 77, 78, 79, 80, 83, 88, 104, 120, 121, 126, 155, 165, 171

Kent & Donna Dannen: 6-7, 41, 107, 113, 114, 116, 122, 130, 132, 133, 137, 138, 181, 184, 188, 195, 197, 198, 203, 204, 206, 214, 216, 217

Kathy and Tara Darling: 42, 123, 131, 136, 153, 163, 170, 173, 186, 189, 190, 191, 199, 202, 207, 212, 213, 219, 226

Daniel Dempster: 157, 160, 224

E.R.Degginger/Bruce Coleman, Inc: 200

Bane and Jeannie Harrison/Close Encounters of the Furry Kind: 8, 12, 20, 106, 112, 115, 118, 119, 128, 129, 134, 139, 162, 185, 193, 194, 196, 205, 215, 218, 221, 228, 232

Gary Kramer: 27, 53

Bill Marchel: 177, 180

Courier & Ives Collection of the Museum of the City of New York: 9, 10, 11, 14-15, 16

Dale Spartas/Spartasphoto.com: 18, 19, 26, 38, 29, 49, 54, 110, 11, 117, 124, 125, 135, 40, 141, 142, 146, 150, 151, 154, 158, 159, 161, 164, 168, 172, 176, 192

Ben O. Williams: 1, 4, 22, 23, 24, 28, 29, 30, 32-33, 34, 26, 40, 43, 46, 56, 57, 58, 59, 64, 71, 84, 86, 87, 89, 90-91, 92, 94, 95, 97, 98, 99, 100-101, 102, 143, 147, 149, 156, 169, 174, 175, 230, 231, 235

Isabelle Francais: 108, 109, 152, 166, 167, 187, 201, 220, 223, 227

ENCYCLOPEDIA
of NORTH AMERICAN
SPORTING DOGS

Written by Sportsmen for Sportsmen

Edited by Steve Smith

WILLOW CREEK PRESS
MINOCQUA, WISCONSIN

TABLE OF CONTENTS

A griffon pup sight–pointing a training quail.

Black and Tan Coon Hound

CHAPTER 1

HUNTING DOGS IN EARLY AMERICA: A BRIEF HISTORY

by Tom Davis

IN 1650, A BRITISH SQUIRE named Robert Brooke sailed across the Atlantic to make a new home in what is now Calvert County, Maryland. He brought with him his wife, their ten children, and no fewer than 28 servants, along with a pack of foxhounds and, presumably, a horse or two. Brooke soon discovered that the native gray foxes of the Maryland tidewater were every bit as challenging and exciting to hunt as their red counterparts of the English hedgerow country, and the American tradition of hunting with dogs for sport — indeed, the American sporting tradition itself — was born.

Fox hunting became a favored pastime of the colonial gentry, beginning in Virginia, Maryland, and the Carolinas and spreading with America's landed aristocracy north to upstate New York, south to Georgia, and inland to Ohio, Kentucky, and Tennessee. George Washington had his own pack of foxhounds by the time he turned twenty (1752), and

when his duties permitted it he rode to his hounds three times a week in clamorous pursuit of "Reynard."

The esteem in which hounds were held by the southern gentlemen-sportsmen of Washington's era — men of "cavalier extraction," as the great New England writer William Harnden Foster put it — is illustrated by a charming anecdote concerning a dog owned by General Howe, the British Revolutionary War commander. In 1777, with the two opposing armies camped not far from one another in the vicinity of Pennibacker's Mill, Pennsylvania, a "sporting dog" belonging to Howe (then as now, it wore a collar with its master's name etched on a metal plate) found its way behind the colonial lines and, as dogs will, began begging for food. Washington took pains to see that the dog was safely returned, and an appreciative General Howe responded with "a letter in the warmest terms."

American Field Sports: "On a Point," 1857
from the Currier & Ives Collection of the Museum of the City of New York

Wild Duck Shooting: "A Good Day's Sport," 1854
from the Currier & Ives Collection of the Museum of the City of New York

While hounds of English origin dominated the early American hunting dog "scene" (such as it was) — and while the British Isles would continue to be the primary source for American canine bloodstock until well into the 20th century — there were a handful of importations from elsewhere in Europe. At about the same time that the young George Washington was assembling his kennel at Mount Vernon, a man named Jonathon Plott emigrated from his native Germany and settled in the mountains of western North Carolina. He was accompanied by several hounds bred to hunt wild boar, but with no boar in the area then (they came later, in the form of domesticated hogs gone AWOL that in the span of a few generations in the wild reverted to tusk-brandishing razorbacks), Plott found that black bears were an eminently acceptable substitute.

Today, the Plott hound is the state dog of North Carolina — and it's still considered the bear dog nonpareil. And while the historical record is sketchy — as it tends to be for virtually all breeds prior to the advent of organized studbooks and kennel clubs in the late-1800s — it's believed that relatively few crosses to "outside" blood have been made in the 250-some years since the hollows of the Appalachian Mountains echoed to the music of the original Plotts when they cut the smoking scent trail of their first bruin.

A few "French hounds" found their way to America as well in the 18th century, including five that were presented to Washington by General Lafayette himself in 1785, and whose voices were described as ringing "like the bells of Moscow." Used in France chiefly to hunt deer and boar, they were noted for being exceptionally cold-nosed — that is, having the ability to detect and follow an old, "cold" scent trail, not just a fresh, "hot" one. The modern bluetick coonhound is thought to be descended from crosses between English-American foxhounds and these early French imports.

But then, virtually all of the large scenthounds that remain useful hunting breeds in America are descended from foxhounds — although, again, tracing every branch of the family tree is at best an exercise in informed speculation. (The qualifier "large" is meant to exclude the beagle, the keen little hare-hunter that began to be imported from Great Britain in large numbers following the Civil War; if anything, the beagle was a progenitor of the foxhound, not a descendent of it.) For example, the redbone ostensibly owes its distinctive coloration to bloodhound forebears, while the modern Treeing Walker is said to derive from a cross circa 1857 between "Virginia strain" foxhounds (also the rootstock of the black-and-tan coonhound) and a dog of "unknown origin" named Tennessee Lead.

Still, the histories of many of the American hound breeds remain murky; the coonhounds, in particular, were typically bred in isolated, rural areas of the South and Midwest by lean, hard, fiercely prideful backwoodsmen who put little stock in "paper" or the dandified notions of slack-fleshed city-dwellers. What mattered was that their dogs could run a coon (or a boar, or a bear, or a lion, or whatever) and sound good doing it, with a ringing bawl on trail and a hard chop on tree (won't do to keep no turkey-mouthed hound, now!); that they didn't fuss with "trash"; and that they came back, eventually.

The ancestry of the American foxhound, on the other hand, is somewhat better-documented, a reflection of the comparative affluence of the land-holding sportsmen who comprised its primary constituency. According to the authors of *The Sporting Life: A Passion for Hunting and Fishing*, foxhounds directly descended from the pack of Robert Brooke continue to make their merry-tailed way over Maryland's green pastures, giving joyful tongue as the scent of their quarry stirs the ancient fires.

It's important to remember, in this context, that distinct, narrowly-defined breeds and so-called "pure" breeding — concepts that we take for granted today — were not embraced to any significant degree in this country until the late-19th century. Function, not pedigree, drove breeding; while there were a number of "strains" associated with particular sportsmen — the Walker family name was first linked to a strain of hounds in 1742, and the Triggs, which date to the mid-1800s, are still a renowned foxhound strain — the breeds themselves existed only in a fluid, generic sense, defined as much (or more) by what they *did* as by what they looked like, or by what someone chose to call them.

Victorian-era notions of "perfectability" served to

American Field Sports: "Flush'd," 1857
from the Currier & Ives Collection of the Museum of the City of New York

change this, along with the rise of pedigreed dogs as status symbols. This led to the adoption of conformation standards, the establishment of studbooks, and the emergence of the individual breeds as discrete, insular entities. "To promote, encourage, and improve the breeding of a superior class of dogs" was the stated objective when the first registry in the United States, the National American Kennel Club Register, opened for business in 1876.

While scenthounds of one variety or another have been popular with American hunters from the beginning, the "sighthounds" (also known as "gazehounds"), dogs of terrific speed and endurance developed to chase (or "course") visible game in open country, were slow to catch on here — with good reason. Few if any areas in the Eastern United States had sufficiently wide horizons or suitable quarry to accommodate this highly specialized style of hunting.

But as settlement expanded westward onto the Great Plains, a handful of sportsmen capitalized on the opportunities these vast, game-filled expanses offered for coursing dogs. (The few contemporary practitioners of coursing are still found there and in the Desert Southwest; greyhounds are the breed of choice, coyotes the preferred quarry.) The most famous — or, depending on your point of view, infamous — of these sportsmen was none other than George Armstrong Custer. Custer adored dogs, hunting dogs in particular; they were in effect the children that he and his devoted wife, Libby, were themselves unable to conceive. And when he was posted to the West following the Civil War — during which his well-publicized exploits had made him a national hero — his gazehounds accompanied him.

Most of Custer's dogs seem to have been large greyhounds and even larger "staghounds," rugged, rough-coated brutes that these days would be identified as Scottish deerhounds. He was almost never without them, and during his various "Indian" campaigns he would frequently leave his column for hours at a time — deserting his command, in effect — galloping off in a cloud of dust to follow the pack as they coursed everything from pronghorn antelope to wolves.

On one such foray in 1867, he was miles from his unit when he accidentally shot and killed his horse while firing at a buffalo bull. (Custer's marksmanship — or lack thereof — remains a hotly debated topic.) Luckily for him — and for his dogs Rover, Lu, Sharp,

Rattler, and Fanny — the Seventh Cavalry found them before the Cheyenne did.

Custer's luck eventually ran out, of course, and many historians believe that when he passed from life into myth at the Battle of the Little Bighorn on June 25, 1876, at least one of his dogs was along. Although its identity has never been conclusively determined, according to some accounts it was a greyhound. If so, there was a certain grisly poetic justice at work: During their "conquest" of the New World in the late 15th and early 16th centuries, the Spanish relied heavily on greyhounds (or large sighthounds of the same basic type) to subdue the Native American resistance.

Indeed, it was these Spanish hounds, not the foxhounds of Robert Brooke, that were the first European hunting dogs in the Americas. But while trained on game, and brought to the New World to help put meat on the table, they soon found a new niche: abetting the conquistadors — whose cruelty was boundless — as deadly instruments of war. As early as 1495, at the Battle of Vega Real on the island of Hispaniola (modern-day Haiti), Christopher Columbus' pack of 20 hounds carried the day for the Spaniards, killing numbers of natives and causing the rest to flee in terror.

And this was only the beginning of the atrocities. "Within a few years," writes Marion Schwartz in *A History of Dogs in the Early Americas*, "public markets sold human body parts for training Spanish dogs to develop a taste for people, and these dogs were pitted against Native Americans for sport." A Spanish missionary reported that "to feed their dogs, they [the conquistadors] ensure that whenever they travel they always have a ready supply of natives, chained and herded like so many calves on the hoof. These they kill and butcher as the need arises."

Enough: As a renowned classicist once remarked of the Roman emperor Caligula (no stranger to atrocities himself), "The less said of him, the better."

In point of fact, however, there were hunting dogs in North America long before the Spanish arrived. About 12,000 years ago, when nomadic peoples crossed the Bering Land Bridge from Asia and began to filter across the heretofore unpopulated continent, dogs accompanied them. And while hard archaeological evidence is lacking, it seems reasonable to suppose that from the beginning these dogs played some role in the hunt.

Hunting was the central act of day-to-day human

Greyhound

Camping in the Woods: "Laying off," 1863
from the Currier & Ives Collection of the Museum of the City of New York

American Field Sports: "A Chance for Both Barrels," 1857
from the Currier & Ives Collection of the Museum of the City of New York

existence; to succeed meant to survive, to fail meant to starve. In the dog, the Stone Age hunter found the perfect ally, a partner whose strengths — nose, speed, stamina, sharp teeth, powerful jaws — compensated for his weaknesses. Whether leading the way to fresh game (or trailing wounded game) that the human hunter could not locate by his own devices, or perhaps simply nipping at the heels of a woolly mammoth and thereby distracting it long enough for the hunter to get close enough to thrust a spear, the dog was capable of making a valuable contribution.

The Coso Range petroglyphs, a series of rock drawings found in California and Nevada, provide the earliest direct evidence of dogs aiding prehistoric Americans in the hunt. Dating to the period 200 B.C.-300 A.D., these drawings depict dogs in pursuit of bighorn sheep, apparently "driving" them toward a line of human hunters. Centuries later — as recently as the 20th century, in fact — ethnographers studying North America's native cultures observed dogs being employed in almost exactly the same manner.

According to the most complete inquiry ever devoted to the subject, a 1920 study by Glover Allen

of Harvard University, there were 17 basic "types" of aboriginal American dogs at the time of European contact. Not all of them were used as hunting dogs, and few if any were used exclusively for that purpose. Most fulfilled multiple roles: hunters, hauling or pack dogs, guards, family pets, and even (gulp) a source of meat for special occasions. The artist George Catlin, who traveled extensively among the Plains Indians in the 1830s, commented insightfully on the deeper meaning of these ceremonial feasts:

Among all Indian tribes the dog is more valued than among any part of the civilized world. They hunt together and are equal sharers in the chase. Their bed is one. On rocks and on their coats of arms they carve his image as a symbol of fidelity. Yet the Indian will sacrifice this faithful follower to seal a sacred pledge of friendship he has made.
I have seen the master take from the bowl the head of his victim and talk of its former affection and fidelity with tears in his eyes...

The majority of these aboriginal dogs no longer exist as such, having been absorbed, assimilated, and all but overwhelmed by the influx of European breeds — a process that began with the conquistadors. And some became extinct through isolation and neglect. This was the fate of a small, terrier-like hunting dog of the Pacific Northwest, the Tahl Tan (or Tahltan) bear dog. In *The Lost History of the Canine Race*, author Mary Elizabeth Thurston quotes an elder of the Tahl Tan people recalling "they were very smart dogs. They could find a bear's den through deep snow and chase up grouse and ptarmigan. They could find rabbits, anything — if you had a bear dog you could find game; if you didn't, you starved."

In other words, the Tahl Tan bear dog — again, like most aboriginal dogs — was a "generalist," an adaptable all-purpose hunter, as opposed to the more specialized European breeds. Sadly, as reliance on subsistence hunting waned in the 20th century and modern firearms replaced traditional weapons, the Tahl Tan bear dog essentially became obsolete. Sporadic efforts to perpetuate it failed, and in 1979, when the last known individual died, the story of the Tahl Tan came to an end.

In contrast to the hounds, the dogs of the "sporting" category — the "gun dog" breeds, generically — were comparative latecomers to the American party. This should not be surprising, given the fact that hunters had been riding to hounds for centuries, if not millennia, by the time that wingshooting began to come into vogue circa 1600 or so. Dogs of the pointer, setter, and spaniel "types" had been developed long before then, of course: They were used in falconry to find and/or flush a variety of gamebirds (including waterfowl) for the peregrines and gyrfalcons of the nobility, while hunters of less lofty status found it possible to cast nets over coveys of quail and partridge whose locations were revealed by a staunch pointer or "setting dogge."

As firearms continually improved and wingshooting caught the fancy of more and more sportsmen, the popularity of these dogs soared — and nowhere more so than in the British Isles, where by the late-18th century dozens of breeders were busily laying the foundation for the modern pointer, the English, Irish, and Gordon setters, and the various flushing spaniels. Although almost no documentation exists, a trickle of imports to the United States seems to have begun in the early 1800s, gradually gaining momentum as increasing numbers of Americans shrugged off the Puritan ethic and discovered the sublime delights of recreational hunting, fishing, and other fieldsports. The first American periodicals devoted to these pursuits appeared around 1830; a few years later, the country's first important "outdoor" writer emerged in the person of a British emigré named Henry William Herbert, whose numerous articles and books were penned under the *nom de plume* Frank Forester.

Herbert's work reveals not only great breadth and depth of knowledge about the sporting dogs of the day, but a tremendous affinity for them as well:

> *After the gun or rifle, the great essential as to the mere killing of game is his dog to the sportsman; but when we regard him as the living, the intelligent, the more than half-reasoning companion, the docile, obedient, enduring, uncomplaining servant, the faithful, grateful, submissive, affectionate friend, and not unseldom the last mourner of the dead master, unmourned by all beside...we must think of him as something widely different from the tool of wood and iron which we fashion, how perfectly soever, merely to be the senseless and unconscious instrument of our skill.*

Herbert was partial to the setter, flatly declaring "First in the list of sporting dogs, without a moment's hesitation, I place the setter." He believed it to be particularly well-suited to American conditions, "where, or at least in the greater part of which, almost all the shooting is either covert shooting or marsh shooting; for both of which branches of sport I consider one setter as equal for the quantity of service to be got out of him to two pointers, and for the satisfactory style of doing the work and the cheerful endurance of the toil without suffering yet more superior."

Most authorities agree that the term "setter" derives from the low, crouching posture, or "set," that these dogs originally displayed upon striking point. (Although a few contrarians argue that it refers to their ability to "set" game; that is, to cause it to hold without flushing until the hunter arrives on the scene.) And according to Herbert's testimony, the setters of Great Britain almost invariably "set" when they winded birds. In 25 years of wingshooting in America, however, he witnessed only two instances in which setters did *not* point with a proud, upstanding attitude — the same attitude that was the defining characteristic of the pointer breed. This phenomenon baffled him; in his words, "it defies conjecture."

The setters found in America during Herbert's

Irish Setter

heyday — the mid-1800s — were rarely if ever distinguishable as "pure" English, Irish, or Gordon. Even in Great Britain, there was considerable intermingling of setter "blood" until the late-19th century, and the early American setter breeders seemed to pay no attention whatsoever to these arbitrary labels. Rather, as noted previously in the case of scenthounds, they focused only on the dogs' abilities in the field, and over time a number of highly-regarded setter "strains" emerged. Among the most prominent were the Mortons, the Gildersleeves, the Ethan Allens, and the Campbells. These strains, and indeed all of the American setters that pre-dated a flood of British imports that began in the mid-1870s (principally from the kennel of R.L. Purcell Llewellin, of whom we will hear more of), would eventually become known as "natives."

Whatever one chose to call them, setters were clearly the most popular gun dog of the 19th century, with the pointer a distant second and spaniels and retrievers (both of which were comparatively rare) bringing up the rear. In his book *The American Kennel and Sporting Field*, published in 1876, Arnold

Burges offered the following observations:

If a man lives in a country abounding in small patches of thick cover and is not a good enough shot to kill his birds therein, let him use a spaniel to drive the birds out; if he lives in a hot, dry country and never shoots elsewhere, a pointer will suit him best; but if he wants a dog for all kinds of work, and over which he can kill every variety of game bird with the least regard to cover, footing, or temperature, let him get a high-couraged, pure-blooded English Setter, intelligently handle and break him, treat him well, and fear no form of dog that can be brought against him. Such a dog I pronounce the best animal for American upland shooting.

Burges noted that setters were well-suited to the needs of waterfowlers as well, a statement that seems puzzling in today's context. Many modern-day setters are indifferent "natural" retrievers, and the setter's coat absorbs, rather than sheds, water. Beyond the consensus that the retrieving instinct was more pronounced in setters then, the solution to the puzzle may lie in the fact that restrictions on open hunting seasons were few and far-between. In other words, waterfowlers weren't necessarily forced to hunt in the raw, wet, blustery late-fall/early winter conditions we now associate with the sport; they could hunt pretty much whenever they felt like it — and in relatively clement weather the setter was up to the task.

The only bona fide retrieving breed with any appreciable presence on the 19th century American scene was the Chesapeake Bay Retriever, and until the advent of the 20th century it was little-known outside of that locale. One of the handful of sporting breeds to originate on this side of the Atlantic, the Chessie's story began in 1807, when a pair of "Newfoundland water dogs" were rescued from an English brig that sank in Chesapeake Bay after taking on a load of lumber. In Britain, the Newfoundland water dog, also known as the St. John's dog, would ultimately evolve into the Labrador retriever; in Maryland, the two "rescuees," Sailor, a male, and Canton, a female, would become the fountainheads of the Chessie breed. Although never mated to one another, their blood, when crossed

with that of other local hunting dogs and mingled through succeeding generations, eventually produced the characteristic Chesapeake type: a big, strong, rugged, densely-coated, all-day retriever capable of handling the very worst Mother Nature could dish out, the perfect partner for the "baymen" whose livelihoods depended on what they could kill and catch.

Burges called the Chesapeake "unsurpassed if equaled at all in the world" as a retriever from water, but added that it was "almost exclusively confined" to the vicinity of Chesapeake Bay. At about the same time that Burges' book was published, one O.D. Foulks, who hailed from Chesapeake City, Maryland, was touting the merits of a retriever called "the Brown Winchester or Red Chester" in the pages of a periodical entitled *The American Sportsman*. Physically, the dog Foulks described sounds like a dead-ringer for the Chessie, and many believe he was simply using the colloquial name(s) by which the dog was known to him. The late Richard Wolters dissented from this view, but then, that outspoken (but always entertaining) showman never passed up a chance to flout the conventional wisdom.

Be that as it may, Foulks' account of this dog's

Chesapeake Bay Retriever

American Water Spaniel

comportment and prowess would do any retriever owner proud. And even Wolters admitted that it "appears to be the first real description of a working retriever at work":

> *This breed of dogs are very swift and powerful swimmers, they will chase a crippled duck one or two miles, and unless the duck is very slightly hit, will catch him in the end. The dogs sits on the shore behind a blind, his color matching so well with the sand and clay that were he even continually moving the ducks would never notice him (this is the reason the color is so carefully bred for). He seldom moves any part of his body except his head, which he continually turns up and down the river, often sighting the approaching ducks before the gunner. When the gun is fired and a duck falls, he bounds to the edge of the water, plunges in and brings it ashore, and then without having received a word of command from his master, carries it up to the place where he sits and drops it... If the duck falls too far out for the dog to see, he takes his direction from the motion of the hand...*

This is the first mention in the literature of a retriever taking a hand signal.

While hard-core waterfowlers in all parts of the country eventually embraced the Chesapeake as their breed of choice, it never became wildly popular. It reached its peak (so to speak) in the 1920s and 1930s, just as the Labrador and golden retrievers — breeds that are generally easier to train, better hunters on land, and more even-tempered than the Chesapeake — were being introduced from Great Britain. They were embraced by sportsmen with an enthusiasm the Chessie never enjoyed, and in the wag of a tail it plummeted from top dog in the retriever realm to a distant third.

Halfway across the continent, another uniquely American breed was taking shape. Like the baymen of the Chesapeake, the hunters and trappers who scratched their livelihood from the Wolf River bottoms in east-central Wisconsin needed a utilitarian canine companion, a dog small and agile enough to ride comfortably in a skiff, but stout-hearted enough to retrieve the occasional goose or face off against a mink.

They found this dog in the American water spaniel. Dating to the mid-1800s (and perhaps earli-

er), its origins are difficult to pin down. But it's thought that indigenous "Indian dogs," the now-extinct English water spaniel, the curly coated retriever, and possibly even the poodle (which was historically an excellent hunting dog) contributed to the genetic mix. In the early 20th century, F.J. "Doc" Pfeifer of New London, Wisconsin, established a large kennel of American water spaniels, advertised them widely, and shipped them to sportsmen all across the country. Male pups went for $25, while the going rate for females was $20.

A portion of the literature Pfeifer mailed to prospective buyers read as follows:

> *The American Brown Water Spaniel is distinctly an American production. Hunters have known this type for years and it was through their efforts that this dog was propagated... For years we have bred only selective stock, breeding for gameness, stability, courage, intelligence, and beauty. They are dogs to admire and trust under all conditions whether in the home circle or in the field with the outdoor man.*

Pfeifer's efforts notwithstanding, the American water spaniel never gained much of a following beyond its home turf in the Midwest. Its influence, however, extended somewhat further afield: Most authorities believe that it comprises the main branch of the family tree of the Boykin spaniel, a breed with which it is physically and functionally almost identical — although it's doubtful that the American was regularly used as a turkey dog, the way the first Boykins were.

Some have even gone so far as to speculate that the "original" Boykin, "Dumpy," the curly-haired brown dog found wandering the streets of Spartanburg, South Carolina circa 1909, was in fact an American water spaniel shipped to the area by Pfeifer and somehow misplaced in transit. The typical unreconstructed Boykin partisan is likely to bristle at the claim that his dog is essentially a Southern-fried version of the AWS, but then, anything of Yankee origin tends to arouse deep suspicion in the people who gave the world B.A.S.S. and NASCAR.

Herbert (Frank Forester) wrote glowingly of cocker and Clumber spaniels, particularly in reference to early season woodcock shooting in dense cover (which is about the only kind of early season wood-

American Brittany

cock shooting there is). But neither of these breeds seems to have earned more than a token following among early American sportsmen. And the English springer spaniel, far-and-away the most popular of the spaniel breeds in America for many decades now, did not arrive in numbers here until the 1920s — the same period in which the Labrador and golden retrievers began streaming into the U.S. of A.

The 1920s also marked the debut of the so-called "continental" breeds on the American stage. (Continental refers to their origins on the European mainland, as opposed to the British Isles.) The German shorthaired pointer and the Brittany, a French breed then known as the Brittany "spaniel" (the spaniel designation was officially dropped in the 1980s), were the groundbreakers; they were followed, in no particular order, by the Weimaraner, the Viszla, the Drahthaar (German wirehaired pointer), and the wirehaired pointing griffon, just to mention the breeds that became solidly established here.

Why this surge of "new" pointing breeds? Well, at

the risk of oversimplification, they met a demand that the pointing dogs available to American sportsmen of the day weren't satisfying very well: the demand for a dog of moderate pace and range, a tractable, biddable, all-day bird hunting companion. For all intents and purposes, the English setter and the pointer were the only pointing breeds to choose from in the United States of the early 20th century, and due to the pervasive influence of field trials — which were conducted on horseback in "big" country and placed a premium on extreme speed and range — they had simply become "too much dog" for many shoe-leather bird hunters.

Another contributing factor was the pheasant. The population of this gaudy import exploded in the early 20th century, and in relatively short order its popularity as a gamebird rivaled — if not exceeded — that of native species such as bobwhite quail, ruffed and sharptailed grouse, prairie chicken, and woodcock. In part because of the nature of pheasant cover and in part because of the nature of the bird itself, many sportsmen found the closer-working continental breeds a better choice for ringnecks than the bigger-going pointer and English setter. (The rise of the pheasant played, if anything, an even greater role in popularizing the Labrador, the golden, and especially the springer spaniel on American shores; in terms of sheer day-in, day-out effectiveness, a strong case can be made that a flushing dog will put more roosters in your gamebag than a pointing dog will.)

All of which begs the question of what happened to the utilitarian type of setter that occasioned the rapturous prose of Herbert, Burges, and other mid-19th century scribes. The answer brings us back to our old friend R.L. Purcell Llewellin. In the 1870s, Llewellin, a Welshman, developed a strain of setters — nominally English, but with acknowledged infusions of Gordon blood as well — that were smaller, faster, and more stylish than anything that had come before. American sportsmen jumped on the Llewellin bandwagon almost immediately, importing the two dogs now considered the most influential sires in the

history of the breed: Gladstone and Count Noble. (Footnote-to-history department: As a boy growing up in Memphis, Nash Buckingham fed cookies to Gladstone through the kennel fence; the dog's owner, P.H. Bryson, lived nearby and was a friend of the family.)

And while Gladstone was defeated by the "native" Campbell-strain setter Joe Jr. in a famous two-day match race held near Florence, Alabama, in 1879 — Joe Jr. had 61 quail finds to Gladstone's 52 (numbers that beggar the imagination in this quail-impoverished era) — Llewellin-bred English setters, by dint of superior speed and range, soon dominated American field trials. Unable to compete in the fast-paced field trial environment, the Irish and Gordon setters fell out of favor, and as their breeding was increasingly co-opted by "show" interests — interests that emphasized beauty while ignoring function — they were all but ruined as useful gun dogs.

The native setter strains pretty much ceased to exist as well, losing their individuality as their blood

English Setter

was absorbed into the Llewellin mainstream. English setters of mixed Llewellin/native ancestry were known as "grades," and regardless of how brilliantly they performed in the field they were dismissed as poor relation by the breeders of the day. This insistence on "100% Pure Llewellin" would have dire consequences; by the time American setter breeders woke up to the realization that the Llewellin blood had gone stale — you can only breed within the same genetic family for so long before problems develop (the Romanovs could testify to this, if the Bolsheviks hadn't killed them all) — the pointer, whose breeders kept their eyes on the ball, had eclipsed the English setter as the dominant force in field trial competition. By 1915, when La Besita, "the last of the great Llewellins," won the National Field Trial Championship, the tide had already turned in the pointer's favor: Only five English setters have worn the crown of National Champion since then.

The pointer, of course, has the reputation for being a rocket on legs, a bird-seeking missile that leaves a vapor trail — not to mention the local time zone — when you turn it loose. While a pointer in the hands of a skilled trainer is capable of finding game and covering ground in a way that makes most other pointing dogs look like they're slogging through quicksand, this reputation is not altogether undeserved. And what made the pointer into this turbocharged machine was the influence of field trials — or more specifically, the influence that the Llewellins had on standards of field trial performance. (Mid-19th century observers typically described the pointer as relatively slow, cautious, and close-working; Herbert faulted it for "inferior dash" — about the last complaint you'd make about a pointer today.)

The first field trial in America was held in 1874 — a black "native" setter, Knight, was the winner — and by the early 1900s sportsmen were already beginning to grumble that the wide-ranging field trial "type" dog was not the kind of dog they wanted for everyday "foot hunting." This — along with the introduction of the pheasant and the increasingly "tight" nature of the American landscape — set the stage for the influx of the Continental breeds in the 1920s and '30s.

Ironically — or perhaps predictably, given the American penchant for tinkering (and thereby screwing up what was perfectly good to begin with) — some breeders have made it their mission to develop Brittanys and German shorthairs that can "run with the big dogs," i.e. pointers and English setters. But that, as they say, is a whole other story. ■

Pointer

German Shorthaired Pointer

CHAPTER 2

BREEDING 101

by David Gowdey

ANYONE WHO OWNS a decent female hunting dog will, at some time, ponder the question of whether or not to breed her. If the inclination is beginning to go beyond the pondering state, and this is your first time, there are some things that you should know before you take the plunge.

The first thing to recognize is that animal shelters are filled with unwanted dogs—many of them pointing breeds. The world has no need for more litters of badly-bred puppies. So unless you are willing to devote the time and effort necessary to breeding superior pups, you are better off not starting at all. Get the bitch spayed.

Breeding pointing dogs is an undertaking that is equal parts science and art. A responsible breeder must have a basic grounding in the science of genetics, as well as a keen eye and gift for assessing and matching up breeding stock. If you are willing to put in the time to do the homework, welcome to the world of breeding pointing dogs.

Starting Out

Every good litter and line starts with a good brood bitch. Most experienced breeders will tell you that the bitch is the most important part of the mix. In golf, they say you drive for show but you putt for dough. In breeding the sire's for show, the dam's for dough.

However, not every female makes a good brood bitch. The hallmark of a good breeder is the ability to make a ruthlessly realistic assessment of a bitch to determine whether she should be bred at all.

To do this requires some time. Only outstanding bitches should be bred. In this regard, pedigree is no substitute for performance. To know whether a bitch is outstanding takes at least two or three seasons in the field or on the trial grounds. Many bitches have come on during their first year like they were going to be in the Hall of Fame, only to backslide during their sophomore year and turn out to be mediocre at best. Waiting until your bitch is at least two — maybe three — before breeding gives you a chance to make a reasonable assessment of her strengths and weaknesses. These strengths and weaknesses are the expressed characteristics of her genes — the genes she will pass on to her pups. If she passes the assessment, if she's worth breeding, then the fun begins.

Genetics (Yikes!)

Genes are building blocks of life. Genes line up on chromosomes that organize protoplasm and gunk into Playboy centerfolds or German shorthairs (pretty amazing, huh?). There are a few things that are important for the novice breeder to know about genes.

Irish Setter

• Genes are "the functional and physical unit of heredity passed from parent to offspring."

• Genes are always found in pairs on chromosomes (very important).

• Genes are dominant or recessive. A dominant gene will always override its pair partner to express a characteristic, but a recessive gene must be paired with another recessive gene to express its characteristic.

• Genes are often linked — so the gene for black hair is always associated with the gene for a black nose in a purebred Labrador, for example. Genes are also often interactive, working together in combination to produce expressed characteristics.

• A dog (or human) gets one half of its genes from its sire, and one half from its dam, which are combined in the chromosomes of each new fetus. How these genes pair determines what characteristics the dog will have. As noted above, genes occur in pairs — one coming from each parent. When different genes (dominant+recessive) pair together, they are known as heterozygous genes. When two genes of the same type (dominant+dominant and recessive+recessive) pair together they are known as homozygous genes. Two parents with identical sets of homozygous genes will produce pups with genes identical to themselves.

Inbreeding (mating two directly related dogs), or close linebreeding (mating two dogs related within two generations), decreases genetic variation and increases homozygosity — which increases consistency among a litter. The more the pups are genetically like their parents, the more likely they are also to be like them in appearance, temperament, ability, etc. This is an attractive quality for big breeders turning out lots of pups — they can be sure of the qualities and characteristics of their pups.

However, increased homozygosity also increases the likelihood for expressed genetic maladies in a litter and line. Most genetic abnormalities and diseases occur on recessive genes. They are not normally expressed in a heterozygous gene pair because the dominant gene cancels them out. All dogs have a great number of these pairs of bad recessive genes masked by good dominant genes. When you increase homozygosity, you increase the likelihood that these recessive genes will pair up — and the pups will wind up with undescended testicles, hip dysplasia, incorrect bites, hypoglycemia, epilepsy, etc. This is why inbreeding and close linebreeding are best left to the experts who are so inclined.

There is a complicated mathematical formula to measure homozygosity called the Coefficient of Inbreeding (COI). This formula is available on some veterinary websites. Many breeders use the COI to help them keep that balance of desirable homozygosity and genetic variety.

Taking Stock

Assessing the strengths and weaknesses of breeding stock is much of what makes breeding an art rather than a science. It requires a keen eye, and an ability to detach oneself from any emotional baggage about an animal and to make an impartial assessment of a dog. It's what makes the great breeders great.

I always advise a novice breeder to use a Zen approach to this aspect of breeding: Close your eyes and envision the perfect hunting dog for the type of hunting you do. How does she move and range? What type of temperament does she have? How does she handle? What type of build and coat does she have? Does she have good conformation within the breed standards?

Assemble a mental checklist of those qualities typically affected by heredity that this ideal dog possesses. The qualities I tend to focus on are (not in any specific order) as follows:

• Natural pointing and retrieving ability
• Nose
• Range
• Conformation
• Temperament
• Biddability
• Intelligence
• Drive

English Setter

Now open your eyes and look at your bitch and make a comparison to that ideal dog. How does your bitch measure up? Assign a number from 1-10 to each of the qualities you've identified, and be brutally honest. Once you've rated your bitch this way, you'll have a good idea of her strengths and weaknesses and where you need to go in your breeding. If she scored well on the checklist, then you are set to take the next step.

The next step is getting a medical assessment of her health. Waiting until your bitch is two gives you the opportunity to have her hips X-rayed for OFA or PennHip certification. Canine hip dysplasia is a relatively common genetic disorder that can be identified through a special review of hip X-rays. For breeds with known problems with CHD, all breeding stock should be certified CHD-free before breeding. Depending upon the breed, screening for a variety of other genetic disorders might be recommended. She should also be tested for brucellosis. It is best to discuss with your vet what tests might be appropriate for your breed.

Now that you have determined that you have a bitch that performs well in the field, has good con-formation within breed standards, is medically sound, and has the personality characteristics you would want in your pups, the next step is to find a stud.

Picking a Stud

Picking the stud is where most amateur breeders fail. Too often they pick a stud that is convenient, or one that is famous, without assessing whether the stud will adequately complement the bitch's traits. The net result of such pairings is nothing more than a gamble — sometimes it works and often it doesn't.

When we were assessing the bitch, we developed a mental image of the ideal hunting dog. Ideally, we want our pups to fit this description. We want to breed pups better than their parents. As we have already assessed the strengths and weaknesses of our dam, we need to figure what characteristics we need in a stud to get us from her to our ideal pups. Surveying our checklist for the bitch should give us some idea of the characteristics we want in the stud. You might want to make a checklist for the stud as well, and then see if you can find a dog to match.

A pair of Brittanys, one pointing the other backing.

If our bitch already fits our profile of a perfect dog, and we want to ensure that the pups are as similar to her as possible, we should consider close line-breeding or inbreeding. By such close breeding, we diminish the genetic variation and increase homozygosity, heightening our chances of getting pups that are very close in appearance and behavior to their parents. On the other hand, we also increase the potential for genetic maladies such as inbreeding depression, hypoglycemia, etc. These risks have to be weighed against the benefits.

Assuming that the bitch is not perfect and has some weaknesses we would want to see improved in the pups, then we need to find a stud that can do the job. The key to remember is that when you breed, genes don't mix like a martini. The pups will be a combination of the genes of their mother and father, not a mix. In a martini, if you have too much vermouth you can add more gin to balance things out. With dogs, if you have a big-running bitch and you want a more moderate range in the pups, you can't breed to a boot-polisher and assume it will wash out. What you will likely get is a litter in which half are big-runners and half are boot-polishers. You have to aim for what you want — not the opposite of your dam.

Finally, you have to make sure that the stud is healthy as well. He should be tested for any potential genetic problems.

Once you've got a stud that you believe has the characteristics you want, you need to take a look at the pedigree and genetic background of both dogs to try and determine if they share enough genes to ensure that he might make a good genetic match for your bitch.

Assessing a Pedigree

The fundamental reason for the existence of canine breed registries such as the AKC, UKC, and the Field Dog Stud Book is to provide an accurate pedigree. A pedigree is a record of the genetic inheritance of a dog. As such, it can be extremely valuable in making breeding decisions. Typical pedigrees contain a record of the ancestry of a dog — generally out to five generations. A good pedigree will list the registered name of each dog and any credentials and titles it might have gained. Some typical abbreviations that you will see in a hunting dog pedigree include FC (Field Champion AKC), CH (Field Champion FDSB/Bench Champion AKC), DC (Dual champion - a champ in both field and show), MH, SH, JH

(Master, Senior, and Junior Hunter).

One word of caution about field trial titles: There are different types of field trial formats, and a dog requires different characteristics to win in these formats. If you are trying to tone down the range of your bitch, you certainly don't want to breed to a line of All-Age field trial champions. FC or CH tells you the dog had the right stuff to win in its format. It doesn't tell you in which format a dog competed for its championship. Nor does it tell you the characteristics needed to win in that format. It's up to you to find out these important facts. Also, don't be put off of a great dog that doesn't have many FCs in its pedigree. Many fine hunting dogs have no FC or CH in front of their names simply because their owners didn't have the inclination or money to compete in field trials.

When comparing two pedigrees to determine breeding suitability, you want to look for common ancestors — hopefully with some titles. These are genetic intersection points — genes that both dogs will have in common and will pass on to the pups. The closer these intersection points are to the proposed pup, the more shared genes it will have. The more shared genes, the more likely a pup is to "throw true," (resemble in conformation, temperament, and ability its parents).

However, the more genes the parents have in common, the greater potential for reproductive problems, and that the pups will exhibit genetic maladies. Therefore, most breeders try to balance the desire for a common genetic foundation to ensure that the pups will throw true, against the dangers of too much inbreeding. In my own case, I try to look for three or four intersection points (common ancestors) between the third and fifth generation, and if these intersection points are DCs, things get better and better!

Mechanics

Normally, if you put a healthy female in heat down with a healthy male, nature will take its course. This is true of the vast majority of breedings. However, there are times when things don't go quite as planned. Sometimes this is a human mistake, sometimes a canine problem, and sometimes it's just an act of God.

The most common human mistake is to put the pair together too soon. Canine estrus has three phases. They are slightly different for each bitch. The first phase, pre-estrus, is characterized by bloody spotting and swelling of the vulva. It usually lasts about a week.

A stylish English Setter on point. The beeper collar
aids in locating the stationary dog.

During this period, a bitch cannot conceive and won't accept the male. The second period is estrus, the time when the bitch is fertile and can conceive. This is characterized by clear or watermelon-colored liquid coming from the vulva, and she will stand and move her tail to one side when you put your hand upon her hips. Estrus normally lasts about a week. The final period is anestrus, in which the bitch moves out of heat if she has not conceived. Traditionally, dogs are put together about 10 days after the first spotting is sighted, and again 12 days after the first spotting. A veterinarian can do hormone tests to tell you exactly when the bitch is in estrus if you have doubts about your own ability to tell.

The most common canine mistakes are caused by inexperience and nervousness. Sometimes a young male, though willing, won't have the mechanics worked out quite right and may need help to hit the bullseye. Other times a bitch may be nervous, or may not find the male attractive, and will refuse to stand. At such times, the owner holding the bitch's head can prevent the male from receiving some potentially dangerous bites. Generally, a rule of thumb is to bring the bitch to the male so she will feel less dominant outside of her own territory, while he will feel more assertive in his own. Finally, if the bitch is still nervous after the tie (dogs remain connected for up to a half-hour), it may be necessary to hold her or tie her up. An agitated bitch can seriously injure a male during the tie.

Finally, there are times when two willing dogs can't seem to tie — or even after a successful tie, the bitch doesn't conceive. Often these are health-related problems, and a trip to the vet can clear up the mystery. Sometimes these problems can be solved — sometimes they can't.

Conclusion

Once you pick the stud and dam — and roll the dice — you won't really know if you've been successful for at least a year or two. That's when you can get feedback from those who bought your pups. If you've hit a homer with the litter, the feeling of pride and accomplishment will more than cover for the hard work and time that you put into creating the litter. ■

A bobwhite quail hunter with all he needs— a bird, a gun, and his Brittany.

Pointer

CHAPTER 3

READING A PEDIGREE

by Amy Dahl

A PEDIGREE IS A FAMILY tree showing several generations of the ancestors of a given dog. The sire and dam appear at the left, the four grandparents in a column to the right of these, the eight great-grandparents in the next column, and so on. Titles and clearances for hereditary disease may be shown for some of the ancestors. Coat colors are sometimes even included.

While it is exciting to see illustrious, titled ancestors in a pedigree, it is important to keep in mind the proportion of the dog's genetic makeup that is probably contributed by each. A close ancestor is expected to have considerably more influence than a more distant ancestor, farther to the right on the pedigree. Every dog receives half of its genes from its sire and half from its dam. Because the particular genes inherited from a parent are a matter of chance, we don't know for certain how many came from each grandparent or earlier ancestors. We can say that on average, 25 percent of a dog's genetic makeup comes from each grandparent, one-eighth or 12.5 percent is contributed by each great-grandparent, and so on. An ancestor in a given generation contributes, on average, a fraction equal to one over the number of dogs in that generation. Since a pup has eight grandparents, the contribution from each is equal to one-eighth. By comparison, since a pup has two parents, the contribution from each parent is expressed as one-half.

Since the closest ancestors contribute most strongly to a dog's heredity, these are the dogs it will most resemble. Thus it is important that the parents and grandparents be good examples of the breed and show the traits desired in a puppy. A pedigree showing titles in the fourth and fifth generation only may indicate lack of selectivity among more recent ancestors. Without selection of the best in every generation, dogs are apt to revert to mediocrity rather quickly.

Although the closest ancestors are most important because they contribute the most, breeders usually prefer to work with pedigrees showing several generations. The additional generations contain information about "depth," or the number of generations over which certain titles, health clearances, etc., have been obtained, and about the degree of relatedness among dogs in the pedigree. Both of these have bearing on the probability that a puppy will closely resemble its ancestors; although, as we will see, they do not tell the whole story.

Weimaraner

Performance vs. Production

The astute reader of pedigrees recognizes that there is a distinction between a good performer (a good hunting or competition dog), and a good producer. Breeding good dogs would be a lot simpler if breeding two good performers consistently produced good performers — but it doesn't. Some studs throw a high proportion of good offspring out of a variety of bitches. These dogs are considered prepotent. At the other extreme are dogs that sire only one good puppy, or several good offspring out of only one bitch, despite hundreds of breedings. While most pedigrees express only performance, the effort to breed and/or identify good producers drives many breeding decisions and so has bearing on pedigrees.

If you are able to identify the great producers in your breed, then by all means seek out pedigrees that are stacked with these ancestors. It is also worthwhile to know some of the strategies breeders use to try to improve consistency in their litters, and that necessitates a discussion of inbreeding.

Inbreeding (also known as linebreeding)

For the purposes of this article I will refer to all breeding of related dogs as "inbreeding," although many use the term "linebreeding" for all but the closest breedings. Inbreeding occurs when the sire and dam of a litter have one or more ancestors in common. If the sire or dam have no ancestors in common, the breeding is an outcross.

Breeders with a plan are usually trying to produce dogs that perform well and breed true, producing offspring that are similar to one another and to the parents. You often hear it said that inbreeding produces greater uniformity (consistency in the offspring). In fact it is the use of inbred parents that tends to produce uniform offspring. Genetics provides an explanation for this. When you breed related animals, both parents (probably) have some of the same genetic material from the common ancestor(s). Thus, the inbred offspring has increased homozygosity — a greater proportion of pairs of identical genes — than the population at large. The eggs or sperm produced by this inbred dog are relatively less diverse, since fewer of its genes offer alternatives, and its offspring in turn are correspondingly less diverse.

Uniformity of offspring doesn't automatically mean they will be of good quality, and yet those rare dogs that seem truly prepotent throw offspring that are consistently good. This suggests that the great producers probably have identical pairs of many of the key genes for performance. Plenty of breeders have noted the potential of inbreeding to produce that great stud dog (or brood bitch), but it must be recognized that most inbred dogs will not have the happy combination of genes and will throw puppies that are uniformly mediocre. The breeder must be extremely critical of the inbred litter, keeping only the individual that most closely approaches his or her standards.

Although the ills often attributed to it are often misunderstood, there is a price to be paid for inbreeding. With increased homozygosity comes an increase in problems collectively known as inbreeding depression, including decreased fertility and resistance to disease, and increased appearance of rare, harmful recessive genes. Therefore, the prospective puppy-buyer has an interest in avoiding the intensively inbred pedigree.

But how much is too much? That depends upon the breed, the breeder, and the family of dogs. Inbreeding is part of the history of every "pure" breed, stemming back to the breed's origin from a small number of individuals. Dependent upon breed and family history, a given inbreeding may or may not involve much risk.

If you know you will never breed your dog, you may try to avoid inbreeding altogether. Remember, if the parents are themselves inbred but are unrelated, their puppies will be outcrosses, and such a breeding may have the best chance of producing good performers that are also healthy. Since many breeders are working toward some goal and hope to obtain future breeding stock from the litter, however, they may do an outcross breeding only rarely — planning to breed the best of the resulting litter back into the family line.

Inbreeding may not always be apparent. Dogs

German Shorthaired Pointer

Labrador Retreiver

may have no ancestors in common in a four-generation pedigree but still share quite a few of the same genes due to the earlier history of the strain. In my experience, Labradors from pure field trial breeding reproduce as an inbred line. Crosses to show-bred Labradors or British imports often produce very nice dogs in the first generation, but these in turn are usually incapable of reproducing themselves. Years ago, Louise Belmont stated flatly, "You can't make a stud dog out of half a pedigree." She was referring to a couple of wonderful dogs my husband John made field champions, DC-AFC Warpath Macho and FC-AFC Jaffer's Blackie, both of which resulted from crosses of field trial-bred Labs to other strains of Labs. Louise had experience with great stud dogs — she owned FC-AFC Air Express, and her husband owned NFC-NAFC Super Chief — and her prediction for Macho and Blackie turned out to be apt. Both dogs were bred and to our knowledge failed to produce competitive offspring.

Health Clearances

Responsible breeders will seek all of the health clearances appropriate for their breed in the interest of minimizing the likelihood of ailments that shorten the dog's life or prevent it from working. Numbers with the prefix "OFA" indicate dogs have passed a screening for hip dysplasia (OFA EL for elbow dysplasia), and those beginning with CERF indicate that the dog has tested clear of a number of eye disorders. It is important to know, however, the limitations of this information. Some hereditary problems important in gun dog breeds may occur even when the breeding stock has been screened, and others may not be included in the standard tests.

The likelihood that puppies will show a trait or defect that is not evident in the parents depends upon the mode of inheritance of the trait. Many of the soundness issues important to gun dogs, such as hip dysplasia, are believed to be polygenic in inheritance. Theoretically, this means the trait is governed by several genes, not just one.

Standard Poodle

Practically speaking, polygenic inheritance has interesting consequences for breeders. One of them is that a dog's potential to throw a trait may be better evaluated by looking at that dog's siblings than at the dog itself. For example, an OFA Fair dog, all of whose siblings earned passing grades from OFA, is expected to be a better breeding prospect for hip joint conformation than an OFA Excellent dog, all of whose siblings failed. Pedigree "depth," that is, several generations of clearances, is widely thought to be desirable but is not nearly as reliable a predictor of soundness as "breadth," or information about the siblings of a dog's parents and grandparents.

Other structural traits and problems are also thought to be polygenic, including elbow dysplasia and epilepsy. Some respected breeders believe pedigree breadth is the key to consistently producing good performers, as well as physically sound dogs.

Since overall working potential is determined by many genes, that idea is consistent with what the genetics experts suggest.

Some genetic diseases are recessive in nature and can appear despite the dogs in the pedigree having been sound for many generations. Progressive Retinal Atrophy (PRA) is such a disease. It has been difficult to select against because many "carriers" have long been impossible to identify. Recently, DNA tests have been developed to identify certain non-carriers in several sporting breeds, including Irish setters and Chesapeake Bay retrievers. We may see this information appearing on AKC pedigrees in the near future.

While it is nice to see health clearances indicated on a pedigree — and it tells you something of the breeder's willingness to screen breeding stock — these clearances fall short of an assurance that the puppies will be free of hereditary disease.

Rhodesian Ridgeback

English Setter

The golden retreiver's undercoat allows it to withstand frigid water.

Titles

Titles, of course, provide some measure of a dog's performance. The advantages of titles are that they represent a measure of the dog's abilities as judged against some kind of uniform standard. They provide more certainty than subjective accounts from people who have shot over the dog, who may have been impressed mainly by the dog's training and manners, or who may not recognize whether or not the dog's abilities were put to the test.

On the other hand, titles, too, are full of pitfalls. A dog's performance in a formal event is a result of heredity, training and handling, and luck. As we consider relatively more demanding titles, of course, there is less room for defects in training or natural endowments. Although many dogs with "good genes" will fall by the wayside, we do know that those who succeed are strong in the traits needed to win.

The other big problem with titles, of course, is that organized events do not always identify and reward exactly the same set of qualities a given hunter is seeking in a dog. I recommend that the student of pedigrees attend a few of the events leading to the various titles and try to understand what traits are being emphasized. A retriever field trial, for example, rewards great desire, bird interest, eyesight, and trainability, but if it is held in warm weather, it tells nothing about the cold-water abilities of the dogs. Since close to 100 percent of the competing dogs have been force-fetched, field trial titles tell us next to nothing about the dogs' inherited tendency to properly handle a bird.

Some people believe that breeding AKC Master Hunter titled retrievers produces calmer, easier-to-train dogs than does breeding field champions, but I question this. Nothing in the structure of Master Hunter tests appears to reward the calm-natured dog, and as many of the dogs earning MH titles are trained by pros using the same methods applied to field trial

retrievers, I doubt the process selects for a difference in response to training. In evaluating the relevance of a title, try to disregard the professed philosophy of the program and look at what the dogs must do in order to win (or qualify). In any case, you can bet the successful breeder makes decisions based on a thorough knowledge of the dog and not just its titles.

There is a lot of information to be gleaned from pedigrees. We can see who the parents and grandparents are and predict whether a dog will closely resemble them. We can learn something about the selection criteria used for a dog's ancestors by looking at the titles and health clearances they obtained, and we can see the extent of inbreeding and other clues to the breeder's strategy. There is also a good deal of relevant information that is not listed — individual characteristics and temperaments of the dogs in the pedigree, and information about siblings of the parents and grandparents. Talking to the breeder is a good way to "flesh out" the summary of information presented in a pedigree and to best understand the genetic potential of a particular dog.

Finally, remember that pedigrees are not created by paper alone. Good breeding decisions must take into account the flesh-and-blood dogs to which they apply. If your breeder consistently produces the type of dogs you like, trust him or her.

Since my experience is retriever-specific, I interviewed (and would like to thank) Harold Ray of Smith Setters to learn about pedigrees and breeding of pointing dogs. I learned that although breeding practices vary, the principles guiding his breeding program are the same as those of the good retriever breeders: Know what kind of dogs you want; select the best in every generation; use dams that possess the traits you like rather than relying entirely on big-deal sires; breed related dogs to maintain consistency; and look at the character of the dog itself instead of just its titles. ■

A field breed Irish, or Red, Setter.

Golden Retriever

CHAPTER 4

HIPS, ELBOWS AND EYES
by Vickie Lamb

GONE ARE THE DAYS when the prospective puppy buyer goes to look at a litter, then picks out a pup, and the two of them live happily ever after. It's just not that simple anymore. Partly due to line breeding and inbreeding practices that have occurred within bloodlines of our favorite retriever breeds — which have also produced many desirable qualities — there are certain orthopedic and eye conditions that must warrant a heads-up when looking to purchase a new pup. These potential problems could cause crippling or blindness in your dog. This pup will be part of the family for the next decade or more; it makes sense to do everything you can before you buy to ensure a sound investment in the new family member, before the family becomes attached to him.

What You Should Know

Today's dedicated breeders usually include some sort of health guarantee when they sell puppies. Examine this guarantee carefully and ask any questions about portions that you don't understand. All guarantees are not the same. In addition, look for information on the pup's parentage that includes information on hips such as OFA or PennHIP, and eye information from CERF.

Orthopedic Concerns

Most people think of the skeletal system as dead twigs supporting soft tissue. However, this system is one of the most dynamic in the body; the skeleton is one of the few systems that can heal without any scarring at all if given time to remodel. Most changes in skeletal structure will occur in the first few months of life, then will slow from that point onward. When the puppy reaches 80 to 90 percent of its adult weight, at about 12 months of age, the skeletal structure is considered to be mature by most veterinarians.

English Setter

Canine hip dysplasia (CHD) is the orthopedic concern with which most people are the most familiar. Another is elbow dysplasia, which is a catch-all term that covers many problems. One elbow compromise is fragmented coronoid process, or FCP. A third is osteochondrosis, which occurs when cartilage thickens. When it develops a flap, this becomes osteo chrondritis dissecans (OCD), a disruption of bone formation. Panosteitis is an inflammation of the lining of the bone.

Hips

Hip dysplasia is the most common form of all developmental orthopedic diseases. Its presence can cause unrecognizable symptoms in the borderline or mild cases to painful crippling in severe cases. The important thing is that puppies start out with normal hips. There are lots of different factors in determining which pups will develop CHD and which will not. That's why veterinarians and breeders use the OFA, Orthopedic Foundation for Animals, and/or PennHIP, a procedure developed at the University of Pennsylvania that measures how much the hips can be moved out of joint, to help in determining canines with inherited hip dysplasia.

Right now there is some controversy between the two available methods. Some contend that during OFA hip X-rays, the hip joint positioning could actually mask certain forms of CHD. In contrast, the PennHIP method is a dynamic measure of laxity in the hips that is coming on strong and, according to orthopedic surgeon Dr. Kyle Kerstetter of Michigan Veterinary Specialists, could very well be the new standard in canine hip evaluation. Both methods, however, indicate hip problems.

The hip formation is a ball and socket joint. PennHIP determines how much laxity — or how much the hip can be moved out of joint — by a distraction index. Certain veterinarians need to be licensed to do this procedure, which is then interpreted at the University of Pennsylvania's facility.

In contrast, a static measure is used for OFA evaluation. This can sometimes cause the joint to falsely tighten up when the dog is positioned for X-ray. Either method usually requires heavy sedation. With PennHIP, the dog is placed on his/her back with the legs extended toward the ceiling; a jig is put between the legs and pushed down pretty hard to try to force a leg out of joint. This jig is made of aluminum with soft rubber coating. Sandbags are placed outside the

dog's rump area. What is measured is the difference between distraction and reduction during this method to determine a distraction index. Dr. Kerstetter cautions that hip dysplasia is a problem with the soft tissues, not a problem with bone, but bone is where the signs eventually show up. If it weren't for laxities in soft tissue, we wouldn't have these problems at all; but this condition will lead to arthritis in varying degrees of severity.

While there are rare cases in which a traumatic injury such as hit-by-car can cause hip problems and arthritis, most hip problems are inherited and can be traced to parents with faulty hips.

Ebows and Shoulders

If you were to look at the elbow joint, it is built like the letter C; at the bottom of this C is the medial coronoid process. Many times the tip of this C is loose. Theories are that the C itself doesn't sit correctly in the joint. This, then, puts pressure on the bottom of this C, where the joint should fit tightly. A growth plate is there, so this may be a form of OCD (osteo chrondritis dissecans), and there's evidence both ways.

Primarily the process goes like this: Cartilage becomes mineralized cartilage and then develops to bone. This process can become de-railed, resulting in a thickened area of cartilage, that leads to a dog having an area of normal bone, thick cartilage, then normal bone. Therefore, it "loads" differently than the bone around it and can fragment and allow fluid to get under the joint. This can start arthritis.

In this condition the beginning cartilage never makes it to the more advanced mineralized state. Says Dr. Kerstetter, "Think of this as the surface of a ball with a focal area. Let's say that this is the surface of the joint and the focal area is the center of the ball, at say, a half-inch circle. All of the surface of that ball is going to be loaded with the same weight-bearing forces, but the problem is that bone loads differently than cartilage. So, this area concentrates all the stresses that this joint sees. That's where cartilage breaks, on that edge. Let me point out, however, that just because you see an area that has thickened cartilage, it doesn't mean that it will always be that way. The dog's body can catch up sometimes. However, once you have an actual fissure, and the cartilage cracks, it's not going to heal back down."

These problems can be manifested in the shoulder, elbow, or even the ankle joint. When a growing animal displays lameness, the first procedure is to rule out other developmental diseases. X-rays can show changes within the bone. However, the real kicker is that all of these orthopedic diseases can occur together. A practitioner could see a dog with one of the elbow dysplasias, and the same dog could have panosteitis, mentioned earlier. (Note: panosteitis is a self-limiting disease; when the pup reaches skeletal maturity he/she is usually done with it. Rarely is this diagnosis made in older dogs.)

What do the professionals recommend as treatment? First and foremost, Dr. Kerstetter states that "nothing helps like tincture of time." From that point, the method is to control discomfort, usually with aspirin. Use of corticosteroids can mess up normal bone growth in the young dog and can be overused; this is a very powerful family of drugs that may be used too often. Basically, exercise restriction and an aspirin or Rimadyl drug regime will show results, often within two or three weeks.

Are elbow/shoulder diseases genetically predetermined? The experts are divided but basically acknowledge that they can't say as yet, although the possibility exists. They agree, however, that the shoulder is more forgiving than arthritis-induced problems in other joints, with the ankle joint being the worst; lesions tend to be largest there. Usually, when dealing with the elbow, knee, hock, or ankle — as opposed to the shoulder — the goal is to make the pain more tolerable to the dog.

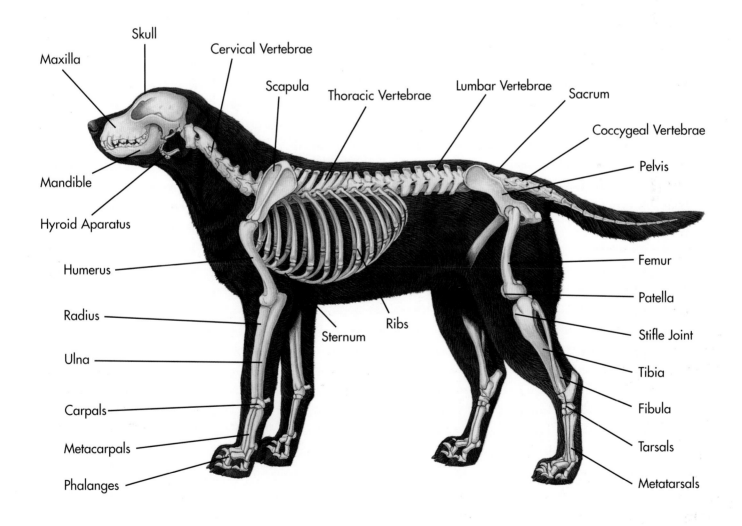

Prevalence of Hip and Elbow Dysplasia Among the Sporting Breeds

The following is a listing based upon 25 years of data collected by the Orthopedic Foundation for Animals (1974 - 1999). The percentages of dysplastic animals detected is based upon 100 or more certifications. Because the breed you are considering does not appear on this list does not necessarily mean that hip and elbow dysplasia are not problems. It could simply mean that there were fewer than 100 certifications.

Breed	% Hip Dysplasia	% Elbow Dysplasia
Clumber spaniel	50.3	—
Boykin spaniel	47.0	—
Sussex spaniel	42.9	—
Bloodhound	25.9	16.5
Chesapeake Bay retriever	23.0	5.4
Golden retriever	21.3	11.1
Gordon setter	21.1	12.7
Field spaniel	21.0	—
English setter	18.7	16.4
Black and tan hound	18.5	—
Spinone	18.2	—
Harrier	17.4	—
Beagle	16.7	—
Brittany	16.3	0.6
Welsh springer spaniel	16.1	—
Curly-coated retriever	15.7	—
English springer spaniel	15.4	16.6
Pudelpointer	15.2	—
Irish water spaniel	15.2	—
Airedale	13.2	—
Labrador retriever	13.2	12.7
Irish setter	13.1	2.4
Munsterlander	13.1	—
German wirehaired pointer	10.1	4.4
Pointer	10.1	—
Wiemaraner	9.4	0.6
Nova Scotia duck Tolling retriever	8.4	—
American water spaniel	8.3	—
Vizsla	7.6	4.0
Cocker spaniel	6.8	—
Rhodesian ridgeback	6.6	6.1
German shorthaired pointer	5.5	1.35
Flat-coated retriever	4.7	1.3
Greyhound	3.4	—

Flat-coated Retriever

Overall Orthopedic View

Says Dr. Kerstetter, "If you were to say to me right now: 'I've got a six-month-old Lab that's lame,' the first things I'd think about would be panosteitis, hip dysplasia, and elbow dysplasia, and will usually diagnose the problem. Now, if you tell me that the problem exists in the front or rear area, I'll nail it down further. Then, we'll proceed: right front end — elbow or shoulder? Usually, we're dealing with one of these orthopedic diseases. Occasionally there are traumatic injuries to the growth plate where your dog might end up with a crooked leg, and sometimes there is a serious bone or joint infection; but those are rare.

"Keep in mind that these developmental orthopedic diseases are predisposed genetically, and certain ones can be further influenced by environmental and nutritional factors. We feel that excess calorie energy can result in too rapid of growth. The role that nutrition plays in the health of the dog is a pretty complex relationship, and one which warrants continual and further study."

Eyes

Canine eyes are plagued with the same problems as human eyes. Although there are cases of glaucoma and cataracts, two eye diseases are of primary concern to the retriever owner. Those are progressive retinal atrophy, (PRA, otherwise known as progressive retinal degeneration, PRD) and retinal dysplasia (RD). PRA is a progressive degenerative eye disease that will worsen as the dog gets older, usually eventually causing blindness. RD, on the other hand, is congenital, meaning that the condition is as bad as it is going to get when the pup is born.

Progressive retinal atrophy can be passed to pups by parents with apparently normal eyes; thus, it is essential to identify such dogs to be able to halt the spread of this disease. As retinal tissue degenerates, it manifests itself in different ways. Some dogs have more trouble with night blindness, others with day blindness, and some simply can't see at all.

In addition, the only diagnostic method available before serious onset of PRA is use of the electroretinogram. In this procedure, the dog is anesthetized and put through a 20- to 30-minute process that is very sensitive and can usually detect PRA. Otherwise, the dog becomes older before symptoms develop, which can also be compounded by the presence of un-related cataracts.

Retinal dysplasia, on the other hand, is not progressive at all. RD is the abnormal development of the retina, or retinal malformation. When primitive layers of the retina don't blend like they should, problems result. With mild RD, there is a slight problem with folds in the inner retinal layer. These dogs may never have compromised vision problems. "Geographic" RD involves larger areas of defective retinal development, and "severe" RD exists when the layers are not together at all and retinal detachment occurs.

With RD, puppies can be checked as early as six to eight weeks for the disease by a certified opthalmologist. However, a re-check is recommended at age six months or older since the pup will be more mature and less likely to wriggle during the exam. The patient has its pupils dilated with drops, then the eye is illuminated and checked for problems. Next, a slit lamp biomicroscope is used, followed by an opthalmoscope. Most retinal problems can be determined during this exam.

In addition, CERF, the Canine Eye Registry Foundation, maintains records on breeds and gives CERF designations to dogs that are free of eye problems. Look for CERF on your puppy's parentage along with OFA and/or PennHIP; if there is no documentation, ask your breeder for an explanation on these things.

Conclusion

There are many means available today to help determine some of the diseases and problems that can plague our canine companions. While even the most careful planning can sometimes result in heartache, it pays to spend the extra effort in doing a little research on the health and soundness of the parentage of your prospective new pup. In addition, thoroughly read any health guarantees or contracts; if there is anything that seems unclear, ask questions before you buy a pup. Waiting until "later" might bring unsatisfactory results. In addition, enlist the help of your local veterinarian. He or she can answer any questions you may have. Most guarantees give 24 to 48 hours for veterinary inspection during which time — if there is a problem detected — the pup can be returned with full reimbursement. ■

Pointer

Love at first sight.

CHAPTER 5

PICKING A PUP

by Steve Smith

THE FIRST DECISION you have to make is what breed you want to go with. That, of course, is the purpose of this entire book, to acquaint you with the various breeds of hunting dogs so you can evaluate and choose. Once you've made your choice, the work starts.

Picking a puppy from a batch of squirming, weeks-old lookalikes is a daunting task, especially for the hunter who will bring the pup into the home to be a valued family member for the next 12 years or more. As a result, a number of sure-fire, puppy-picking techniques regularly become all the rage and then sink into obscurity. It's almost as though some of us ask the pup to pass a multiple-choice exam before he or she can go home with us.

While there are a few things you can do to ascertain the sort of dog your pup will come to be — before he comes to be your pup — the most important task is to pick the litter — the bloodlines possessed by the parents. In fact, it is more important to

pick the litter than to have the pick of the litter.

The dilemma, sleepless nights, and ulcers that arise when picking your puppy can be virtually eliminated if you've done your homework in finding the right breeder. There are reasons to worry when it comes to the "backyard" breeder or an acquaintance who suddenly has a litter of pups on his hands, not the least of which are dogs of poor health with mean temperaments. If you want to enjoy your dog with a minimum of concern, you owe it to the him or her to find a reputable breeder, one who cares about the breed, cares about the puppies, and wants to see them go to good homes.

If you want that dog of yours to shine in the field, make sure you look for good hunting bloodlines, with the sire and dam having either field championships or hunting titles in the pedigree. Elsewhere in this volume is a section dealing specifically with pedigrees. Suffice it to say that instincts and temperament have a way of filtering down through the gene pool.

A new pup in the house will gravitate toward the older dog, no matter the breed or sex.

You may come across a breeder who assures you that, even though his dogs are from show stock, they "really like to hunt." There are some differences between show breeding and hunting-bred dogs. The show dogs tend to be bred for conformation and temperament, while the hunting dogs — though great companions in their own right — usually have more drive. Some might say hunting dogs have almost hyperactive personalities when compared to their show-ring cousins, although that assessment is not fair. Inversely, I have seen a number of show dogs that would and could hunt all day long, do it well, and have to be coaxed back into the truck as the sun went down. All things being equal, however, opt to get a hunting dog pup from hunting dog stock. With some breeds, this is relatively easy because the preponderance of those breeds come from hunting stock or have hunting backgrounds. Others breeds have to be thoroughly investigated.

The process of picking a breeder should be done well in advance of picking the puppy. You may have to wait several months for the litter to be born, but this will give you ample time to shop around and find the right breeder. Above all, don't choose a puppy on impulse — do your homework!

Clubs and organizations, hunting magazines, or full-fledged kennels devoted to a specific breed are great places to start looking. Stay away from the breeder advertising a litter of pups in the paper for $40 each. If your friends have dogs that you like, it may be just a simple matter of going to their breeder and putting your name on the waiting list.

Once you have found a breeder who takes the business of producing, raising, and placing puppies seriously — above just the urge to make money — you should go and meet him or her and see the breeding environment. It's a definite plus if the breeder belongs to some sort of club or organization that is devoted to the breed. This shows that he cares about the betterment of the breed, and that he is constantly gathering information and talking with other retriever fanciers about how to produce the best litters. If you want a hunting bloodline coursing through your pup, then it helps if the breeder can display competent hunting skills in the parents, either through pedigrees, hunting titles, or actual demonstrations with the sire or dam. The breeder, if he or she is raising gun dogs, will often make noise around the pups — bang some pans and rap on the whelping box — as a way of guarding against later gunshyness. He is not trying to frighten the pups, but is guarding against their being fearful later on in life.

The parents of the pup should have certifications for their hips and eyes, and ideally, their hearts too. It's a big plus if you can see both of the parents, not just the bitch. The breeder should even have X-ray copies of the parents' hips so you can see that there is no hip dysplasia. Certifications for hips come from the Orthopedic Foundation for Animals (OFA) or PennHip, and as many generations back as possible should also be OFA certified. Their eyes should be certified against retinal dysplasia and PRA (Progressive Retinal Atrophy) by a veterinary ophthalmologist within the previous year (Canine Eye Research Foundation — CERF — certification). The breeder should also provide a four- to five-generation pedigree for each parent.

The breeding environment should be clean. There is no reason to fear the "outside" litter, but one that will be born, whelped, and raised inside will probably have more human contact. And it is imperative to ask how much human contact the pups will get once born. Though the hunting breeds are genetically predisposed to associating with humans, nothing replaces actual human contact in those first few weeks of life. It is vital that they have the exposure. Also, you can get a good indication as to the temperament of the puppies by looking at the dam. You should almost want to take the mother home — she'll be the best litmus test for the pups.

When the pups are born, the breeder should provide documentation of shot and de-worming records, as well as feeding, training, and care instructions, an AKC, *Field Dog Stud Book*, or UKC registration card, contacts for local clubs, and perhaps magazines or books to help you out. And don't forget a written receipt of sale. You should even be allowed to have 30 days to get the pup examined by a certified veterinarian; if there are problems, get your money back before you get too attached to the dog.

Pups raised together will too often bond with each other rather than their people.

A golden retriever with her pups. The young dogs should leave the litter
at about seven weeks of age for the most successful training.

A tough choice—they're all cute. But which one will hunt the best?

Don't be afraid if you get quizzed as to your candidacy to take one of his pups home — in fact, you want this test. It shows that the breeder cares about where his pups are going. Again, this is going to be true more often with the less-popular breeds. The breeder should ask you what kind of dogs you've had before, what your intentions with the dog are (hunting, show, family, etc.), if the dog will be an inside or outside dog, how much time you plan on spending with the pup — typical nervous parent-type questions. Based on your answers, some breeders will even choose the puppy for you, based on their observations of the litter through the first seven weeks. Though this is fine, it is nice if you can pick him or her out on your own.

When it comes to price, now is not the time to be stingy. Just accept the fact that, varying by state and location, you're going to pay more to the meticulous breeder who has been breeding for good hunting stock. Though you may find cheaper puppies, you pretty much get what you pay for, and you could end up paying more in medical costs over the dog's short-

ened lifetime. Better to fork over the extra $200 or so on the front end. You may have to put a deposit down, and if you're the first to inquire, this could get you pick of the litter. Otherwise, the pick of the litter right will cost you extra.

When the puppies are around five weeks of age, the day arrives when it is time to go pick out your puppy. At this age, the pups are beginning to explore more and are really starting to thrive on human contact. In most cases, you won't be able to take the pup home until at least the seventh week — or 49th day — but you can pick out the pup now.

The first question you need to ask yourself is male or female? Answer that based on your intentions. Though you should be extremely careful in deciding if you want to breed your dog and should not enter into that situation lightly, female dogs carry more responsibility when it comes to having and raising pups. If there are no intentions of breeding, it is recommended that all males be neutered and all females be spayed. Not only will it help control their sexual urges and cycles, it will diminish the occurrences of certain cancers and lead to overall better health for your dog.

Like most species of mammals, males may tend to be more aggressive and females may be a bit more laid-back. Males can be a tad tougher and more high-strung when it comes to training — tougher as in they can take it more — while females may require a more gentle hand. Of course, nothing is set in stone; it's better to pick the sex based on your individual preferences. By and large, though, males will err on the hyper side, females on the relaxed.

When you first see the litter together, they should mob you, absolutely thrilled at the sight of people, and new people at that. But just stand back and observe the pups for a few moments. Is there one in particular that sort of hangs back and doesn't get in the mix? Is there one that is continually shoving his littermates out of the way? You'll want to stay away from the overly-aggressive puppy, and the shy, withdrawn pup hiding in the corner. Look for the one that gets active, but sort of just stares at you.

First look at the puppies' coats, teeth, eyes, ears, and overall appearance. There should be no evidence of any disease or discharge, nor should there be any bald spots, obvious sores, or evidence of any adverse reactions to recent shots.

Next, take a few of the prospects off away from their littermates. Shy away from the puppies that immediately want to return to the whelping box and look distressed in their new surroundings; look for the pups that start to explore their new environment, or are precocious to the point of getting into trouble. Take a duck wing or pheasant tail and tease the puppies with it. Some will immediately be fixated on the feathers and chase it around constantly, even picking it up when you toss it. Other pups will not care one way or the other what's tickling their nose.

To get a *very subjective* idea of how hard the dog will be to train, roll the dog over on his back and hold him down with your hand. The pup that struggles constantly might be one tough cookie when it comes to training; conversely, the pup that immediately lies still with a frightened look could be extremely soft, equally as hard to train as the blockhead. Try to find the pup that struggles for a few seconds and then lies quietly. This dog is indicating that you can use some pressure in training and not frighten the dog, yet you won't have a battle on your hands. Also, carefully pinch the puppy's toes or his ear to see how quickly he'll yip. One that immediately whines could be a soft dog; others will look at you with a, "Is that the best you can do?"

When you pick up the puppy, he shouldn't constantly struggle to get down; instead, he should sit comfortably, content in your presence. Don't expect him to stay that way for too long, but you want to see a little calmness. You also don't want to see the puppy that is constantly biting or growling. Look for the pups that like to hold things or carry them around, and those that respond when you clap your hands or whistle. You should be able to entice a youngster to follow you.

Once you've picked out the dog, you'll have to wait a couple more weeks to take the new family member home. Now is the time to buy puppy supplies, make the veterinary appointments, check back with the breeder to make sure the dog gets the last series of puppy shots from him, and prepare your household for the invasion.

Take a crate to the breeder for the puppy's ride home, sign all necessary forms, and be sure to get that receipt. Make sure the breeder says it's all right to call for questions about the bloodline, breeding, or the puppy in general; but you don't want to be pestering him at every turn. If you've been extremely satisfied in your puppy-choosing experience, then be sure to tell the breeder that you'll give him a good recommendation. That's vital to their operation, and reputable breeders help the breed in general. Don't be surprised to hear that the breeder may call in a few months to see how dog life is treating you.

As indicated earlier, picking the breeder is the trick, not picking the puppy. If you've done your homework thoroughly, have gotten many references and recommendations, and have been impressed with the breeding environment and conditions, then you can just about close your eyes, reach your hand into the box, and pick one out. To paraphrase a close, late friend Gene Hill, you'll end up doing all those puppy selection tests, carefully watching the dogs and selecting the breeder, and then go home with the one that chews on your shoelaces.

What's with those sentence-long names? Yellow Thunder Josie, Jet of Zenith, Magic Marker of Timber Town, Smitty's Rocket Gal, Floodbay's Baron O'Glengarven. Why not just "Roscoe"? Well, part of that stems from the registration process, a need to give each dog its own individuality, instead of being "Abby 92." Most breeders or kennels will attach their kennel name to the dog right on the registration form, with you left to fill in the name of what you'll call the dog. Others leave it entirely up to you. There's really no science or a right or wrong way to do it. Just have fun.

Be sure to register your new pup with the breed registry you feel the most familiar with. There are registries for all the breeds, and the breeder can help you here because you should have received a registration card from the breeder showing that the pup came from a registered litter, that is, a litter conceived by two registered parents. But it's up to you to register the pup as an individual. Simply fill it out and send it in along with the registration fee. You'll receive a card with some puppy information in a couple of weeks.

Tied in with registration is the new idea of tattooing your puppy or inserting a microchip under the dog's skin. Both are done to identify the dog should he become lost. They contain a code that refers to a file in a registry. The microchip, the size of a grain of rice that can be inserted between the shoulder blades when the puppy is seven weeks old, does not have batteries, but it shows up under a scanner. A code in the microchip relates back to the registry, providing information as to the breeder, owner, phone numbers, even feeding schedules in some cases. Talk with your veterinarian about the advantages and disadvantages of each method; however, it is not a requirement that your dog be traced in these ways. A microchip won't fall off like a collar, though, and it will provide some level of comfort if your dog should get lost.

In all, picking a pup is a multi-step proposition:
• choose the breed you want
• choose the breeder
• make sure all is in order in terms of parents' registrations, bloodlines, and health certifications
• pick the sex you want
• pick out the pup
• take the pup home and register him or her
• start the regular health care that will be a regular part of the dog's life

Puppies socialized with humans while still in the litter make the best citizens.

The Hunting Dog Pup at Home

As you walk in the door with the puppy in your arms, pause briefly at the threshold and take a long, last look about you. Your house and indeed your very life will never be the same. Not just because of the toys that you'll trip on or the pup that will always be underfoot or the gobs of dog hair and muddy paw prints, but your home will never again feel as empty, not as long as your new pup lives and breathes, and brings his or her own special character into your life. The squirming puppy in your arms will, from now on, be as much a family member as it is possible for an animal to be, and you will love every minute of it. Well, almost every minute.

This starts the pup's first experience with training and discipline, at least discipline as meted out by someone other than his mother. Here, we should discuss a little canine psychology and social structure. Only recently, geneticists have been able to identify the genes that go together to form this creature we call a dog. What they found was that dogs are actually wolves at the genetic level, Hence, their scientific name was changed from *Canis familiaris* to *Canis lupus familiaris*, *Canis lupus* being the wolf.

Although there are a myriad of species of dog — *canids* — in the world, only the wolf had the sort of social structure, such as it was, that people had developed at the dawn of human history: small family groups, nomadic hunters and opportunists, the rules and behavior patterns dictated and enforced by the dominant male and female — the Alpha pair. It was no wonder, then, that wolf pups readily fell into the ways of human society — it was like their own, the one their genes told them was the best way to survive.

This is a roundabout way of saying that dogs — and especially pups — not only require discipline, they want it. You, throughout the dog's life, will be the alpha animal — unless you abdicate the position and allow the pup to do as he pleases, something neither of you wants. A pup normally wants to please, the same way he or she would want to please their mother, and the same way those *Canis* genes would require them to be subservient to the alpha male or female in the pack. You, quite literally, have become the leader of the pack, and pack leaders maintain their rank and pack order through discipline. Fair and gentle, yet firm, discipline is genetically required by the animal; it is not mean or cruel — only methods are cruel. Making and enforcing rules and being consistent actually comforts the young dog; it makes him

feel at home and in his proper place within this new pack. There's more on this later in this chapter.

The Young and the Restless

For the first four or five weeks after you bring him or her home from the breeder, the pup has three things that he must learn: that the inside of your house is not his bathroom (housebreaking), what "no" means, and his name. During that time, you should also mold his desire to retrieve, bond with him, and let him explore and be a puppy. However, the housebreaking and "no" command are vital if you are to enjoy your pup, and if he is to enjoy you. The act of learning his or her name will come in time, provided you are constantly using it and helping him understand that his name means you want his attention. For instance, instead of saying, "Good boy," when he does something right, say, "Good Roscoe," or "Good Maggie."

After setting the new family member down on the floor, you will be in a constant state of readiness for the slightest indication of the puppy's full bladder. If the little rascal is ever going to be trusted in the house, the pup is going to have to learn to go to the bathroom outside, the all-important lesson of housebreaking. Though it may not seem like it at first, the pup will eventually learn that a full bladder means go to the door. Just be patient.

Housebreaking a puppy is easier if you train yourself to recognize the signs. Watch for the pup that suddenly becomes uninterested in a chew toy, perhaps starts exploring a little too eagerly, or just abruptly looks uncomfortable. Puppies sniffing the floor, especially in a circular motion, are good candidates for going outside quickly, as are those little scoundrels that all of a sudden just disappear as if they are on a secret mission; they are.

There is no use in dragging the pup back to the dirty deed and shoving his nose in it if you haven't caught him in the act. The older dogs become, the more they'll remember; for now, they can't get the hang of their name, much less remember that they wet the floor 10 minutes ago. So if you stumble upon the scene of the crime, accept the blame for not keeping an eye on the pup or taking him outside after he was done roughhousing.

However, if you see the precursors to a puppy having to relieve himself, scoop him up while you say, "Outside!" There may not be time for you to snap a leash on him, but don't worry — at this age, you can usually run him down if he starts to scamper away.

Don't let him back in the house until he goes to the bathroom, and when he does go, praise him thoroughly. He has to learn that as soon as he goes, he gets to come back in; the longer he holds it, the longer he has to be out there. Incidentally, this a very good reason why housebreaking in the winter usually takes less time than in the summer: if the pup is freezing his bare belly off, he'll hurry up so he can go back in the warm house; if it's warmer, he'll want to explore more. Also, as you pick the dog up to take him outside, be careful not to lift on his tummy, or you'll be treated to a warm surprise down your leg.

While the pup is doing his business, try adding some commands. Saying, "Hurry up!" as he is urinating, or, "Go potty!" will eventually make the dog relieve himself on command. This is very useful on trips, if you and the dog are staying at a hotel, or when the mercury dips dangerously low and you're freezing. You should notice how once he gets his toes in the grass he seems to settle in, maybe wiggling around a bit. Once you see him start to get comfortable, the evacuation will follow — this is a good time to tell him, "Hurry up!" and soon you'll be able to stimulate that sensation simply by the command. It's a nifty trick and can save a lot of time in strange places when the dog is more interested in the smells about him instead of bodily functions.

If you catch the pup in the act of going on the floor, now is the time for a scolding. Grasp the pup gently by the scruff of the neck, reprimand with a sharp, "No!" and gently shake her, repeating, "No!" There is no need to swat her behind — a scolding and a gentle shake will get the message across. Quickly take the pup outdoors while you say, "Outside," again, and stay out there with her until she finishes or goes again, praising her when she finishes.

In addition to recognizing the signs of when a puppy has to go, you should understand the times when he'll probably have to empty his bladder. The old saying that puppies are nothing more than a hollow tube you pass food through is very true. Almost immediately after mealtime, take the dog outside. What is your first stop when you get up in the morning? It should be the pup's, too, and that goes for after midday naps. If the pup has been quite active for a while — chasing the tennis ball, another dog, or tearing into a rubber chew toy — chances are he's going to have to go when he starts to calm down or gets on his feet. Tell him, "Outside," or whatever command you want to use to tell him it's time to go out to the bathroom; be consistent, though, and use the same command every single time you take him outdoors.

Don't get used to the notion that you're going to bring the puppy home and be able to sleep through the entire night. He or she is simply not going to be able to hold it that long. About every two hours, you're going to need to take her outside, even if she hasn't woke up already. Set the alarm for every two or three hours for the first week or so, wake her up, and take her out, repeating the "outside" command. At first, she might want to play when you bring her back indoors, but she'll soon learn that nighttime is the time to restore the energy she'll need to plague you during daylight.

As the pup gets older, start moving the nighttime bathroom breaks back a half hour. Then an hour. Soon, after about two weeks, you might only have to take the little rascal out once or twice. Be sure to always let him go outside if he gets up himself and starts whining — he may have to go again, or his bladder just didn't take three hours to fill up. It's imperative that whenever the dog whines or is trying to get your attention about an impending bladder release, that you get up and take him out. This is precisely what you want him to do — get your attention. You don't want to ignore him or tell him to shut up and go back to sleep.

But how do you recognize the difference between "full bladder" whines, and "I-want-to-get-up-in-your-bed-and-play" whines? That takes practice, and every dog is different. Some puppies will absolutely insist that they sleep with you, others will be more nocturnal than bats. With repetition and practice, you'll eventually switch the dog to your schedule. But for now, remember that this puppy just got separated from his mother and littermates, and is in a strange home with strange people and strange smells. The first thing he'll bond to will be another dog (if you have one), and then you. Therefore, it makes sense that when the lights go out and everything gets quiet, he might get scared and want to be near you. Use your discretion as to how much of this aid and comfort you want to give, but realize that the more you give him, the more it will take to break him of it.

Puppies that don't seem to get the hang of being able to hold it until they go outside may be indicating that there's another problem, in particular a bladder infection. This is when the dog feels like he has to go all the time — and usually does. Look for the early signs of a dog that is constantly squatting, even if nothing is coming out. This condition can be cleared up a visit to the vet.

Housebreaking takes time. You need to be patient, and always be consistent in your discipline, praise, and commands. Always use, "No!" when scolding, and repeat, "Outside!" whenever the pup goes to the door, makes the telltale signs, or finishes with one of the aforementioned events that usually culminates in a full-court evacuation. And when the dog goes outside, be sure to tell him how wonderful he or she is.

Puppies will eventually understand; in the meantime, it is wise to have a selection of carpet cleaners within close reach for those times when he — or you — wasn't quick enough. Check to see if the carpet cleaner is colorfast or will bleach the carpet if you forget about wiping it up right away. In most pet food aisles of the grocery store, there are carpet cleaners specifically designed for the new dog owner, with formulas that work magic not only on your carpet, but also on the smell. You should also find cleaners or odor protectors for the adult dog smell.

While your new puppy is learning the ins and outs of the house, her new family, and this housebreaking thing, you'll start to fear the she's going to think her name is "No." That will be the one word that you will use more than any other in the first few months of dog ownership, yet it is the one word she must learn — and quickly. "No" will stop her from biting, chewing, wetting, barking, yapping, yowling, digging, destroying, leg-humping, and otherwise being a menace to society.

You want to be firm when you say, "No." Stare the dog down and bark the command. If the little ingrate is biting the hand that feeds him, grab his lower jaw, shake it, and say, "No!" Lifting the dog off all fours is also a good way to get the message across that you mean business. A dog likes to have his paws on something, to have some sort of foothold. If you take that away from him, he'll freeze and stiffen, and usually, his ears will open up. He'll begin to stop doing the things that will lead to him being off his feet. However, this will get more difficult as your dog starts to put on weight.

The feeling of grass between their toes urges pups to do their business.
Using the same spot speeds housebreaking.

When pups are around, the lifespan of shoes and boots shortens dramatically.

Puppy-Proofing

Much the same way you may have had to "baby-proof" your home, you'll have to "puppy-proof" it. Closing the door behind you will be the most important thing you can do to keep the puppy out of trouble. Trouble not only means the dog getting into things you don't want destroyed — slippers, papers, your dirty laundry — it also means he's safe from the things that can harm or kill him — poisons, detergents, antifreeze, medicines, sharp or hot objects. And whenever you close the door behind you, not only make sure you didn't shut the puppy inside, make sure that it latched. I almost lost a dog — not even a puppy — to a box of rat poison because I thought I had pulled a garage door tight, when in fact, I hadn't checked to be sure. She pushed it open with her nose and ate the poison. That's the day she was introduced to Mr. Stomach Pump at the vet's office.

Other barricades that are effective are pet gates or baby gates. These come in all shapes and sizes, and they are indispensable for keeping the dog in or out of a room. They especially are useful in a stairway, keeping him upstairs or down in the basement. But realize that some stubborn dogs will not be deterred by a simple gate. Some will lunge over the top; others will chew right through. Use the gate as a form of control, but include times when you can let the dog wander on his own or go into a room (with you) that he's normally not allowed in. If he's always kept out of a certain area and not taught the proper way to behave in those places, then he'll always be a puppy when it comes to that room (or wandering the house). In order for him to behave well with freedom, he has to experience freedom.

A Place of His Own

That being said, though, leaving a new puppy free in the house while you leave is, of course, nonsense; some dogs will take years of proving themselves before you can trust them to behave themselves without supervision. And the best way to confine the dog when you leave is with a kennel or crate.

These literally come in all shapes and sizes, but if you think you'll do any kind of traveling with your dog, be sure to get one that is airline approved. They will have more secure fastenings on the side instead of just simple latches that can be easily removed or unfastened. Unless you want to buy a different-sized crate for each size the puppy grows to, buy the one he'll fit in as an adult.

I'm sure you've heard the all-important dog training rule of never using the crate as a form of punishment. You want the pup to enjoy going into his kennel, to see it as his little "bedroom" or his "place." Every time you go somewhere and have to put him in, you don't want him cowering in the corner; if you use the crate in a callous manner, that's exactly how he'll react when you move him toward it.

A way to get him to enjoy his kennel is to feed him in it. Leave the door open, but place his food in there. Toss treats in there for him to run in and get. He'll soon learn to associate the crate with something he craves — food. Leave the crate in an accessible area so that when he starts chewing on a toy, you can direct him there; or if he falls asleep, gently pick him up and place him in his kennel — with the door open. As you progress, close the door, then eventually latch it. You can use the kennel at nighttime, provided it's not tucked away in a basement far away from the ones he loves. Putting him in his kennel when you travel — something all dogs grow to love — will help him to understand that the kennel can mean good things. And every single time you put him in his crate or if he goes in on his own, say, "Kennel," or whatever command you want to use.

Whatever you do, be sure to let a quiet puppy out of his kennel, and ignore one yapping his head off. He must not be allowed to think he can bully you into doing what he wants.

Sometimes, no matter what we do, the crate is going to seem like punishment. Some days, the little yahoo is more than we can handle, and so we stick him or her in the crate so we can get a little peace and quiet. If he's been on a tear — having one of those days — there's hardly any way to put the pup away in his place without having it look like punishment. Just remember to crate him with a cheerfulness that you don't feel. His crate should be a good place.

Make sure you put the crate in someplace warm, especially for little puppies. Don't leave it out on an unheated porch in January in the North; conversely, don't leave it in the only non-air-conditioned room in the house. Keep the climate mild for the dog. And while the pup is young, try to keep the crate in an area where he can see you when he's in there. At first, he'll be quite noisy because he'll want to be with you; only when he quiets down should you let him out.

Your puppy will shred any bedding you put in with him or her, be it a towel, kennel pad, or blanket; that's just a fact of life. That leaves the hard kennel

A pup asleep where he dropped—exhausted from play.

floor. Usually when you buy your kennel crate, there will be thin foam kennel pads available as well. Be mindful, though: puppy pee will soak right through, and unless you want to keep washing it, it might be best to remove it until the puppy has displayed some degree of bladder control. Until then, lining the bottom with newspapers will make some of the inevitable cleanup faster.

It's a good idea to leave a chew toy in there with the dog so he has something to play with. If there's nothing with him, he'll turn those puppy teeth to something else — in a bad case exemplified once again by our wonderful model pup, her own leg. She gnawed on her foot, developing a nasty sore that had to be treated by a veterinarian.

Partitioning off half the kennel will help in house-breaking. When the pup starts to view the crate as home, she won't want to soil it anymore than you'd want her to. If she has room to roam in there, she'll simply go in the corner; if it's blocked off, she'll have to lay in it. Dogs will learn how unpleasant that is

very quickly. To block off half the kennel, wedge in a piece of wood. You can also use a box or a milk crate, but the puppy may flip these over, either on herself or trapping him over on the other side. Something sturdy and firm that can stand up to puppy pressure — and that you don't mind if it gets chewed — will work. This, in effect, shrinks the size of the crate, so if the dog goes in the crate, it's all over him or her. Dogs are normally clean creatures and dislike being near their own waste, so they'll hold it. Listen to the pup's yammering, and determine of she's bored or has to go outside. Crates really help with housebreaking.

Crates are indispensable travel companions. It's nice to put her in there with a toy. The riding will be more comfortable for her, and she won't bounce back and forth or be thrown forward too hard if you have to hit the brakes. Be careful about leaving one in an open-bed pickup truck. Make sure it is strapped down somehow so it doesn't slide around, and be mindful that objects on the road may fly around and hit the dog in the crate.

That First Night

Ah, it's finally bedtime for the hooligan, his first night's sleep in his new home. You've got to be bushed. Time to crash and call it a night just so you can get up in the morning and do it all over again. I certainly hope you don't think it will be as easy as drifting off to thoughts of your little misfit all grown up and bringing back a pheasant, catching a Frisbee, or launching himself off a dock. It won't be that easy.

Though I already addressed some of the housebreaking issues you'll have to deal with at nighttime, there are also the sleeping arrangements that must be reconciled. And be careful — puppies that seem to take weeks to understand their name, months to grasp the meanings of *sit* and *stay*, and never quite get the hang of roll over, will learn, in absolutely Guinness Book material time, that if they whine once, they get to come up on the bed with you. If you don't mind the adult dog sprawling out on the bed next to you, then by all means, let the puppy sleep there. But as soon as the pup sleeps there once, you'll be astonished at how quickly he'll insist on sleeping there permanently.

So, you must decide where you want the adult dog to sleep, and begin there with the pup. If you're going to require that to be in his crate in the basement, then start there. But here's fair warning: because he's not going to be near you, he'll work those vocal cords to the max, and you'll be amazed at how long the pup will be able to stay awake. It will take much longer for him to sleep through the entire night. What most people prefer is to have their dogs sleep on the floor in their bedroom. If that's the case, then bring his crate in there with you. When he can hear and smell you, he'll settle down much quicker; if you already have an adult dog on the bedroom floor, put his/her blanket or pad next to the puppy's crate. And, as mentioned before, you'll be able to hear when nature calls and he has to go.

There are myriad types of dog nests and pads on the market, available through all of the hunting, outdoor, or pet supply catalogs. Though you probably won't want to trust a puppy to sleep on one until he's housebroken, it's a good idea to let older dogs have one. Not only will it be more comfortable, it will provide a haven for them to go and lie down throughout the day, much the same way you tried to instill that "den" attitude about their crate when they were small.

The pads with a tough, Cordura-like covering will resist teeth a bit longer than some of the cotton blend ones. Some other covers are made of corduroy, fleece, denim, or other materials. Always take into consideration how the pad will feel in the extremes of temperature. You don't want him sleeping in something he's going to cook him in the summertime, and something that will quickly get cold in the winter. Most covers are washable, and you will usually be able to buy replacement covers should the pup chew or soil it beyond saving. Choose a color that means you won't be constantly staring at dog hair — dark for dark dogs, light for light dogs. The hair is still there; you just won't see it.

Inside the pad will be the stuffing. Some brands will have the lining itself inside another bag so that you can wash the cover; other brands allow you to put the entire pad in the washing machine. Stuffing comes in the form of cotton/polyester batting, cedar shavings, Styrofoam beads, foam mats like the kennel pad, or a combination of things. While the batting and cedar mix is usually cheaper, cedar can hold odor a bit longer, and the bed will quickly flatten under your dog. The Sytrofoam beads will bounce back to shape, providing a fluffier nest longer, but they are usually more expensive. Gauge your choice based on price, how often you think the dog will use it, and aesthetics.

You may want to stay away from the nests that look almost like dog boxes or beds, the kind with a raised rim around most of it. Dogs like to sprawl out when they sleep, and unless you can find one big enough to accommodate a stretched out 75-pound dog, stick with the traditional pad and let the dog sleep in whatever fashion suits him. On hot days especially, you may find that he likes to have half his body on the pad with his head and neck on the cool linoleum floor.

Itchy Teeth

You certainly don't want your new little charge to make a toy out of your antique coffee table. In fact, while he is young, it might be better to put that antique coffee table in a room where he can't get at it. But the best way to give those puppy teeth something to sink into, besides your hand, is to shower him with toys. The more options he has, the more he'll stick with the toys instead of moving on to the furniture or carpeting.

Dog supply catalogs look like a Toys-R-Us store for canines. There is just about every kind of toy imaginable: those that help the dog's teeth, those that help his breath, rubber, plastic, cloth, fleece, balls, Frisbees, stuffed animals, the list goes on. There is really no science to picking a toy — some your dog will cherish and carry around like a security blanket, others he'll never touch. Most are made of material that, should you have a destructive chewer on your hands and he swallows portions of it, will just pass right through his system. Still, you'll need to monitor his chewing and toss out things that he's seriously tearing into. No matter what you choose, it's hard to go wrong — it all depends on the size of your dog and to what sort of chewer he is.

Toys will help keep a bored puppy occupied, especially if he has to be in his crate for any length of time. Some toys will have cavities where you can place a dog treat, and the pup will spend the next hour or so absolutely obsessed with getting it out. This is a great way to occupy him when guests are over and you need a dog-free zone for a while.

If you have a retriever pup, you can — and should — also use the toy to start to introduce the game of fetch. You can toss anything to her and start to coax her back to you with it, but tennis balls and fleece toys work the best. If you want to have that dog of yours be a reliable retriever, then you should never

play tug-of-war with her toy. If she thinks that giving the object to you turns into a game, then you'll soon be fighting over a prized duck or pheasant. Whenever the puppy has something that you want, gently pry her mouth open — or tickle the back of her tongue with your finger — while you say, "Give," or "Release," whatever you choose; I've seen some trainers use, "Thank-you," as they take the object from the dog. Then praise her lavishly when she gives it up. Soon the pup will learn that if you throw it so she can chase it, and if she brings it back to you, you'll throw it again so she can chase it again, then you've got a game on your hands and have started a retriever down the right road. Soon, she'll be spitting out the ball in your direction for you to throw again.

The supposed indestructible rubber kongs and their variations are great toys for puppies; those with small protuberances, grooves, and edges will itch gums and clean teeth. And they'll usually last a long time. Choose a size that's right for the pup's age, one that he can carry around into his kennel, onto his pad, or to a favorite sunspot on the carpet.

The retrieving urge is genetic in golden retrievers, even as pups.

Be mindful of the toys that have noise-makers inside. If a pup is chewing on a fleece-shaped bone and it squeaks, he'll be fixated on finding out what exactly is making that noise. Some dogs will simply chew the toy and make it squeak (and drive you crazy); others will not rest until they've ripped the toy open and exposed the innards. Make sure you choose your toy wisely; you don't want to have to supply him with a fresh one every few days.

Some toys that look good at first but usually evolve into something stinky and slimy are the chewable rawhides and rope toys. They start off nice, but soon they dissolve into a blackening mass or a soggy lump of some unidentifiable substance. If you don't mind seeing it around the house, then these toys will captivate a youngster's interest, especially the rawhides. Be forewarned, though: if you walk around barefooted and step on one, it's an unforgettable experience.

The Alpha Concept

Although you chose wisely and didn't pick the most dominant puppy in the litter, you'll still need to establish the pecking order of the household. As alluded to at the beginning of this chapter, dogs are pack animals, with chains of command, the leader being the Alpha dog. You are the Alpha, the dog's leader. The quicker you establish this, the easier training will be, and the quicker the dog will bond with you. Now is not the time to try to negotiate with the animal. He must respect your leadership and follow; he'll enjoy a battle of wills as much as you do — which is to say, not much at all.

Signs that point to a dog that thinks he is dominant over you are: growling when you come near, aggressive biting as you try to pet him, ignoring you (once he knows his name and some commands, of course), and just an overall stubborn attitude. These avoidance behaviors manifest themselves in other ways: yawning, looking away, rolling on the ground and fighting a leash, head-shaking, and more. If you get the feeling that he is trying to manipulate you in some way, don't be fooled and think, "Isn't that cute how he keeps nudging my hand to be petted?" He telling you, "Hey, I didn't say you could stop petting me!" You need to do things on your terms, not the dog's.

Introduction to the leash.

Therefore, you'll need to establish that you're the leader. You don't want the dog to be completely submissive to the point of being unable to work with or have him cowering in the corner. This will happen if you try to establish your dominance with force. You need to use commanding yet calm forms of leadership, ones that don't frighten the dog into thinking he's going to be hurt. He needs to feel he can trust you to ensure his survival.

One of the best ways to establish that things will happen on your terms is at mealtime. First of all, feed the dog after you've eaten. While the puppy is feeding, get down on all fours with him. Pet him, talk to him, and above all, don't let him growl or bite at you when you get near his food. If he should do this, command, "No!" in a loud voice and take his food away. You should be able to get to the point where you can open his mouth up and physically take the food out of his jaws with him letting you. Sticking your head near the bowl and making sounds like you're eating also works; escalate that maneuver into taking the bowl from him and pretending to eat it all yourself. He should sit by and watch patiently for you to finish or give it back to

him. If he starts to bite at you or barge his way in, you'll have a fight on your hands. A dog that nips or acts threatening to people when food is around is not to be tolerated. Everybody these days knows a good lawyer, and you have no guarantee the dog won't someday chomp down on a visitor or a child.

But don't expect too much early on. Remember, he's just been competing with his littermates at mealtime. Expect some competition at first. What you don't want is an aggressive, mean puppy demanding his food back.

If you already have another dog in the house, one that you've established dominance over, then watch what that adult dog does to the puppy. And above all, let the older dog establish its dominance over the youngster. There may be some nasty moments as things get sorted out — don't worry. Unless you have real reason to fear that the older dog will seriously harm the puppy, let them sort it out. The older dog will realize how small and fragile the puppy is and won't do anything to severely hurt him. A right smart nip, judiciously administered, usually gets everyone on the same page of the playbook.

Final acceptance—after a struggle.

75

Making your pup listen to you, keeping him or her in one place for a period of time, always going through a doorway before her, crating when necessary, and various postures will establish that you are the leader. Getting down on all fours and placing your neck over the pup's and giving a soft growl is a dominance move; if the puppy fights you and tries to get out from under you, be careful. Those teeth and nails are sharp! Once the puppy sits there and accepts you over her, you're on your way to being Alpha.

Another move that helped with our puppy, and one that we tried when picking her out, was rolling her onto her back. If the puppy fights nonstop with you, be prepared. We actually grabbed our puppies throat in our teeth — gently! — and growled. She held still instantly. That is a dominance move that all canids understand, even if they've never experienced before. It harkens back to the time when their wolf ancestors were establishing pack order. Holding the dog's throat in your teeth and growling says, "I've got you right where I want you, and all I have to do is close my jaws." If you do it properly, you'll find the puppy will hold still instantly.

If you establish the pecking order early, you'll find very few instances when you'll have a combative dog on your hands. As the pup matures, he'll test you to see what he can get away with, and you may have to reinforce your leadership role; but the dog should immediately remember that you're the boss. And the dog that has been correctly taught the subordinate role will not be a submissive pile of jelly. He'll love having his job! He'll have less to worry about, less that he'll feel he has to do to ensure survival. He'll accept training in a manner that says, "What can I learn next?" instead of, "Oh no, not this again!" The more you instill in your dog the feeling that he can trust you to keep him healthy and occupied, the more you'll establish yourself as the leader.

Socialization

Nothing is worse than taking your young dog over to a friend's house and spending the entire time apologizing for his behavior. Sure, new puppies will be handfuls, but there will be a point when the behavior is obnoxiously bad. For this reason, you need to properly socialize your dog — with other dogs, people, and environments. Socialization is simply teaching the dog how to behave in human society — how to comfortably and confidently live in your world.

This is done in one simple way: include your dog in everything! Take him places, let him explore, let him feel his way through his new world. And at first, it's important to let the pup experience these new things on his turf — bring your friends and other dogs to him. As he starts to get bolder, then take him to new places. Insist that your friends don't let the puppy get away with things you don't want him to do at home, especially biting. But also be sure they reprimand him the same way that you would. That is another way for the dog to understand that he is not the leader in your absence, that other people are also dominant over him.

Playtime with other dogs is invaluable. You want the pup to be able to romp with other dogs and not have every encounter with another animal turn into a brutal fight. The best way to ensure this doesn't happen is by exposing him or her to plenty of other dogs, especially those her age. Supervise him or her to be sure they don't get hurt or that two curious pups don't get into something harmful; but just let them play.

Puppy obedience classes are an excellent venue for socializing your dog, as most of these are gatherings of people and their dogs with little strict training. As the pup matures, there are Canine Good Citizen tests, where dogs will be expected to behave in the presence of strangers and other dogs. If your dog is intended for the show-ring or field trial work, getting along with other dogs is imperative. Once, while judging a hunt test, I had to ask a handler to pick up his dog because it was more intent on fighting with the dog he was supposed to be honoring than the task at hand; it ruined the handler's day, and it didn't do much for the owner of the innocent-victim dog, either. For now, though, just get the puppy acquainted with the great big world around him.

Now is also the time to expose the pup to different surroundings, especially to water if it's a retrieving or versatile breed. Be sure that the ice didn't just melt when you take him for his first swim. You always want the water to be a positive experience.

When the water is warm enough, at least 50 degrees or warmer, take him down to the shore and just let him romp. He'll soon wader into the water. He'll probably jump back at first, unsure of what that stuff is, but the more you show him how fun it is to be in there, you soon won't be able to keep him out. If you have an older dog that loves the water, take that one along — dogs readily learn by example.

Always let the dog go in on his own; never pick him up by the scruff and toss him in. Put on some waders or boots and go out into the water, coaxing him to come in after you. He'll probably just sit there and stare at you, so take one of his toys, one that he absolutely cannot resist. Tease him with it, splash the water, do whatever it takes to get him to come to you, but let him come on his own. At first, the pup will only go as far as he can go and still touch bottom. Once he realizes that the water won't hurt him, he'll run and play in the water as long as he can still touch bottom.

Now is when you get him to use those legs to keep him afloat. If the pup is pretty proficient at chasing things you throw for him, toss his toy in the water and let him get it. Keep tossing it farther until he eventually has to swim for it. Now is when a slight nudge off his feet into deeper water is not harmful, provided that the dog already likes the water when he can touch bottom. He'll have a terrified look on his face the first time he's pumping those legs to stay afloat, but with plenty of praise and congratulations, he'll quickly think it's fun. Once he's done that, he'll be busting through the waves for a swim.

The pup will look like a carp out of water at first, probably flogging the water with the front paws and swimming almost vertically. Don't worry; he'll settle down into a champion swimmer. Some dogs won't get

the hang of it quickly, though. You can't take a dog to swimming class, but you can just give him plenty of exposure to water and let him figure it out on his own.

When the pup is little, you also want to get him used to being groomed, in particular around his toes, his ears, and his mouth; the vet will be looking at those things during regular checkups, and you want a cooperative animal — so does the vet! Very gently, stick your fingers in his mouth and rub his gums and hold his teeth. Don't do anything to cause pain or anxiety. A puppy comfortable with your hands in his mouth will let you clean his teeth much easier. You'll get those fingers of yours bitten fairly regularly at first, but the pup should be getting used to being touched on his lips and guns.

Also, gently rub the fur between his toes. Dogs will naturally be ticklish there, but you don't want him to be dancing around when you come at him with scissors to trim the flowing, uncontrollable hair, or toenail clippers when he needs them. The younger he gets used to having his feet and other groomable areas touched, the easier it will be to keep him looking nice.

Meeting the neighbor.

A golden fulfilling its destiny.

Introduction to feathers—the earlier the better.

If the pup is to be a bird-hunting companion, then you also want to introduce him or her to feathers. These can be in the form of duck wings or pheasant tails, frozen pigeons that you've shot, or birds you've brought back from a hunt. Let the pup experience the tickly feathers in her mouth, toss a frozen pigeon for her and let her tussle over it. As long as you don't let her sit down and completely devour something with feathers on it, you're laying a good foundation for later exposure to birds.

Oh the Weater Outside Is Frightful

Although it's been established that our hunting dog breeds are people dogs and just won't be entirely happy unless they're at your feet, there may be a variety of reasons that you must have your dog outside. You could be allergic to pet dander, your landlord may frown upon an inside dog but not mind one in a kennel, or you may have too many precious things to trust around an excited, thrashing lead pipe of a tail.

The outside kennel the dog will stay in should give him at least 10 to 20 feet of room to trot around in, and have a concrete floor that is sloped. This will help in cleaning up, but it will also keep soil-born bugs and mites from infesting the dog. There should also be some form of shade, either in the form of a dog house or a kennel cover, and the fencing should be at least five to seven feet high — you'd be amazed at how well these dogs can climb. And above all, have a padlock on the kennel door. There are thieves out there, and most of our gun dig breeds are not the greatest at recognizing dangerous people.

You must have ample water available to the outside dog, as he will probably drink more if he's constantly in the sunshine and heat. Not having sweat glands, dogs cool by breathing on through the nose and out through the mouth, depending upon moisture in both to carry away excess heat through evaporative cooling. You drink when you're thirsty; dogs drink when they're hot and thirsty. If you use a pail, clip the handle to the chain link with a fastener so that it won't get tipped over by the dog. In the winter, you may have to switch to an electronic dog watering system, one that has an internal heating mechanism so that the water doesn't freeze.

If you make the commitment to have a dog but need/want him to be outside, you must not neglect him in times of weather extremes. Pay attention to the pet warnings on the local news or radio broadcasts. In cases of extreme hot or cold temperatures, they'll recommend bringing any outside pets into the house. You can usually throw his blanket or kennel pad into the basement and keep him down there; if he has some house manners, you should be able to trust him in the house with you. Just always be mindful of the weather, and realize that when *Canis familiaris* was domesticated, he lost touch with much of the physiological and behavioral traits and characteristics that helped him survive in the wild.

Order Are Orders

I already went over how to introduce some commands, in particular "outside," "hurry up," "no," "kennel," and "give." Your pup is going to be mobbed with orders and commands throughout his formative weeks; don't expect him to start learning them until you begin to train specifically for those commands. For instance, don't expect the pup to plop the tennis ball in your lap at eight-weeks of age the first time you say, "Give."

However, you can begin to lay the foundation for those commands before you begin to specifically train for them. Say, "Give" each time you take something from the dog's mouth, with a prying open of the jaws if necessary; command, "Sit" each time it looks as though the dog is going to sit on his own; say, "Stay" if the pup is just sitting by himself and staying there. Whenever you place the dog in his crate, say, "Kennel," so that when you begin to train for that particular command, the word is familiar to him. Whenever the dog bounds toward you, say, "Come," or "Here." In all instances, be consistent and use the same word each time, and make sure that other family members also use the same words.

Above all, you must have patience when it comes to getting the dog to follow your orders. If you're quick to lose your temper, then you shouldn't have brought a dog into your life. Dogs, especially puppies, will test that temper at every turn; they'll make you understand just exactly what patience is all about.

To create an effective gun dog, the handler must have ultimate control.

Repetition is how you eventually win the battle; getting angry and flying off the handle at a dog that doesn't know what you mean by "come" will set him back and hurt his chances for understanding. There will be times for discipline and a scolding, but above all, patience and repetition will win out.

To help come training time, make sure you get the desired behavior out of the dog when you're first introducing him to the commands. This is also a good way to further establish your dominance. But if the pup has a ball, and you say, "Give," and hold out your hand and then let the puppy just wander off with the ball, you're laying the foundation for a tough training regime. When you say, "Give," even if the puppy has never heard the word before, open his mouth for him and take the toy, praising him when you have it. Every time you say, "Sit," don't let the pup walk away as if he has better things to do than to listen to you. Make him sit. You don't have to be mean about it, just demand compliance. But in that demand, remember that the puppy has no idea what those words mean. You are laying a foundation of commands so that he'll recognize, even if just slightly, the words when we begin to train.

Retriever breed or pointing breed, retrieving is important and using toys and playtime when they're puppies to bring out and mold that training instinct is invaluable. You may find it difficult to get the pup to come back to you once you toss a toy. He may pick it up and go somewhere else, lie down and chew on it, or just ignore it.

When you first toss it, let him chase it madly, but say the command you'll later use to release him for a retrieve. This could be, "Fetch," or her name. To get him to come back to you, keep whistling, clapping, calling his name, saying, "Come!" while you move into a different room, out of sight. Most often, the pup will come tearing around the corner to see where you've gone, and most often, he won't have the object with him. That's okay — once you get a few puppy retrieves out of him and praise him lavishly, he'll start to learn that he needs to keep the object with him when he comes to see you. But moving out of sight will help get the pup back on his feet and running to you. Also, if he is attached to his kennel or has an otherwise "favorite spot" that he always runs to with his toy, get between him and that spot. That way, he'll scamper right at you on the return trip; you can scoop him up, praise him, and keep the game going.

Even if you don't have plans on hunting the pup and aren't worried about gunshyness, you should get him used to loud noises. This will help especially when a thunderstorm rages outside or the neighbor kids are shooting off firecrackers. To accustom the pup to loud noises, make the noises go hand-in-hand with something he likes, i.e., his food or his toys. While he's gobbling up dinner or chewing his fuzzy guy, clap your hands once or twice and then praise him; escalate to banging a pan or slamming a cupboard door. Do it only once or twice; he doesn't need to feed to a cacophony of pans, doors, and applause. If you do plan on hunting him, eventually escalate the noise level to firing a blank pistol far away from the dog, and gradually move closer to him, and incorporate loud noises when you play fetch with him. Whatever you do, never frighten a pup with loud noises — don't wake him up with a stomp on the floor, sneak up on him from behind and pop a balloon, or pound on his crate with him inside.

The Inner Creature

It goes without saying that you must always have clean, cool water available. But the question of what to feed a dog is one of the most controversial topics in the dog world, mainly because there is a lot of money to be made by the various companies; the pet-food business is a several-billion dollar annual enterprise.

First, understand that gun dogs fall into the category of large breed. Specific dog food companies are now starting to categorize their blends into large breed, small breed, senior dog, and so on. For the most part, any of the commercial brands on the market have proven themselves time and again. Brands such as Purina, Pedigree, Sunshine Mills, and others have been widely accepted by pet owners, and most have been developed and thoroughly tested by veterinarians and scientists. It is hard to go wrong in following the different blends and feeding schedules for your dog's age and weight.

Some of the more expensive foods — Eukanuba, Iams, and Science Diet to name a few — may have blends that are more specialized; for instance, a puppy large breed formula. Some are designed for hunting and active dogs, those that require a bit more protein during their active times.

When it comes to dry versus canned dog food, I've found that dry food produces firmer stools and cleaner teeth. For small puppies, it is important that you soften dry food with warm water because their tiny teeth and jaws are not strong enough to crunch the kibble yet. Mixing canned with dry food is also a good way to soften the food and make it easier to go down the hatch.

The biggest food controversy comes on a couple of topics. First is the question of whether a puppy formula will cause the dog to grow too fast, thereby causing bone and joint problems. There is some scientific basis for these claims, especially for the large breed dogs. And a diet especially high in protein can be a factor in these developmental problems, as well as too much calcium and other nutrients. But many foods have formulas that are balanced for all puppy breeds, with adjusted feeding rates depending on how big the dog will reach at maturity.

Another hot topic is the theory that poor food causes skin and allergy problems. Though this has been hard to pin down with scientific evidence, the dog's diet should not be ruled out as a cause in a dog suffering an allergic reaction to something.

It is important that you get as much information as possible when it comes to the proper nutrition for your dog. Don't just limit your conversation to veterinarians, though they do have the most experience dealing with all kinds of dogs and food. But lifelong dog owners are a fountain of information, as is the Internet and the different dog food companies themselves. (Don't worry — most will not just try to sell you their particular brand but will have useful information.) As far as nutrients and food ingredients are concerned, you first want to look at the protein. For an active large-breed dog, the range for an adult should be somewhere between 21 to 26 percent, depending on the season (more during active times; less in the off-season). You can switch to a higher-protein diet come hunting season when the dog is older, but don't overload a puppy with protein. A pup that seems to be growing unbelievably fast could be developing structural problems as a result.

Remember: dogs are omnivores, but particularly carnivores. Therefore, don't insist that he become a vegetarian; look at the animal matter contents of the food as these provide most of the amino acids necessary, remembering that the first ingredient listed is the largest by volume in the blend. There should be at least a few different animal products (lamb, chicken, beef, fish) in the food, balanced with byproducts and cereal grains, which deliver the amino acids the animal products don't. Try to stay away from foods that have many variations of the same type of grain (especially rice products).

Next, look at the fat content. Unlike humans, dogs thrive on fat. It helps their coats, is a great source of energy, and it facilitates a better-tasting food. You must be careful, however, as fat in extreme amounts will lead to obesity. A food with eight to 10 percent crude fat content will deliver the necessary requirements for an adult. Remember to guard against this with the pup, as you don't want him growing at an alarming rate. If using a food with less fat than this, you can try mixing a teaspoon of vegetable oil with it every so often. This is especially good to do during his working season.

Be aware that changing foods many times until you find something you and the dog like won't be the best for your puppy's stomach and could lead to diarrhea or a finicky eater. Try to find a good brand and formula and stick with it. If you do find yourself switching brands, incorporate the new formula slowly, mixing it with his normal food first, eventually switching completely over to the new diet. You can move to an adult food when the puppy is around six months old. In the end, it is hard to go wrong by choosing a respected brand and following the schedules published right on the bag.

There are many different types of feeding dishes on the market — plastic, stainless steel, ceramic. Some are even raised off the floor to promote better digestion. Whatever you choose, you may want to shy away from the plastic food dishes. With ravenous eaters such as most gun dogs, they may eventually get small plastic splinters in their chins, in much the same way as plastic chew toys. A ceramic bowl is easy to clean and heavier, so the excited pup won't push it all over the floor. Stainless steel bowls will stack easily for travel.

Now you've finally decided on a brand of puppy food, and it's actually time to set the dish down. First of all, you're making the right decision by setting the dish down. For large breed dogs, it is unwise to allow the dog to be a self-feeder. If we constantly have the pup's bowl full, The pup will constantly be full. Though you've probably heard exceptions to this, there are very, very few things that can go wrong if you set up a feeding schedule; if you allow self-feeding with a dish that constantly has food in it, the number of problems that can occur rises drastically. Better to be safe and set a schedule.

Puppies will need to be fed often while they're young, but usually no more than three times a day; try your hardest to stick to the same times each day, which helps with housebreaking. For instance, just after your mealtimes are the perfect way to remember. This means that you may have to come home from work at lunchtime for a while, but you should anyway to let the dog out of his crate to go to the bathroom. Usually, feeding times of around 7a.m., noon, and 7p.m. work best.

When he reaches about four or five months, start to make the middle meal smaller and smaller, putting more food into his first and third meals, until you can phase out that second meal completely. Then, you'll be on a good, two-meal per day schedule. And don't forget to follow the label on the food bag closely — you don't want to be feeding him three cups of food per meal when it said per day. Is once a day feeding okay? Yes, and millions of dogs are happy as clams with that schedule. If you do feed once a day, make it the evening meal; a full dog relaxes and rests better.

Aside from helping to control weight, setting a feeding schedule assures that the pup will be hungry when you put the food down. You'll be grateful for this when you're on a trip and you must feed at a certain time. If he's used to having to gobble his food in

A puppy's initial introduction to game can be as simple as it is fascinating. The scent of goose arouses immediate interest and stirs the hunting instincts in this young Lab.

five or 10 minutes, he'll be prepared for when you set the dish down instead of lingering over it. Setting a schedule will also help in housebreaking. You won't have the food constantly moving through the puppy; you'll know when it's in there and about when it has to come out. The pup will begin to learn that right after mealtime means going outdoors.

When you've done it properly, you should just about be able to set your watch to his stomach. He'll start to come get you when his tummy grumbles; for this reason, don't get him started eating too early in the morning. You want to be able to sleep in at least a little on the weekends!

Guard against the obese puppy. You want to be able to see the pup's ribs, and when you look down at him from above, he should have a distinct hourglass shape. A profile view should show his deep chest rising up to a thinner belly. The more effort you take to control his weight right from the begin-

ning, the better off you'll be when he grows into his bones. He'll look gangly at first — all puppies do. But if he just looks abnormally shaped (extremely gaunt, a round ball, etc.), pay attention to his diet. Growing puppies do require more protein and fat than adults, and a reputable puppy meal will deliver the balanced diet necessary for the dog, no matter the breed.

Keep the puppy on dog food; don't get him into the habitat of begging from the table. Also, and very importantly, don't allow the pup to romp or swim right after eating. This can lead to something called gastric bloat, where gas is trapped in the pup's stomach and then it twists, trapping the air. It is a truly life-threatening — usually fatal — situation. Therefore, you may need to crate an especially hyper puppy to keep him calm after mealtime. Also avoid excessive exercise before his meal for the same reason. ■

A pointer pup's first curious point.

A pointer suiting up for the day's training session.

CHAPTER 6

GENERAL TRAINING AND OBEDIENCE

by Jake Smith

UNLESS YOU'D PREFER to have your new pup do whatever they feel like whenever they feel like, you'll need to train him. And though they may eventually claim quite an extensive vocabulary, the foundation of all training is rooted in four commands: *sit, stay, come,* and *heel.* Some trainers like to combine *sit* and *stay,* or even *come* and *heel* into one word for both commands; I'm going to use them singularly because I feel it provides better emphasis to the dog. If you use *sit* to mean "sit and stay," then how do you reprimand the pup when he sits but doesn't stay? He followed part of the command — how is he to know which part he is doing wrong? Others use one command to mean both and do a good job of it; they are probably better trainers — or have smarter dogs!

Training should be administered with equal parts insistence and praise. Insist the dog do it right, and then praise him when he does. Comfort the afflicted and afflict the comfortable, in a way.

As with all training, these four simple commands need to be practiced over and over. The famous Labrador retriever King Buck, two-time National Field Trial Champion, was trained on *sit, stay, come,* and *heel* every day, even after he had filled the trophy case at the famed Nilo Farms where he made his home. Remember, repetition is the key, and it usually need be no more than five or 10 minutes a day, maybe a morning and an evening session, starting when the pup is 10 to 12 weeks of age. The dog will learn much more quickly in short bursts of success than in long, drawn-out battles of will. Keep the sessions fun, positive, and rewarding, and the pup should be well on his way to laying a firm foundation for future, and more specialized, training.

There has been much debate over the question of whether you should use food rewards while training. By food rewards, I mean dog biscuits, treats, hot dogs, or other tidbits that are not the dog's regular meal.

Brittany

Keep training sessions fun, positive and rewarding, but
above all, be consistent and firm in your commands.

While food rewards do help to get the message across faster — the quickest way to a dog's brain is through his stomach — it can become a nuisance, especially after you run out of dog bones. Rewarding the pup every fifth or sixth time with a small treat usually works the best as it keeps him guessing — "Maybe this will be the time I get the biscuit!"

Using food is also a good way to teach the dog to depend on its nose to help it find things. My daughter taught her retriever to find a dead bird, a useful hunting command, by hiding pieces of hot dog in the grass in her backyard. She first made it easy for the dog to find the food when she was teaching the command, then once the dog knew that *dead bird* meant that she had to get her nose down and find the hot dog, the hiding places became more difficult. As the dog matured, *dead bird* didn't mean hot dog anymore — it meant a duck or pheasant or grouse or retrieving dummy that was concealed.

One instance where food is a natural training tool is at the dog's regular mealtime. Because the pup is going to be fed anyway, you can usually withhold the food until he obeys a given command. It's a "no dessert until you clean your room" type of thing. Just don't fall into the habit of only saying the command at mealtime — every time you say, "Sit," you don't want Old Roscoe to start salivating for his food.

Before we begin our discussion with training, it is important to remember some training "lessons" — for you, not the dog. First, be consistent. If you want the pup to remain seated at the word *stay*, then stick with that. Don't use *stay* one day and *freeze* the next. If *come* is used to call the dog, don't expect him to race toward you when you holler, "Here!" Second, be firm and blunt. "Sit" means *sit*, not "come-on-boy-sit-down-come-on-you-can-do-it-sit-boy-come-on." It's, "Sit." It's very confusing to throw in unnecessary words, expecting the dog to pick out the one you want him to follow.

Next, unless the dog has a hearing problem, he'll hear the one word *sit*. Don't get into the habit of repeating the command until the dog obeys. Sure, it's

A thorough training program will develop the
instincts perpetuated by bloodlines.

all right to maybe say it a second or a third time, especially if it's pretty obvious that a young pup is not
paying attention to you. But be firm — if the pup
doesn't sit after one or two commands, show him how
it's done while giving the command again. If he's
wandering off as you holler, "Stay," don't turn it into
a shouting match, sounding like a broken record.
Corral the dog, sit him down, and say, "Stay" — even
if you only gave him the one chance to follow.
Repeating the commands is necessary when teaching
them for the first time, but after you're sure the pup
knows what you mean when you say, "Heel," she
should follow the first time you say it.

This command and control system is much easier with a leash or checkcord — a six-foot-length piece
of quarter-inch rope attached to a collar is plenty. A
so-called "choke chain" collar is handy as well. This
collar is misnamed; it should be called a "pop collar"
instead, because the way it's used, you simply pop the
dog with a quick flick of the wrist or a slight upward
pull. The chain will tighten and then loosen quickly,
administering a little discomfort and showing the dog
that you are calling the shots. For example, the dog
has on the collar attached to the checkcord:
"Come,"(dog ignores you) — contrarily, "Come,"
pop, "Come." He'll come.

At first, any dog worth his salt is going to fight
the leash and collar. He'll roll over, bite the leash,
wrap it around your legs. Just stay patient and let him
sort it out. When he realizes that he can't do anything
except cooperate, he will. Good training and discipline are often a simple matter of eliminating the
dog's options so that he has no choice except to obey
— you got the leash, you got the hammer!

It helps to get on the dog's level when you begin
training. You won't be such an imposing figure if
you're on your knees looking the pup in the eyes
instead of towering above him. You've already established who the leader of the pack is, so he'll respect
you no matter where you are. But by being eye level,
you take yourself out of a threatening position and
put yourself in his zone.

At the end of a hard day, Brittany catches a snooze.

This Brittany has been placed on "sit," where he waits until the next command.

It's also imperative that you know how to praise and how to discipline. When just starting out with commands, don't even think about getting angry with the dog — the pup has no idea what you're trying to teach him, so there's no point in smacking him across the bottom. And while praise is important, overly praising the dog can be just as detrimental, with the dog forgetting what it was he did right to deserve the hugs and kisses. A simple "good boy," or "good Roscoe" will do, along with a rub on the neck or a scratch behind the ears. Spend a second or two praising him and petting him, and then get back to business.

Once the dog knows the commands and has proven he can follow them, discipline will get the message across that disobedience will not be tolerated. But discipline does not mean a beating. A quick ear pinch, or a firm scolding will usually be all it takes. By the way, in the litter, when Mom wants to discipline the pups, she does so with a nip on the ear. Dogs accept this form of pack discipline without holding a grudge. The *canids* do not as a rule smack each other around or paddle each other's backsides, so this form of discipline is usually much less effective than the kind they are genetically engineered to understand. And instead of disciplining the dog while you're teaching a command, just give him a firm "No" when he begins to disobey, and start over (see Stay below).

Finally, though many people may handle the dog and give him commands over the course of his lifetime, it's best to train the dog one-on-one. That's not to say that a few people can't train the pup (as long as they also use the same commands you started with and train in the same manner); but during a training session, you don't want your spouse, children, and the odd nosy neighbor hollering commands at him. Take the dog off by yourself and work with him. If your spouse wants to train, let him or her, and don't poke your nose in. A popular saying is that dogs are just children with fur; their attention spans are about the same. The pup will pick up more quickly on commands if he only has to pay attention to one voice giving the instructions.

Sit

Sit is a good command to start with — it's easy, the dog usually masters it quickly, and as you'll see with just about anything you want to teach the dog, you can use his appetite to your advantage. However, it's best to start off without the food and show the pup what you mean when you tell him, "Sit."

With a leash on the pup's collar (if the pup is fairly big) or by grabbing the slip link in the pop collar, pull up at the same time you push down on his bottom. As you do this, command, "Sit" in a firm but not threatening voice. When the dog has his rear end planted, praise him, scratch his ears, or rub his neck. Using the leash or collar again, get the pup back on all fours, maybe walk him around a bit, and then repeat the pull up-push down maneuver, repeating, "Sit" each time you do so.

As the pup progresses with this command, incorporate a short delay between when you issue the command and when you pull up-push down — give him a chance to do it himself. But don't expect him to do it properly after only a few repetitions; after perhaps the third or fourth training session and a few-dozen repetitions should you give him the opportunity to respond on his own. Don't get angry if the puppy doesn't do it — or do it quickly enough for you. Remember the thing about patience we talked about in the previous chapter. This is a brand new world to him, with new people, smells, surroundings, and lessons.

Once it's obvious that the pup is starting to get the hang of things, mealtime is the perfect opportunity to see success and give a nice reward. Stand up with the full food dish, the dog facing you, and command, "Sit." If the dog doesn't obey right away, hold the dish out and move it back over his head, forcing him to lean well back. When it looks like momentum and gravity will push his bottom down, repeat, "Sit." He should easily sit. Make him stay in that position for a second or two, and then praise him and give him his food. When the pup learns that the sooner he obeys, the sooner he gets something nice, you've got him. As he matures, the "something nice" will be another throw of the tennis ball, a warm feathery duck or pheasant, or the kind tone in your praise.

Stay

Stay is the next natural command to teach, as it builds upon and helps to reinforce *sit. Stay* and *come* can usually be taught at the same time, but when starting out, stick with one command and use some other cue to let the dog know that it can move again. As stated elsewhere, some trainers do not teach *stay*, making the valid point that *sit* means "sit until you are told to do otherwise." But for those who wish to use *stay* as an additional command, here's how it's done.

The pup should be sitting reliably before you move on to *stay*. *Stay* is best taught, at first, with the checkcord on. Once she is in place, command, "Stay," holding your hand up in front of her in the "stop" position like a traffic cop. This is an important command, and you must be firm. *Stay* may one day keep the dog from bolting in front of traffic, stop her from mobbing guests, or keep her out of broken glass or another kind of danger.

After commanding, "Stay," move a few paces away — so she can still see you — repeating "Stay" after a few-seconds pause. Most of the time, she'll sort of look at you with a cocked head as if saying, "Just exactly what are you saying?" As soon as you see the pup begin to move, you might clap your hands, whistle, or do something to tell her that it's all right to move, and also get down on her level. She'll usually bound toward you if she's been paying attention. If she's not looking at you as you're teaching, you're wasting your time. You need to get her attention first before anything good can happen.

Increase the time you require the pup to stay in one place as you progress, and increase the distance you move away before you let her off the hook. When she starts to hold in the *stay* position longer, correct her when she moves. As she gets up say, "No," take her by the leash back to the position where she started, tell her "Sit," and repeat, "Stay." Each time she moves without permission, say, "No," take her back to the starting point, and begin again. You'll soon get an indication as to how long she'll hold in one place on her own before she gets fidgety. Time your release command just before she starts to move.

If you don't want to use *come* to release her right away — and when you just start out, it's best not to — clap your hands, whistle, or make some noise to let her know that she can come running and see what's up. But after you command, "Stay," and you want her to stay put, be silent. It's not very constructive to set the dog up to fail by throwing in distracting conversation before she has the commands down pat. When the pup matures in her training, you should be able to tell her, "Stay" and carry on with your business; but for right now, it's best to make the sessions as easy for

Even in the field there are times when you'll want the dog to stay in one place.

her to succeed as possible. Not only will she learn faster, but she'll bond with you quicker because she'll begin to see just exactly what she has to do to make you happy.

Come

You can begin introducing the command *come* or *here* whenever you're playing with the pup, taking him out for a bathroom break, at mealtime — whenever. But don't expect results until you start working specifically on the command.

To get the pup to come reliably, he'll need to be focused on you. Therefore, trying to teach the dog *come* while he's chasing butterflies, wrestling with another puppy, or terrorizing the neighbor cat will be futile. The best way to have the pup focused on you — or to get his attention on you — is by having him *sit* and *stay* consistently, and with a leash and collar.

Teaching the dog *come* is nothing more than adding the command to move after the *stay* command. Instead of getting him to bound toward you from the stay position by whistling or clapping your hands, simply substitute the command, "Come." As soon as you see him start to break the *stay* command, tell him, "Come," and praise him. It's all right at this point to add in some clapping while you give the command, but try and just use the word as soon as possible. Repeat the *sit* and *stay* routine, move away, and again command, "Come." Soon, you'll be able to correct the pup for breaking the *stay* command without it confusing him — he won't think he's getting punished for coming as long as you don't say the command while you're reprimanding him. Remember, it's just a "No," lead him back to where he was supposed to stay, walk back to where you were, pause, and command, "Come."

At first, don't be surprised to see that the pup will only come to you from that stay position. Don't worry — he'll mature and soon come when he's called no matter what he's doing. Use the leash to help guide the dog to you; don't drag him kicking and screaming. More than likely, if he is good at staying, you'll need the leash to get him started when you say, "Come." Up to this point, you've been making a gen-

A disciplined hunting dog is a happy dog;
he knows the limits and feels comfortable within them.

eral commotion when you want him to come; now you're just using one firm word. The pup will need a little encouragement to get started, and a soft pull on the leash to pull him up on all fours will do the trick. Keep repeating and increasing the distance you move away from him.

If you practice this indoors, try moving into another room where the pup can't see you — most times, he'll get anxious to see where you've gone and come looking for you. As soon as you suspect he's moving, say, "Come," and clap your hands so he can find you. He'll have a most relieved look on his face when he comes around the corner and finds you there.

Heel

Heel is a vital command if you want to enjoy taking the pup for a walk without it being a tug-of-war. The *heel* position is also where the retrieving breeds start when making formal retrieves on marks and blinds. But he'll need to be a little older before you begin teaching *heel*. The pup will need a good foundation of *come* and *sit* before you can expect him to be a good citizen at your side.

With the leash on, start walking with the pup, commanding, "Heel." If he trots up next to you and starts walking by your side, congratulations; but you haven't won yet. He is just following the leash or following you, and not responding to the command at all. Once again, this skill requires repetition.

As you walk, and as he keeps walking by your side, repeat the command, "Heel." Pause and give a rub on his side with a "Good Roscoe" while he's in the correct position. If he starts to bound ahead, hold the leash firm and let him run to the end of it — don't jerk him back! The pup has a fairly fragile neck, and you don't want to snap him around by it. Just hold tight and let him jerk himself off his feet. When the pup gets to the end of the leash, say, "No," turn away from him, and command, "Heel" again, guiding him back into position. If the pup lags behind, say, "No," lead him into position, and command "Heel" again when he gets into the right spot. Just keep walking and saying "Heel" whenever he's by your side.

Getting ahead of you or behind you is easier to correct with the leash than the dog that wants to bolt off left or right. In those cases, find a handy wall such as a house or fence, and heel the dog between you and the wall. This really cuts down on his options. Properly, the dog's head should be even with your knee — no farther ahead or behind than that. For the dog that gets ahead, pop him back with the leash. For the dog that lags behind, hold the leash in your off hand (the side opposite from the dog), and let it pass across the front of your legs to the dog's collar. Now, every time you take a step, your leg will push the leash forward, pulling the dog forward. They catch on to this pretty quickly.

Whether you want he pup to heel to your right on left side is entirely up to you, but be consistent. Most hunters like to have the dog heel on the side opposite where they carry their gun so the dog won't bonk his head on the barrels. Keep repeating the *heel* command until the pup will walk nicely next to you. Scold if he lags behind or lunges forward, but don't forcefully yank him back with the leash. Soon, use the *heel* command to put the dog into position when he comes to you. Put all four commands together in this sequence: *sit* the pup down; command "Stay" as you move away; wait a few seconds; say "Come" to get him to move to you; and as he gets near, command "Heel" to get him to your side. When he does, finish it off with another "Sit" and you've got it — a dog that will *stay* when told, *come* when called, and *sit* at *heel*. Whew!

Progressing with the Four Commands

When the pup has displayed at least some level of cognizance of all four commands, work from the heel position. While he's walking on heel, stop while commanding, "Sit." You may have to pull up on the leash and push on his butt to remind him what it means. With many repetitions of this, you'll be able to stop walking and have him sit without your saying a word. After he sits, command "Stay," walk away, and say "Come" to get him to you. If you want him to move into the heel position, tell him, "Heel" and guide him with the leash; once there, say "Sit" again to finish it off. Start your walk again, and keep repeating these commands in any sequence you like. Again, doing this training near a fence or the house, with the pup in the middle, will help keep him straight.

When the pup really has the commands mastered, you should be able to tell him, "Sit," and keep walking. At first, the dog will want to keep up next to you; just turn around and tell him, "Sit" again, and "Stay," and keep walking after he's in position. This will take a little while to perfect, because the dog has been taught to keep up with you during heel training. Now, you're asking him to stay put while you keep walking. It's confusing, and he's likely to look and act bewildered. Don't despair; keep at it, and he will pick it up — just not in the first five minutes.

A good day on the prairie. The flushing Labrador is a popular upland bird dog.

This sort of performance comes from good genetics and intelligent training.

Whistle Training

Most hunters and trainers use a whistle to give instructions to the dog when it's at a distance that makes shouting difficult or impossible. Whistles also carry much better through the wind, and the dog can pick up the high trill much better than your voice. Whistle training is not difficult, and you can start it at a young age, but only after the dog understands the spoken command.

The *whistle-sit* is one such whistle command — there are others — used as a substitute for the spoken command. It is introduced the same way as the other whistle commands. The *whistle-sit* command is normally one sharp blast on the whistle, while a *come* whistle command is several short, quick blasts.

When the pup can sit with confidence, introduce the whistle. Command, "Sit" and as he starts to sit, give one sharp blast on the whistle. It'll ring your ears at first, but a sharp blast is the same as a firm spoken command; a wimpy whistle will be like you're asking the dog if he wants to sit instead of telling him. Use the whistle just after you say, "Sit." Even though the pup will sit reliably, it's nice to remind him with the

pull up-push down maneuver when you give the whistle. After many repetitions, start to phase out the verbal "Sit," and just give the whistle blast. You'll be surprised how quickly he'll understand that there are now two things that mean *sit*.

Some Final Basic Training Words

Throughout your training sessions, there are going to be times when the pup doesn't feel like doing anything productive. Ever have a bad day at work? This is the same thing; this is the dog's job — to learn and to listen to you. There may be a variety of reasons — he could be sick, having some growing pains, maybe he's tired. More than likely — like the kid he is — he just wants to play and not pay attention at that particular moment.

As trainers, we need to read our dogs. We need to recognize those times when the pup just seems to be a sponge and will soak up anything we tell him; and we need to see the times when our commands, no matter how loud we shout them, are just bouncing off his skull. When the dog is young, we must capitalize on those sponge times, and play and bond during the

That's enough for today, boss.

other times. When the pup matures, we should be able to make him listen when we want him to.

Before mealtime — an hour to an hour and a half, not a few minutes before — is a good time to train. The pup usually isn't hearing his grumbling stomach, and he's probably already had his afternoon nap. It's easy to mold a playing session into a training session if you've been keeping everything fun for him. If training sessions are like physics class, he'll like learning *heel* as much as you liked to learn about the laws of inertia.

You also need to be able to read the pup so you can know when he's had enough. The five- to 10-minute rule is about the maximum for young puppies; older dogs can go longer, but regardless of age, keep training sessions short in hot weather, even the simple obedience training we've been discussing. Whatever the length, be sure you end on a positive note, but don't sacrifice a couple of bad experiences to get that positive note. For instance, let's say the pup is heeling, coming, and staying like a pro, and you want to get one more good series out of him. But the next couple times, he didn't come right away or sit when

you told him to, and you had to reprimand him. Because you really want to end on a positive note, you keep drilling it into him, forcing him to obey the commands when it's obvious that he's finished for the day — he's punched out and thinking about a cold beer. You've entered the law of diminishing returns. If you get into this situation, pause for a few seconds, let the pup romp, and then give him a simple *sit*, helping him with the pull up-push down maneuver. When he does it, praise him and let him chase you back to the house for dinner.

What you should have done, though, is recognize the signs that the pup was getting ready to quit. Sometimes, he may not come to you as quickly, or he'll sit a little slower after the command. Perhaps he didn't hold his stay as long, or you don't get the eye contact you were getting earlier. If you start to see those signs, wrap it up. It's best to keep the dog wanting more and enjoying himself instead of going through a few sharp disciplines before calling it a night. You want him bounding at your side when you grab your whistle and his leash, not curling up in a ball and yawning.

The electronic collar in the right hands is a great training tool.

Electronic Collars

Of course, no discussion of training would be complete without a view of the use of electronic training aids — electronic collars. Although these gadgets have reached an incredibly high level of reliability, many people see them as cruel and unusual punishment. I would agree only with the "unusual" part of that — not the "cruel" or the "punishment."

If you're not familiar with them, these collars are fastened around the dog's neck with studs protruding that make contact with the dog's skin. The transmitter, held by the trainer, is capable of giving off a low-level to higher-level impulse — some would incorrectly call it a "shock" — with the push of a button. Properly used, they are a great training aid; improperly used, they can be dangerous. Do you know anything else like that? How about your family car? Or a steak knife? Or a shotgun? Or... you get the picture.

What the collar is, is this: It's a long-range tap on the shoulder in which the trainer is saying, "Hey — remember me? I can reach out and remind you of what you should be doing even though I'm a couple-hundred yards away, if I have to." If, as a friend of mine once commented, you use it as a "two-by-four with a long handle," you are headed for trouble.

The amount of electric current that the good trainer uses is almost imperceptible to human touch if you put your fingers on the probes and push the button. In fact, the only way you can tell a dog is being "impulsed" is to watch carefully his eyes or ears for a flicker or twitch. If the dog "gives voice," that's too much. But, if you have a dog that persists in running deer or other game, fighting with the neighbor dog, or chasing cars, the higher setting will almost instantly give him religion — "The boogie man is out there and when I'm bad, he bites my neck."

If you have a hot temper and tend to be a punishing trainer, I would not advise that you use the electronic collar. But then I would also advise that you not even own a dog. I have seen trainers who regard the collar as cruel who discipline by kicking and punching these great animals. Troglodytes like that give collars — and hands and feet — a bad name. One more disclaimer: a jillion dogs have been trained very well without these collars, and most of the animals that win in hunting and field trial competitions have been trained with them. It is your choice. That's why I am including tips on both types of training in this book.

Essentially, the best form of using the electronic collar to train for compliance or obedience — "collar training" — is when the dog herself controls the collar's impulse. One of the easiest ways to introduce the dog to the collar is with the use of the crate. Here's how it works. The dog, wearing the e-collar, is given a very low level of stimulation, such that you notice that the ears move or the eyes flicker. This is the level to start with. The dog, wearing the collar, is led to the crate and given the command, "Kennel." At the same time, this low level of intensity is given on a continuous basis until the dog makes her first positive move to comply with the command, at which point you let up on the button. The dog, uncomfortable with but unharmed by the impulse, has learned to turn the collar off by complying with the command.

Another instance. The dog — same collar setting — is in the heel position. She has already gone through the formal heel training as described earlier — the leash and the wall and the whole drill. Now, that training is reinforced with the e-collar, which is an important concept. Dogs are trained the old-fashioned way; the e-collar is used to reinforce the training. At heel, the dog starts to wander. You tell her, "Heel," and impulse her at low level until she returns to the proper position. You establish a proper "zone" around you where you want the dog to heel; when she strays from that zone, she "turns the collar on"; when she returns to the proper zone, she turns it off. She is in control.

It works the same way for all training — what doesn't work through "attrition," doing it over and over in a more and more simple matter until the light goes on, will often work with the e-collar. Let's take *stay*. By now, you see how it works. As long as the dog stays where she was told, the collar stays off; when she gets up without permission, the collar goes on. You repeat the commands "sit - stay," and when she complies, she turns the collar off.

Electronic collars are not cheap, but they can be used to train an infinite number of dogs. They are rechargeable, and the companies that manufacture and sell them are run by first-class people who know dogs and employ professional trainers on their staffs as advisors and field-testers. In all, e-collar training is very efficient, and certainly not a cruel way to train. ◾

A pointer in full battle gear; electronic and beeper collars.

Labrador Retriever

CHAPTER 7

THE RETRIEVER BREEDS

by Steve Smith

RETRIEVERS ARE A BRANCH of the sporting dog breeds that were bred specifically for the purpose of retrieving to hand game, primarily birds, shot in the field. They also hunt upland birds in the manner of many of the spaniel breeds, as close-working flushing breeds. While the hounds track or chase game absent the sportsman, who appears on the scene when the animal is brought to bay, and while the pointing dog hunts the field or forest with his human counterpart many yards away until the dog contacts game and points it, the retriever, operating in the purest sense, can do nothing until the hunter shoots a bird. Then he performs his function. Because of this, the retriever breeds seem to form closer bonds with human beings than do the other breeds.

Because of the true partnership they share with their person, retrievers seem to their fans to be more willing to please than other breeds, and their temperament is often more pleasing to humans than are the other breeds. The Labrador retriever, for example, is by far the continent's most popular breed, and owes his immense following to these very traits. Most non-hunting Lab owners have no idea that they owe their dog's engaging personality to his hunting heritage.

Today, hunting retrievers in the United States and Canada hunt in two basic ways: as retrievers of waterfowl, and as flushing dogs for upland bird hunting. As waterfowl dogs, retrieving ducks and geese shot over water or land, the dog waits with his human until the bird is shot. Then, on command, he swims or runs to the place where the bird lies, scoops it up in his gentle mouth, and returns it to his owner. If the bird is crippled and tries to escape, the dog's eyes and nose aid him in the bird's capture.

If the bird is shot and the dog does not see it go down, the human partner directs the dog's path to the bird, using hand and whistle signals that have been taught and trained into the dog in long hours of practice and repetition. Often, the dog must see and remember multiple birds that have been dropped, so good retrievers have good memories, a trait that makes their training easier. A bird or object the dog must retrieve after he sees come down is called a "mark," while one he must retrieve that he has not seen is called a "blind."

As a flusher of upland birds — pheasants, any of the grouse species, quail, or partridge — a well-trained retriever covers the field or woodland in an even pattern, using his nose to scent hidden birds. He must do this in fairly close proximity to the hunter because, unlike the pointing dog that will find, point, and hold his bird until the hunter arrives on the scene, the retriever will keep after the bird on the ground until it takes flight. Then the hunter shoots, and the dog retrieves. But since the effective range of a shotgun for all practical purposes is about 40 yards, the entire enterprise must be carried out at close range or the effort is wasted. In this case, the dog must naturally be trained to hunt within that range.

There is a dichotomy, here, in these two types of hunting. In waterfowling, the dog waits for game to come to him; in upland hunting, the dog goes out to find the game on his own. In waterfowling, the hunter's shot marks the beginning of the dog's activity; in upland hunting, the shot marks nearly the end of the dog's activity. In waterfowling, the dog remains sitting until the hunter directs the action by sending him for the retrieve; in upland hunting, the dog is "in charge," because nothing happens until he locates a bird. In waterfowling, the dog's sight is the most important sense; in upland hunting, he depends upon his nose.

As a result, retrievers that are effective in both types of sport are smart animals, ranking very high on intelligence scales for all dog breeds. This intelligence makes them trainable, tractable and, in the opinion of many, is one factor leading to their overall friendliness toward people and, in a family situation, what seems to be their well-developed sense of humor. ■

AMERICAN WATER SPANIEL

The American water spaniel (AWS) is one of the very few breeds to have been developed in North America, specifically in the Midwest (it is the state dog of Wisconsin), by market-hunters of that region. It is also one of the smaller of the retrievers.

- **Area & Date of Origin:** United States, 1800s
- **Function:** Bird flushing & retrieving, gun dog, water dog, field trials
- **Height & Weight:** 15-18"; 30-45 lbs (male); 25-40 lbs (female)
- **Colors:** Solid liver, brown, or dark chocolate
- **Coat:** Can range from marcel (uniform waves) to close curls, with a dense undercoat
- **Standards:** Broad skull; square muzzle; long, wide ears with close curls; slightly rounded eyes, color harmonizing with coat; black or dark brown nose; sturdy back; straight, strong forelegs feathered with waterproof hair; tail slightly curved and carried near the level of the back; tapered tail has moderate feathering; well-padded feet with closely-grouped toes
- **Life Span:** 10-12 years

■ Appearance and Temperament

As mentioned, the AWS is one of the smaller retrievers, with both sexes being 15 - 18 inches, the males weighing 30 - 45 pounds, and the females 25 - 40 pounds. These are fairly wide ranges. Colors are liver, brown, and dark chocolate, often with some splashes of white, especially on the feet and chest. The coat is either in tight curls or wavy, and these dogs have a double coat for warmth.

The AWS is a tough dog, with a high pain threshold, and many — especially the males — attempt to dominate or assume the Alpha dog position with other dogs or people. There can also be a problem with "food possession," and this has to be guarded against, especially with small children about. Some of these dogs are regarded as being somewhat stubborn.

On the positive side, they are loyal and intelligent and very much eager to please. They are also sensitive and, like some other rare breeds such as the flat-coat, are slow to mature.

■ History

One of the few breeds developed in the United States, the American water spaniel was developed as a market-hunter's companion around the 1860s, possibly from some of the other curly-coated breeds and spaniels. It was developed in the Wolf and Fox River Valley region of east-central Wisconsin where a tough, small, water dog was needed. The AWS was the first American breed to be developed to hunt from a boat, hence its relatively small size for a retriever. Possibly due to its rough-and-tumble beginnings, this dog's instincts are often at the elemental level.

In 1920, the UKC registered the first AWS, "Curly Pfeifer," named after Dr. F.J. Pfeifer, the first person to register the dog. The breed was not recognized by the AKC for another 20 years, in 1940.

■ In the Field

The AWS is an excellent waterfowl dog and also functions well as an upland flushing dog, particularly on grouse and woodcock in tight cover. It may get "rangy" if not controlled.

■ Trainability

Training an American water spaniel is something of a challenge. The dog is smart and sensitive to the point of being "soft," but it also has a stubborn streak and a drive to do things its own way. This, when combined with its slow rate of maturation, has turned some away from the breed. Hard methods, including the electronic collar, are not for this dog. An AWS must be dealt with gently, and early and reinforced obedience training is a must to establish your place as the leader.

■ Strengths/Weaknesses

The dog's innate drive and inbred skills and intelligence allow it to do a fine job in uplands and lowlands. Some of the problems outlined above in terms of personality, however, mean that this dog will never be a breed for everyone. But for the discerning sportsman with a gift for gentle training, he is a wonderful piece of American waterfowling history.

Like most of the other retriever breeds, hip dysplasia can be a problem, and a pup's eyes are subject to some inherited problems, so a CERF certification is essential.

■ The Show Ring

Very few of these dogs ever find their way to the show ring.

BOYKIN SPANIEL

The Boykin spaniel is another of those rare breeds that is, like the American water spaniel, a product of the New World, specifically South Carolina. Moreover, it is the latest breed to be developed for water-fowling — not appearing until the early 1900s.

- **Area & Date of Origin:** United States, 1900s
- **Function:** Gun dog, water dog, retriever
- **Height & Weight:** 15.5-18", 30-40 lbs (male); 14-16.5", 25-35 lbs (female)
- **Colors:** Solid, rich liver or dark chocolate
- **Coat:** Flat to moderately curly, of medium length; legs may have light feathering
- **Standards:** Medium-sized, sturdy; strong, straight, level back; well-developed chest; dark yellow to brown eyes; high-set ears have rounded tips; strong, straight legs; tail docked to 2.5-3"; round, firm, well-padded feet
- **Life Span:** 10-12 years

■ Appearance and Temperament

The Boykin spaniel is a smallish dog as retrievers go, the males being 15½ - 18 inches and 30 - 40 pounds, and the females 14 - 16½ inches and 25 - 35 pounds. The wavy, fairly curly coat ranges from liver through red-brown, to chocolate. The tail is docked in the tradition of some others of the spaniel tribe.

■ History

The breed was developed by Mr. L. Whitaker Boykin in South Carolina, who took in a dog named Dumpy from its owner, his friend Alexander White, in the early part of the 1900s for training. Boykin used Dumpy as the rootstock and is thought to have outcrossed with Chesapeake Bay retrievers, springer spaniels, and American water spaniels, among others.

The Wateree River in South Carolina was a popular sports-men's destination. The shores of the river teemed with game, and these shores were accessed by take-apart boats called "section boats." Because these boats were carried to the river in wagons in their unassembled state, they were small and didn't hold much gear. The result was little room left for a big retriever — hence the development and popularity of the pocket-sized Boykin.

In the Field

Although not necessarily overly-sensitive to cold water, the Boykin has a high tolerance for hot conditions, making them a good dog for the dove fields, where early season shooting can put a bigger breed in danger of overheating. They are also good flushing dogs, especially in close cover, and some have even been trained to trail deer where it is legal. Some Boykins find jobs as the pick-up dogs on the quail wagons of Southern plantations, retrieving the birds first pinned by the pointers and shot by the guests.

Trainability

These dogs are at their best when they are encouraged and when training is made fun or like a game. Like the rest of this family of gun dogs, they want to please their handler master. As a pure hunting dog, they take to the sport readily with no "show blood" to overcome.

Strengths/Weaknesses

One major strength is their compact size for the hunter who wants a dog that "doesn't rock the boat." They are also friendly and cheerful. Foremost, they are hunting dogs that have always been bred for such.

Weaknesses include hyperactivity and aggressiveness in some bloodlines, as well as incidences of hip dysplasia, skin allergies, and cataracts.

Other Uses

These dogs make fine family pets as well as hunting companions.

The Show Ring

Although recognized by the UKC in 1985, these dogs are not recognized by the AKC, so they do not compete in the show ring.

CHESAPEAKE BAY RETRIEVER

The Chesapeake Bay retriever is a strong, powerfully-built breed that is generally regarded as the hardiest and most rugged of all the retriever breeds. Although adept as an upland hunter on land, this breed is most at home in the water, and can handle the most brutal conditions that waterfowlers encounter.

- **Area & Date of Origin:** United States, 1800s
- **Function:** Retriever, gun dog, water dog, field trials
- **Height & Weight:** 23-26", 65-80 lbs (male); 21-24", 55-70 lbs (female)
- **Colors:** Any color of brown, sedge, or deadgrass
- **Coat:** Oily, harsh outer coat and dense, fine, wooly undercoat (sheds profusely in spring)
- **Standards:** Broad round skull; amber or yellowish eyes; small ears set well-up on head; powerful hindquarters as high or slightly higher than shoulder; medium-length tail straight or slightly curved, with light feathering; webbed hare feet with rounded toes
- **Life Span:** 10-13 years

■ Appearance and Temperament

The dog (male) is 23 - 26 inches at the shoulder and weighs 65 - 80 pounds; the smaller bitch (female) is 21 - 24 inches and 55 - 70 pounds. They occur in several color phases: deadgrass, sedge, browns (light, medium, and dark) and, more rarely, liver. White spots or patches may appear, especially on the feet or underside of the dog. The coat is wavy and oily, helping to prevent cold water from penetrating to the skin.

The Chesapeake suffers from some unwarranted bad press concerning its temperament. Happy, intelligent, and fiercely loyal, these animals bond with a person or family and are quite protective of people and property. They do not present a danger to children (with whom they are excellent) or strangers, although they do not display the "instant friendship" with strangers that the Labrador does. For all of their hardy fearlessness of the elements, these dogs are soft-hearted and respond best to kindness. The novice trainer should be aware that these dogs have a mind of their own, however, and are strong-willed and often stubborn. This combination of complex traits has made the Chesapeake perhaps the least understood and appreciated of all the more popular retriever breeds. They are not usually recommended for families seeking a retriever as a pet only. For those who have a gun dog in mind, the Chesapeake does better as a house dog than as a kennel dog.

■ History

The Chesapeake Bay retriever was developed, as the name implies, near this Eastern body of water. Waterfowl market hunters needed a dog capable of withstanding the heavy seas and cold temperatures of the open Bay, a dog capable of retrieving dozens, perhaps more, birds shot in a day. By selectively breeding for a strong conformation and a brown coat (for camouflage), the "Chessie" came to be, probably with its roots in the St. John's dog — also part of the Labrador's early beginnings. Other dogs were bred to produce the breed, including the curly-coated retriever and the various water spaniels.

It is said that the Chesapeake's protective nature came from guarding his master's gear — boat, decoys, guns, bagged birds — against theft after the hunt when his master was away fetching the horse and wagon. The story goes that the market hunters valued this trait and bred for it, creating the perfect combination of helpmate, companion, and guardian.

In 1878, the Chesapeake Bay retriever was the first breed to be recognized as a distinct, separate retriever breed by the American Kennel Club, predating AKC recognition of the other retriever breeds by four decades.

■ In the Field

The Chesapeake is first and foremost a waterfowl dog, and not one for beginners or those who dabble in the sport. This is a serious dog that requires serious work to stay fit and happy; consequently, it is not usually best as a "first dog." Chesapeakes have excellent eyes and memories, making them superb markers of fallen birds.

On land, they do not, as a rule, possess the speed, slash, and fire of the Labrador, nor the beauty of the hunting golden retriever. But they have outstanding noses and a nearly neurotic drive to find downed game. They are especially good on crippled birds. Methodical in their ground coverage, they hunt close to the gun with proper field training.

Most serious upland hunters seeking a flushing retriever do not seriously consider a Chesapeake. The dog's first love is the water — and the person who takes him duck hunting.

■ Trainability

The Chesapeake is best trained by his owner rather than a professional trainer. Part of the stories of bad training experiences with the breed stem from the handler trying to force the dog into the same training regimen as used on a Labrador. The Chesapeake's stubbornness and desire to do things their own way can frustrate a handler unaccustomed to the breed. They do not respond well to heavy-handedness, and they quickly get bored with repetitive drills. It is said that in training a Labrador, you give orders; with a Chesapeake, you negotiate. It is imperative with all breeds — but especially this one — to know when there's been enough for one training session and it's time to quit.

■ Strengths/Weaknesses

The breed's strengths include an insatiable hunting drive, wonderful nose, superb eyesight, intelligence, and loyalty to owner and family members. Among the weaknesses are some training difficulties, stubbornness, and an aloofness with strangers that is often misinterpreted as bad temper.

There are also some health concerns, namely the dreaded hip dysplasia, elbow dysplasia, and PRA (Progressive Retinal Atrophy), which afflicts the eyes. Buyers should check into the health certification of registered parents before purchasing (see the "Hips, Elbows, and Eyes" chapter on page 48). Like the Lab, the Chesapeake is not exceptionally long-lived; a dog older than 12 is an old dog indeed. In addition, the robust life some of the harder-working dogs lead often results in aches and pains in old age, limiting mobility before their time.

■ Other Uses and the Show Ring

Unlike the Lab and the golden retriever, Chesapeakes are not in high demand for such tasks as guide dogs or therapy dogs. They are first, last, and always hunting dogs and devoted family members.

Due to their limited numbers compared with Labs and goldens, there has not been a split into show-bred and field-bred Chesapeakes, and a number of Dual Champions (both field and show championships) are sprinkled among them. A puppy buyer purchasing from a show dog litter has a better chance of getting a good hunting Chesapeake than with any of the other retrieving breeds.

CURLY-COATED RETRIEVER

The curly-coated retriever is one of the more under-represented retriever breeds in America. It is both a show dog and a hunting retriever with a small but dedicated group of breeders and devotees.

- **Area & Date of Origin:** England, 1700s
- **Function:** Retriever, gun dog, water dog, field trials
- **Height & Weight:** 25-27", 60-70 lbs (male); 23-25", 60-70 lbs (female)
- **Colors:** Black or liver
- **Coat:** Dense mass of tight, crisp curls lie close to skin and cover entire body
- **Standards:** Head longer than wide, wedge shaped; long, strong jaw; almond-shaped eyes are not prominent; tight lips; small ears hang close to sides of head; deep, broad chest; tail fairly straight and covered with curls; round, compact feet
- **Life Span:** 10-12 years

■ Appearance and Temperament

The curly-coat is quite distinctive, having a coat of tight, water-resistant curls on most of the body, the lower legs and face excepted. A large dog (males 25 - 27 inches; females 23 - 25 inches), some specimens can weigh in at 100 pounds or more. They are black or liver in color. In temperament, the curly-coat is an intelligent, loyal companion. Like the flat-coat, he is slow to mature. He is gentle with children, and tends to be aloof with strangers in the manner of the Chesapeake Bay retriever. He is something of a rarity among retrievers in that he is a good watchdog and a good protector of the family. Like virtually all the retriever breeds that were bred to hunt *with* people, the curly-coat does better in the house than in the kennel, and needs a lot of exercise.

History

The curly-coated retriever is one of the oldest retriever breeds. Developed in England where it was a favorite of English gamekeepers, the curly is probably descended from the 16th century English water spaniel, retrieving spaniel, and the Irish water spaniel. The breed was first exhibited at England's Birmingham dog show in 1860. It was first recognized by the AKC in 1924, and by the UKC in 1960.

In the Field

The curly-coat is a fine retriever on land and water, and a good flushing dog for upland game. Prized for its innate field ability and great stamina, the breed will work tirelessly all day. Its coat protects it from the iciest waters. Many do well in hunt tests, though they are rarely seen at retriever field trials.

Trainability

Because he matures slowly, this dog must have obedience training well ingrained to prevent mischief. The prolonged adolescence also means that training must proceed slower and longer. Like the Chesapeake, they do not do well with repetitious training regimens, and do better with gentle rather than harsh methods. Overall, however, the curly is very smart and highly trainable.

Strengths/Weaknesses

This breed makes a wonderful all-around gun dog for those who hunt waterfowl and enjoy hunting with a flushing retriever. They are companionable animals with a desire to please, and will do as they are asked if they understand the task. They make fine pets in the home, but there are few of these dogs available, so you may have to wait for a pup.

The breed's slow maturation process, however, often means that these dogs are not ready for the field for two or three seasons, unlike the popular Labrador, which can hunt its first year. This breed, like so many others, can be plagued by hip dysplasia and eye problems. CERF clearance for eyes and OFA or PennHIP clearances for hips are essential. In addition, some curly-coats develop pattern baldness, a malady of the immune system that can also, in extreme cases, stunt growth to a certain extent. In some dogs, the baldness can appear and disappear completely or reappear later.

Other Uses and the Show Ring

Curly-coats are found in the show ring, and a few have found work as service dogs. However, their low numbers have made them rare in these pursuits.

FLAT-COATED RETRIEVER

The flat-coated retriever is one of the more rare retriever breeds. It is also rare in that, unlike the golden and to a certain extent the Lab, the forward-thinking breeders of this dog have not allowed separate "show" and "field" lines to evolve, despite the breed's beauty. In fact, many show champion dogs also hold hunt test titles, and breeders want this tradition to continue, feeling the hunting instincts contribute to the breeds overall talents and personality.

There is a caution, however. The flat-coat is in most cases not the breed for the first-time retriever owner. They offer an exuberant playfulness that can exasperate trainers, but they do not respond at all well to the heavy-handedness that some trainers may employ in response to the dog's skylarking.

- **Area & Date of Origin:** England, 1800s
- **Function:** Retriever, gun dog, water dog, field trials
- **Height & Weight:** 23-24.5" 60-80 lbs (male); 22-23.5" 55-70 lbs (female)
- **Colors:** Solid black or solid liver
- **Coat:** Thick, flat, shiny, of moderate length; ears, front, chest, backs of legs, thighs & underside of tail well-feathered
- **Standards:** Deep chest; long, well-molded head with gentle stop and deep muzzle; almond-shaped, dark brown or hazel eyes set wide apart; small, hanging, thickly-feathered ears; strong, straight, well-feathered legs; fairly straight, flat tail, carried near horizontal; round, strong feet
- **Life Span:** 10-14 years

■ Appearance and Temperament

The flat-coated retriever is a moderately good-sized black or liver dog, the males 23 - 24 inches high and 60 - 80 pounds, and the females 22 - 23 inches and 55 - 70 pounds. One of the more handsome retrievers, the coat from which the breed draws its name is dense and flat — non-wavy — with feathering on the legs and tail much like an English or Irish setter.

The breed's temperament deserves some space to fully explain. These dogs have a prolonged adolescence, often up to 2½ years of age or longer. They are happy-go-lucky dogs and often appear immature when compared with other breeds. They are extremely people-oriented, thriving on life in the house, not the kennel. They are fine around children, but their activity level and size may not make them the best choice for a home with a toddler. They are sensitive and can go into a shell at a harsh word. Because of their high intelligence and high energy level, if you are not there to entertain them, they will entertain themselves — and not always in a constructive manner! The flat-coat does best in an environment where his people do their best to wear him out every day of his life.

■ History

The genesis of the flat-coat can be traced to a single individual, a Mr. Sewallis E. Shirley of England, who developed the breed in the 1870s from a blend of wavy-coated retriever, St. John's water dog, various water spaniels, collies, and possibly the English setter. Mr. Shirley, who bred the dogs for hunting, also happened to be the person who founded the Kennel Club and who loved show dogs, hence the dual hunting and show careers these dogs have enjoyed, the only retriever breed to have been bred for and maintained as dual purpose dogs.

The breed was admitted to the AKC register in 1915, but by 1918, its popularity was overtaken by the Labrador retriever, and by the end of the 1920s, by the golden retriever. During the two World Wars, registrations dwindled to very low levels.

■ In the Field

The well-trained flat-coat is a solid performer in the field, and arguably may look better doing it than any other breed. None of the skills a hunting retriever needs are beyond this dog's abilities, including upland hunting, which requires a keen nose. However, the upland flat-coat has to be watched carefully to make sure its ground pattern keeps well within gun range.

■ Trainability

The flat-coat responds best to gentle-handed training, not always an easy task given the dog's view of his world. The electronic collar is not usually recommended for this breed. Of vital importance is early, thorough, and repeated obedience training. It is a good idea with any retriever to start each field session with a review of *sit, stay, heel, come,* and *down*, but especially with the flat-coat.

■ Strengths/Weaknesses

Among the strengths the dog possesses are a sense of humor and a desire for human companionship, as well as an exuberance for life. In addition, the dog is at home in both the show ring and the duck blind, and the breeders specializing in flat-coats are small in number, dedicated, and knowledgeable, meaning your chance of getting a good dog are excellent. However, demand for pups almost always outweighs supply, and you may have to go on a waiting list to get one.

The breed's primary weakness can be its prolonged adolescence (although many find this an endearing trait). Left unsupervised and unentertained, these dogs can be industrious chewers, diggers, and eaters of their own stool, an activity in canines that no one has ever been able to adequately explain.

■ Other Uses

Aside from show, field, and pet use, flat-coats are not found among the ranks of service dogs as are some of the other retriever breeds such as Labradors and goldens.

■ The Show Ring

Dual champions — field and show — are numerous because of their original development and the continued breeding programs.

GOLDEN RETRIEVER

The golden retriever is one of America's most popular dogs of any breed, ranking second only to the Labrador retriever in American Kennel Club registrations. Like the Lab, this breed is popular as a pet and companion, and its high intelligence and pleasing disposition make it one of humanity's most valued workmates. As a family dog, the golden perhaps has no peer among the retrievers – unless you don't happen to like long, golden hair on the good furniture.

- **Area & Date of Origin:** Scotland, 1800s
- **Function:** Retriever, gun dog, field trials, assistance, obedience, guide dog
- **Height & Weight:** 23-24″, 65-75 lbs. (male); 21.5-22.5″, 55-65 lbs (female)
- **Colors:** Various shades of gold
- **Coat:** Dense outer coat is straight or wavy and lies close to body; heavier feathering on front of neck, backs of thighs, and underside of tail; coat on head, paws, and fronts of legs is short and even
- **Standards:** Broad skull, slightly rounded, with well-defined stop; powerful muzzle; large black nose; dark eyes set well apart; rather short ears hang with slight fold; muscular neck with loose-fitting skin; abundantly-feathered forelegs; well-muscled hind legs; thick, muscular tail at base, carried near horizontal; round, compact feet
- **Life Span:** 11-14 years

■ Appearance and Temperament

The golden, like so many hunting breeds, has suffered from its own beauty in that breeding for the show ring has diluted the hunting drive in some strains of this dog. However, there is a rule of thumb that can be applied when looking at a golden retriever. In general, the better hunters — and goldens are superb hunters — are darker in color than the very light, sometimes nearly white, show-bred dogs.

There are exceptions to this both ways, of course. But the discussion here is for those who are considering a hunting golden retriever, so bear this in mind when selecting a breeder, and make sure the breeder you use breeds for hunting and not the show ring.

In general, and like all retriever breeds, the male (dog), at 23 - 24 inches and 65 - 75 pounds, is larger than the female (bitch) at 21 - 23 inches and 55 - 65 pounds. The coat can be, as noted above, anywhere from nearly white to a very dark bronze. A thick, wavy topcoat resists moisture and weather, while the soft undercoat provides warmth. The legs, tail, and underside grow "feathers," but these are usually kept trimmed on hunting dogs.

The dogs have a pleasing face and happy eyes, denoting a bubbly and upbeat personality — the original happy warrior. Golden are great with children and do best as house dogs, quickly falling into the routines of family life. They are watchful and alert, making a racket when there's a knock at the door or a strange sound in the night, but their disposition ranks them quite low as watchdogs or personal protection dogs. They are far from wimps, however; in a battle with another dog, a male golden retriever is a devastating fighter because of his superior quickness — the fastest-reacting of all the retriever breeds. In general, male golden retrievers are not as aggressive as are the males of many other dog breeds.

History

The golden retriever was developed as a hunting retriever in England and Scotland in the late 1800s, a period that saw the development of a number of the retrieving breeds. It was an era of country shooting estates and house parties, and picking up the shot birds — sometimes many hundreds in a day — required a talented retriever. The golden also "looked the part," having been bred for beauty as well as ability. Interestingly, it is one of the few breeds that was developed solely by one person, Lord Tweedmouth.

It is believed that the golden retriever came from the ubiquitous St. John's water dog, Irish setter, and a pinch and a dash of several other breeds, the primary ones being the Tweed water spaniel (from which came today's water spaniels) and the wavy-coated retriever (a progenitor of today's flat-coat). They were first shown in England in 1908, where they were listed as "Flat Coats (Golden)." The breed was first registered with the AKC in 1925, and with the UKC in 1956.

In the Field

The golden retriever is an energetic and intelligent hunter in the fields and wetlands. In the marsh when used for waterfowling, he learns quickly, is an excellent marker, and is a rugged companion. In the uplands, he covers ground well and quickly, thorough in his ground search with a lot of "hunt."

Though it is sometimes disputed, there is the legend of the "golden nose," reputed to be the finest of all the retrieving breeds, enabling the dog to follow a scent trail on both land and across water, which helps in locating hidden cripples.

Trainability

Owing to its high intelligence, enthusiasm, and willingness to please, the golden learns quickly and retains his training well from session to session. Some goldens, however, are "soft" in comparison to the Labrador (considered the standard for training comparisons), and therefore should not be trained with a heavy hand. Where you can demand from a Lab, and negotiate with a Chesapeake, you *ask* a golden. If the dog will not do as you ask, rather than being defiant, the chances are near 100 percent it's simply because he does not understand what you want.

Strengths/Weaknesses

The breed's strengths, as alluded to above, are its friendly disposition, its intelligence, willingness to please, beauty, and its skills as a service dog. As a hunting dog, they are underestimated by those who are used to other breeds. As commented, they have an incredibly fine nose.

The golden is an active sporting dog, and as such does not do well in confined situations such as apartment living. If you don't like gold hair on the furniture, your clothes, and in wisps in the corners regardless of how tidy you are, you need to own a different breed. Goldens shed, especially in the spring.

They are also subject to such medical maladies as hip dysplasia, Progressive Retinal Atrophy, cataracts, and a heart problem known as Subvalvular Aortic Stenosis. As with any ultra-popular breed, a golden's line should be thoroughly investigated before a litter is chosen.

Other Uses

Goldens are popular guide dogs; service and therapy dogs; sniffing dogs for drugs, explosives, and contraband; and search and rescue dogs, roles they share with the ever-popular Labrador retriever.

The Show Ring

Goldens are popular show ring competitors. As a result, lines of show dogs are being bred that have far less of the hunting drive than they once had, but which the hunting lines still enjoy. While virtually all show Chesapeakes are worthy hunters, and many show Labs are, very few bench show goldens can perform in the field or marsh. It is necessary to know the background of the pup's parents; if the parents do not hunt, look elsewhere, regardless of any assurances you may receive.

IRISH WATER SPANIEL

The Irish water spaniel is one of the oldest of the sporting breeds, and one of those few kept "pure" as hunting dogs. It is also one of the most rare. Those who hunt behind this dog are few, but intensely devoted.

- **Area & Date of Origin:** Ireland, 1800s
- **Function:** Water retriever, gun dog, field trials
- **Height & Weight:** 22-24", 55-65 lbs. (male); 21-23", 45-58 lbs (female)
- **Colors:** Solid liver
- **Coat:** Double coat of tight, crisp ringlets; smooth coat on face, throat, tail end, and rear legs below the hocks
- **Standards:** Strongly-built and well-boned; lightly rectangular body with deep chest; cleanly chiseled head; top knot is characteristic of the breed, and consists of long loose curls growing down into a well-defined peak between the eyes and falling over the tops of the ears; low-set, long ears abundantly covered with long curls; "rat" tail, thick and covered with curls at the base only, tapering to a fine point at end, carried nearly level with back; large feet covered in hair both over and between the toes
- **Life Span:** 10-12 years

■ Appearance and Temperament

Always liver in color, the Irish water spaniel is one breed of retriever that sports a tightly-curled coat combined with a dense undercoat for warmth and protection from the elements. The males are 22 - 24 inches and 55 - 65 pounds in hunting trim, the females 21 - 23 inches and 45 - 58 pounds. They have a "topknot," a key characteristic of the breed, that grows between the ears in loose curls and extends downward to a widow's peak between the eyes. The breed also has a smooth, relatively short "rat tail."

In temperament, it is people oriented, like all the retrievers who have been bred to work in harmony with humans, with a strong desire to please. This dog bonds well with all family members but not necessarily other family pets unless introduced early in life. One particularly nice trait is that they are not known as "barkers."

History

Although the exact history of this breed, like so many others, is not known, it wasn't until the 1830s, in Ireland, that the breed was developed. Research suggests that common ancestors include the north country water spaniel and the south country water spaniel, breeds that no longer exist, along with the poodle and the Portuguese water dog. Justin McCarthy, in the mid 1830s, is credited with selective breeding to "fix" the breed type.

Interestingly, in America in the 1870s, the IWS was the third most popular sporting breed, and in 1900, it was the most registered breed in America. It has retained type for over 150 years, and is still very popular in Ireland.

In the Field

The Irish water spaniel is a fine hunter of both waterfowl and upland birds, possessing a good nose and tractibility. Early training is essential, something that is true of all the sporting breeds.

Trainability

With their eagerness to please and alert demeanor, the IWS trains well. They do not seem to get bored as easily as some of the other breeds, adhering to the task at hand. They are excellent markers of downed game, the best indication of fine eyesight.

Strengths/Weaknesses

Like so many of the more rare and obscure breeds, the IWS's weakness is its strength: the low numbers mean that getting a pup may be difficult and the gene pool not as broad, but the breeders have adhered to the dog's true origin and have not bred for the show ring. In fact, very few IWS's compete on the show circuit.

However, these dogs are susceptible to a variety of medical problems, many of them genetic, including canine hip dysplasia to a moderate degree, immune system problems, seizures, reaction to certain veterinary drugs, cancer (especially for those with immunity deficiencies), hair loss, hypothyroidism, and others. A potential buyer must be aware of these potential problems and consult with the breeder carefully concerning the longevity of his line before buying.

Finally some owners report that individuals of the breed are prone toward stubbornness.

Other Uses

Besides being an able hunting dog, the IWS is a fine family dog, either in its own right, or for the 10 months a year when he is not hunted.

The Show Ring

Very little use in the show ring.

LABRADOR RETRIEVER

If you are looking for an all-around hunting dog, one that doubles as a family pet and companion as well as a source of entertainment in the off-season, you may want to do what hundreds of thousands of others have done — begin and end your search with the Labrador retriever. The Lab is America's most popular dog and has been for the past decade, ranking Number One on virtually every canine registry that includes retrievers.

- **Area & Date of Origin:** Newfoundland, 1800s

- **Function:** Retriever, gun dog, field trials, guide dog, search-and-rescue, narcotics detection

- **Height & Weight:** 22.5-24.5", 65-80 lbs (male); 21.5-23.5", 55-70 lbs (female)

- **Colors:** Solid black, yellow, or chocolate

- **Coat:** Short, straight, and very dense with a soft undercoat

- **Standards:** Strongly-built and athletic; clean-cut head with a broad backskull and pronounced stop; kind, intelligent eyes; deep, broad chest; well-boned, straight forelegs; tail very thick toward base, with a rounded "otter-like" appearance, carried in line with topline; round, compact feet

- **Life Span:** 11-14 years

■ Appearance and Temperament

Ranging in size from 50 pounds to more than 100 (show-ring Labs are held to more exacting standards), the hunting Labrador retriever comes in three recognized colors — black, yellow, and chocolate. When looking at litters from hunting bloodlines, you will find them in that same order of frequency as well — the blacks outnumber the yellows, which outnumber the chocolates. There are color phases of the yellow that appear as "red Labs" as well, but these are quite rare. At one time, the black dogs were considered the best hunters, but no more. However, American and British field trials continue to be dominated by black Labs. All versions possess webbed feet, a coat that easily repels water, and a thick "otter" type tail that makes a dandy rudder in the water.

There are two essential Lab conformations seen in the field: the stocky, shorter-legged dog and the longer-legged, lanky style. Known roughly and respectively as "British style" and "American style," they share a hunting drive and exuberance for life unmatched in the canine world. The average Lab is active without being hyper, incredibly bright, easy to train, and willing to please — in fact, they almost literally live to please. The dog (male) is typically more ingratiating than the slightly aloof female (bitch). Although the male is a better protector and guardian, no one should ever buy a Labrador as a guard dog — they are just too friendly. They will, however, bark and put up a fuss if something is not right, making them a passably good watchdog.

Importantly for hunters and show-ring competitors who use their dogs in the company of other animals, Labs are friendly to other dogs as well as humans.

■ History

The Labrador retriever's roots are in hunting. First developed in Newfoundland from an earlier breed, probably the St. John's dog that itself came from the English water dogge to help fishermen retrieve floats, nets, and the occasional cod, one version of the dog, called the lesser St. John's dog, was taken back to England where it was developed as a game dog by several members of the aristocracy for their shooting pleasure (the other version — the greater St. John's dog — stayed behind to become the Newfoundland breed). The dog became a recognized breed in England in 1903 and in the United States in the late 1920s, when only a handful were registered with the AKC.

Interestingly, the other retriever breeds — golden retrievers, flat-coated retrievers and others — share the Lab's ancestry, making them relatives in the distant past.

■ In the Field
In England, the dog was and is used primarily as a picker-up after driven shoots or as an adjunct to the pointing breeds in "rough" — walk-up — shoots. In North America, the breed's most recognizable role is as a waterfowl retriever. That's not to say that it isn't a great and very popular upland dog, because it is, working as a flusher much like a spaniel, and with the ability to locate and retrieve downed game second to none. As this is being written, gaining in popularity is the "pointing Lab," a Labrador with the pointing instinct that all *canids* possess, developed through breeding and training to a relatively high degree.

While the classic Labrador retriever gun dog hunts waterfowl and flushes upland birds, in the latter case, it is much more effective on birds found in the open — pheasants, especially, and prairie species such as sharp-tailed grouse, Hungarian partridge, chukars, and prairie chickens. On birds normally found in thick cover, such as ruffed grouse and woodcock, most hunters find a pointing breed superior, offering more warning before a shot is presented.

■ Trainability
The Labrador retriever is a highly-trainable, quickly-maturing animal often ready for the rigors of the field before his or her first birthday. Further, Labs seem to continue to learn throughout their lives. As active dogs, they thrive on work, and seem proud of a skill once mastered.

Labs have been bred for the ability to remember. This trait is vital for remembering where each bird is on multiple falls. This highly-tuned memory helps the Lab retain his training skills with regular brush-up sessions.

Labs are best trained with affection and praise. Though they can take a certain amount of heavy handedness, they respond best when they see themselves as part of a team. When a Lab fails to execute a command, the chances are 99 out of 100 it is because he does not understand, rather than he is refusing to obey.

■ Strengths/Weaknesses
Among the Lab's many strengths are intelligence, a willingness to please, adaptability, a loving demeanor, a fine nose, an intense drive in the field, loyalty, and playfulness.

The breed's weaknesses show up in the area of health. Labs are especially prone to hip dysplasia and elbow and retinal problems. Any dog as popular as the Labrador retriever is too often bred from stock not suitable for producing healthy puppies; there is a ready buyer awaiting each pup.

Like most large breeds, they are not especially long-lived, a 12-year-old dog being pretty close to the end of its lifespan. They also require a lot of activity and therefore are not the perfect pet for the apartment dweller. Most hunting Labs are also house dogs, despite their size, and whoever does the vacuuming will attest to the fact that they are prodigious shedders when kept indoors.

■ Other Uses
Labrador retrievers serve society as search and rescue dogs, therapy dogs, guide dogs for those who are visually impaired, assistance dogs for the physically- and hearing-challenged, and as drug- and arson-detection dogs. Their ease of trainability, unique disposition, and keen senses make them extremely valuable in helping humans with the jobs we can't do as well ourselves.

Those who adopt a Lab soon learn that there is a wide culture devoted to these animals: books, videos, support organizations, training groups, clubs, and registries abound. So do competitive situations, especially hunt tests and field trials, both at the professional- and amateur-trainer levels.

■ The Show Ring
At present, the standards considered by show-ring judges call for a dog with a blocky head, short coupling, shallow chest, and short legs — long-legged, American-type Labs need not apply. Such conformation would not give a dog the stamina it needs in the pheasant fields of the Midwest, however.

At the present time, there is no hard evidence that show-ring breeding has dimmed too much of the hunting drive in these great animals like it has other breeds, such as the Irish setter. However, very few dual-champion (bench and field) Labs have been seen for a number of decades. Prospective puppy buyers need to know that their pup comes with a hunting, not bench, pedigree.

NOVA SCOTIA DUCK-TOLLING RETREIVER

The Nova Scotia Duck-Tolling Retriever – "toller" – is one of the most unusual hunting dogs, certainly the most unusual waterfowling dog, in the world in that he actually participates in the decoying of ducks. He was designed to "toll," or lure, and retrieve waterfowl. The breed is also one of the very few developed to take advantage of the natural curiosity of its prey; in this case, to lure ducks close enough to the hunter for a shot.

- **Area & Date of Origin:** Nova Scotia, 1800s

- **Function:** Gun dog, waterfowl flusher (toller), retriever

- **Height & Weight:** 23-24.5", 45-50 lbs (male); 17-20", 35-45 lbs (female)

- **Colors:** Any shade of red, ranging from golden red through dark coppery red

- **Coat:** Medium-length, water-repellent doublecoat; may have slight wave on back but otherwise straight; soft featherings

- **Standards:** Medium-sized, compact, powerful dog; strong, straight, short back; clean-cut, slightly wedge-shaped skull; almond-shaped eyes set well apart; high-set triangular ears with rounded tips; well-feathered tail is broad at the base and held high in a curve when the dog is alert; strongly-webbed feet

- **Life Span:** 12-14 years

■ Appearance and Temperament

The toller looks much like a large fox in coloration and movement, and indeed this is the object. The males are 23 - 25 inches tall and weigh 45 - 50 pounds, the females 17- 20 inches and 35 - 45 pounds. The dog has a double coat of orange or red. Often, and perhaps desirably, there are spots of white, especially on the tip of the tail, the feet, and the head. The tail itself is long and bushy and waves enticingly as the dog runs. These dogs have a sprightly manner about them as they move.

In temperament, these dogs are warm and willing companions that take well to training and family life. They like activity and a robust lifestyle, and they make a good pet for homes where there is a lot of coming and going, especially in homes with young children.

History

The toller was developed, as you would expect, in Nova Scotia, in the 1800s, possibly starting with a European breed called a cage dog, an extinct breed that had the same color as the toller and was used to lure waterfowl into nets, although it was not also a retriever. It is thought that the present breed was developed by crossing a variety of others, including but probably not limited to the St. John's water dog, golden retriever, Chesapeake Bay retriever, the collie, the flat-coat, and the cocker spaniel. The end result is a fine if unlikely looking retriever. The dog was recognized in 1945 by the Canadian Kennel Club (CKC), when the present name became the breed designation.

In the Field

It should be stressed that the toller functions well as a traditional retriever, and probably this is the major use of the breed, especially in the United States. However, it has been a well-known fact for centuries that a hunting technique of foxes is to prance back and forth on shore, appearing in brief flashes behind cover. Curious ducks swim closer for a look, whereupon the fox pounces. The toller was bred to replicate this technique and the look and movements of the fox. The flashes of white on the billowing coat and floating tail add duck-attracting flashes that get ducks aroused.

In the old days, tollers were used to lure ducks into wire or mesh traps. Today, the sportsman hides in shore cover and simply plays fetch with his toller, tossing a tennis ball or stick so that the dog runs along the shore, disappears into cover, reappears with the object, and disappears again to deliver the ball or stick to his master. When the curious ducks swim close enough, the hunter stands, the ducks flush, and he takes his shot, after which the toller makes the retrieve in the usual manner. Other breeds, especially those reddish or light in color, can be used for tolling, but the toller does it best.

Trainability

Traditional obedience and retriever training work well with this breed, although they are somewhat slow to mature. The tolling itself does not have to be taught — the hunter is merely playing fetch with his dog.

Strengths/Weaknesses

Like all the retriever breeds, this dog's happy personality and willingness to please are its greatest assets, along with its intelligence. The dog is hardy in cold water, and is also used for upland hunting, although infrequently.

Among its weaknesses are a few special medical problem, including some cases of deafness late in life, PRA, some problems with the immune system and thyroid, and hip dysplasia. Compared with other breeds, however, elbow dysplasia is virtually unknown. Getting a puppy is a problem because of the limited number of these dogs, and there seems to be show stock as well as hunting stock, although the differences are not as pronounced as they are in some other breeds.

Other Uses

Tollers make wonderful pets, and some are used as therapy dogs because of their friendliness. The dogs also compete in UKC and NAHRA (but not AKC) hunt tests.

The Show Ring

Although these dogs are not recognized by the AKC, the CKC and the UKC recognize them and they appear regularly in shows sponsored by these registries.

STANDARD POODLE

Of all the retrieving breeds, none has been bred for as many different sizes and colors as has the poodle, from the Germanic pudelin – or "splashing" dog. While the dog's distinctive cut, especially as a show dog, gives him something of a delicate appearance, looks are deceiving. Standard poodles are honest-to-goodness hunting dogs in the best sense of waterfowling tradition.

- **Area & Date of Origin:** Germany and central Europe, 1500s
- **Function:** Water retriever, gun dog
- **Height & Weight:** Over 15" (usually over 21"); 45-65 lb
- **Colors:** Any solid color
- **Coat:** Curly, harsh, and dense
- **Standards:** Long, fine, chiseled muzzle; slight but definite stop; oval eyes; level topline; tail straight and carried up, docked; small, oval feet
- **Life Span:** 10-13 years

■ Appearance and Temperament

The standard poodle is a dog of varying weight and to a certain extent, height, running approximately 21 - 26 inches at the shoulder. Various shades of gray, brown, and black are acceptable, the coat curly and wavy. The well-known poodle cut probably originated as a means of keeping joints and vital areas warm in cold water.

In temperament, this is one of dogdom's more delightful breeds, having a high intelligence and a ready sense of humor. They are very people oriented and make human friends quickly. They are also sensitive to the moods of people and even other dogs around them. However, standard poodles have a tendency to remember if you unfairly discipline them.

History

Poodles are one of the world's oldest dog breeds, with canines similar in type to today's poodles carved in Roman tombs as far back as 30 A.D. They can also be seen in paintings of the Middle Ages. Originating in Germany, the breed took its name from the German word "pudel," which means "to splash in water." They grew to popularity in France in pre-Napoleonic times, hence the misnomer: French poodle. They were among the first hunting dogs developed, possibly from herding dogs, and actually predated the use of gunpowder in sporting weapons.

The first poodles in England were known as "rough water dogs," and they served primarily as hunting companions. Poodles were first brought to the U.S. toward the end of the 19th century, although the breed did not become popular until after World War II. From the mid-1950s to the 1970s, the poodle was the most popular breed in the United States. Today, the standard poodle is differentiated from the miniature and toy varieties.

In the Field

Developed originally as a water retriever and herder of ducks into net traps, the poodle is used today as a waterfowl retriever and upland flusher. In both the uplands and the lowlands, however, they demonstrate something of a reluctance to barge into cover or leap into unknown waters with the abandon of some of the other breeds. They are also sensitive to cold water, despite their coat.

Trainability

Because of some of the sensitivities outlined above, these dogs have to be trained to do some things that other breeds do naturally, such as bust brush and lunge through emergent water plants. However, their willingness to please and their intelligence makes them good training candidates, including good candidates for electronic training devices.

Strengths/Weaknesses

These dogs are people-oriented; in fact they become single-person dogs in the field with their trainer, so they are perfect candidates for the person who wants to bond with his dog during training. They are bright, creative, and naturally friendly. For those owners suffering from allergies, poodle hair is usually not an irritant, and their devotees claim they "don't shed." (All dogs shed; poodles are just light shedders.)

On the downside, poodles must be groomed regularly, and they are susceptible to a number of maladies of the hips, eyes, and thyroid, as well as some other rare medical problems. They are not as rugged in the field or water as some other breeds, but they are enthusiastic once trained in a task.

Other Uses

These dogs rival even the Labrador in their uses by people. Poodles make great service dogs, especially as guides for the hearing- and visually-impaired (in fact, there are records of poodles being used as seeing-eye dogs as far back as the 17th century). They are proficient in agility competitions and the show ring.

The Show Ring

Standard poodles are a mainstay of the conformation ring; however, the AKC requirement for these dogs is 15 inches maximum in height.

The Spaniels are some of today's premier upland flushing dogs.

CHAPTER 8

THE SPANIELS

by Jason Smith

THE SPANIEL'S PRIMARY FUNCTION is as a flusher of upland game. Over time, some spaniel breeds, such as the American and Irish water spaniels, have become more valuable in water environments, rivaling some of the retriever breeds as dedicated waterfowl hunters. Today, those "spaniels" are classified among the true retrievers. Other breeds, such as the cockers, are spaniels; one other, the Brittany was once named "Brittany spaniel" but is a true pointing breed.

By and large, the spaniel's original job description was to seek out and flush game — both feathers and fur — that were then driven into nets, and later, with the advent of the armed pursuit of game, put up before the hunter to be shot.

This upland hunting was done within shotgun range (less than 40 yards) of the human hunter so that flushed game could be easily bagged, and the dog has, over time, developed a natural tendency — augmented with training — to work a hunting field in a zig-zag pattern, a process called *quartering*. Here, the dog shows its natural hunting instincts by using the wind to its advantage and pursuing game — both by scent and sight — relentlessly until flushed. All spaniels are expected to retrieve the game back to the hunter's hand; some may need more formal instruction in the retrieving arena, however.

The tough coat of all the spaniel breeds is a product of their function, that of busting through tough cover or water in any weather condition to fulfill their duties as finder, flusher, and retriever of game. Dense, feathery coats provide a suitable barrier to much of the brush encountered by the dog.

These coats, though, have also been the reason some of the breeds have seen their primary function switch from the field to the show-ring, with a resulting loss in hunting drive and sensual acuity. Some breeds, primarily the cockers, have their coats groomed to long, lavish finishes for beauty's sake, coats that would be snarled into a mess five minutes into the cover. Others, such as the field spaniel and Welsh springer, however, have followed strictly in appearance the guidelines set forth by their hunting ancestry; many make both good show-ring and hunting dogs. In any case, it is recommended that if you intend the dog to be a hunting spaniel, you seek out bloodlines that consistently produce hunting dogs.

Today, spaniels mostly pursue upland birds, leaving the fur to hounds or the versatile breeds. Many dedicated pheasant hunters look no further than an English springer spaniel to fulfill all of their pheasant hunting needs. They have also seen action on ruffed grouse, woodcock, quail, and the prairie birds.

Some spaniels are befallen with orthopedic problems, in particular the Boykin spaniel — one of the spaniels used more for waterfowl than for upland work — which has a high incidence of canine hip dysplasia. As with all hunting dogs, it is wise to buy puppies only from those breeders who have demonstrated a genetic soundness in their dogs; most hunting dogs will typically develop joint problems and arthritis over the course of time simply from their athletic work. There is no need to compound the pain by having a genetic problem to begin with.

Perhaps more than anything else, however, spaniels will become a willing and affectionate part of any family when given love and affection in return. Also, by being competitive in the show-ring, intelligent and trainable to take part in agility testing, and having a wonderful temperament so as to function in many service areas, all breeds of spaniels fill a wonderful segment of the community. They can give their owners many different areas in which to enjoy them. ∎

CLUMBER SPANIEL

Though its full name ends in "spaniel," the Clumber spaniel doesn't look much like the other flushing dogs. Its function is the same, however — which is that it is a flushing dog that works through heavy cover. The versatile Clumbers are currently enjoying a resurgence in the U.S. in several categories of use, among them, hunting, agility, show, obedience, and as companion dogs.

- **Area & Date of Origin:** France, 1700s
- **Function:** Bird flushing & retrieving, gun dog, versatile hunting dog, field trials
- **Height & Weight:** 18-20", 70-85 lbs. (male); 17-19", 55-70 lbs (female)
- **Colors:** White dog with lemon or orange markings usually on the ears and/or face (the fewer the markings on body the better)
- **Coat:** Straight, flat, soft, and dense
- **Standards:** Long, low, substantial dog; has the appearance of great power; massive head with heavy brow; well-developed flews; nose colored any shade of brown; eyes large, deep-set, diamond shaped, deep amber color; low-set triangular ears with a rounded lower edge; well-feathered tail can be docked or left natural, carried near horizontal; large, compact feet
- **Life Span:** 10-12 years

■ Appearance and Temperament

If you haven't seen a Clumber spaniel before, imagine a cross between a bloodhound and a St. Bernard, which is one theory of how the breed came to be. Unlike the smaller, quicker, more nimble spaniels — English springer spaniel, English cocker spaniel, American cocker spaniel, and field spaniel — Clumbers are big, slow dogs with sad eyes, large skulls, and modest feathering along their legs, chest, buttocks, and docked tail.

Their soft, dense, straight coat is mostly white with brown or orange flecking throughout; it is naturally weather-resistant, making the dog able to withstand many hunting conditions. Clumbers are short for their bulk, standing approximately 18 to 20 inches at the shoulder; males weigh in the range of 70 to 85 pounds, females 55 to 70.

The temperament of the Clumber is that of a big loveable schmo, which has led to its use as a companion dog, a calm, even-tempered dog able to be with strangers. They are affectionate family dogs, and their easy trainability, which makes them able to perform so many functions, helps them find a genuine place in the household.

History

The history of the Clumber spaniel is a much-debated topic among Clumber fanciers. It is thought that the breed originated in France, making its way to England in 1768 in the way of a gift from Duc de Noailles to the Second Duke of Newcastle, who housed them in a kennel at Clumber Park. According to paintings, our modern Clumbers show very little difference from those of the late 18th century.

Two other theories hold that Clumbers developed in England from a cross between the Alpine spaniel and basset or Saint Bernard, or that it developed from the Blenheim spaniel. Whatever path the Clumber took to the present day, it has only recently enjoyed a resurgence of popularity. It was one of the first ten breeds recognized by the AKC in the late 1800s, but it has only been since 1968 that the Clumber has established a foothold in the U.S. Now they are a relatively popular breed at dog shows, and they are increasingly common in other venues.

In the Field

It has only been recently that hunters have really begun to see the potential of Clumber spaniels for the field. They are a spaniel through and through, tracking, finding, and flushing game, and then retrieving reliably to hand. They may be hardier waterfowling dogs than some of the other spaniels, but their predominantly white coat makes them difficult to conceal. The same coat certainly shows up in the uplands.

Clumbers are slow dogs, though, so expect a slower pace when hunting behind one. Also, the Clumber spaniel was bred to go through thick cover in England — woodlands, hedgerows, thick ferns — and therefore hunts with its head low to the ground, fastidiously sniffing out any trace of scent at a much slower gait. The English springer and other spaniels, by contrast, were meant for slightly lighter cover, hunting with their heads up and at a quick pace.

Trainability

Clumbers are easily trainable, as evidenced by their many functions. They can be trained for agility tests (the first Clumber to earn this title was only recently in 1999), obedience tests, hunting trials, the show ring, and tracking tests. They are truly a versatile dog, and in that regard will pick up lessons easily, but firm, compassionate compliance will get

through to this family-dog-at-heart faster than forcing. Though Clumbers may retrieve naturally, a good training regime on fetching will get them to be splendid retrievers.

Strengths/Weaknesses

The versatility of the Clumber is a major strength, but its slower pace in the uplands may be hard for some hunters to deal with. Also, its white coat, unless covered with camouflage, will hurt the waterfowler. Its feathered coat, like the other spaniels, will require a modest amount of grooming prior to the hunting season to assure the dog isn't festooned with burrs in one short trip afield.

There is little noted in the way of health problems associated with the Clumber spaniel, but it can be assumed that it suffers from the other ailments typical of the spaniels — hip dysplasia, eye problems, etc. There may be more in the way of joint problems and arthritis because of the dog's larger frame, especially for the hard-working Clumber.

Other Uses

As mentioned several times already, Clumbers can be used for a variety of purposes. Currently, there are numerous Clumbers with titles in either obedience, tracking, hunting, agility, and of course, the show ring. They are also a valued family dog, and as such, may be trained for companion or therapy work.

The Show Ring

The show ring is still where the Clumber shines, specifically with his distinctive form, color, and gait. Some show lines may be heavily groomed and lack the hunting instinct; it will require some research to find a line of working, active Clumbers to fulfill your field needs because of the abundance of show Clumbers.

COCKER SPANIEL

The cocker spaniel – referred to overseas as the American cocker spaniel – is most easily confused with the English cocker spaniel; in fact, the two became separate breeds only after selective breeding for a few minor differences. American cockers have the show ring as their primary goal, but many hunting lines for this flushing dog still exist.

- **Area & Date of Origin:** United States, 1800s
- **Function:** Bird flushing & retrieving, gun dog, field trials
- **Height & Weight:** ~15" (male); ~14" (female); 24-28 lbs
- **Colors:** Black variety: solid black or black and tan; ASCOB (Any Solid Color Other than Black) variety: cream, red, brown, and brown with tan points; Parti-color variety: any of the allowed solid colors broken up on a white background; also roans
- **Coat:** Silky, flat or slightly wavy, not overly long; short and fine on the head; ears, chest, abdomen, and legs are well-feathered
- **Standards:** Sturdy, compact body; alert, soft, and appealing expression; rounded skull with pronounced stop; long, low-set, lobular ears; topline slopes slightly to rear; tail docked and carried in line or slightly higher than the topline; large, round feet
- **Life Span:** 12-15 years

■ Appearance and Temperament

The American cocker spaniel (or just "cocker") is the smallest of the AKC's Sporting Group. Cockers stand 14 to 15 inches at the shoulders, and they weigh on average in the 20 to 30 pound range. Their heads are more rounded with a more pronounced forehead than the English cocker, and the feathering along the legs, ears, chest, belly, and docked tail may be longer than the English cocker's. Big, round, sad eyes are also characteristic of the breed.

Color markings on the soft flat or wavy coat can vary from any solid color (most often black, brown, cream, buff, rust, or shades of these), to those colors with tan markings in the facial area or legs and feet, to mixtures of any of the colors and white; they also have roan variations with the color flecking "peppering" the white patches.

Cockers make excellent family animals because of their size and temperament — an affectionate dog with no "mood swings" when encountering strangers. They may be slightly reserved, but are most often docile, which makes them excellent candidates for obedience tests and therapy work. They are great dogs to have around small children, though their excitability (based on its hunting history and eager-to-please attitude) should be monitored.

■ History

Cocker spaniels as a group (including both the American and English cocker spaniels) developed at the same time as the English springer spaniel. In fact, some history suggests that these breeds were at first merely dogs from the same litter — smaller pups were used for hunting the smaller woodcock (cockers), and larger pups were used to spring or flush game from cover (springers).

The cocker spaniel encompassed both the English and American versions until 1946, when the English cocker was recognized as a separate breed; differences were primarily in size (bigger) and skull shape (more elongated). So when the English cocker was separated out from the group "cocker spaniel," the American cocker spaniel was left to be referred to as "cocker spaniel," at least in this country. Abroad, the American cocker spaniel has the designation, while the English cocker spaniel is simply "cocker spaniel."

The cocker spaniel, presumably including both versions, have been exhibited in the U.S. since the late 1800s, and the American Spaniel Club (the parent breed club of the American Cocker Spaniel) has been in existence since 1881. Though its reason for being was as a flushing dog on the English countryside, like all the other spaniels developed around the same time period, the cocker spaniel owes much of its preservation and popularity to the show ring. There are still several lines of hunting cocker spaniels, able to hunt upland birds very well, but most will be groomed to a lavish finish for conformation shows.

In the Field

Cocker spaniels were developed as flushing dogs, and cockers that hunt today remain fixed in that function of their ancestors. They quarter in front of the walking hunter at a close range, use their good noses to find and flush birds, and then are expected to retrieve the downed game — no matter the conditions — after the shot. Because of their smaller size and perhaps delicate nature, they find scant — if any — use in waterfowl hunting, though they are expected to retrieve birds from the water should that be where they fall. Their lustrous coats — while not as manicured as the show ring cockers — will attract burrs and debris quite efficiently, so regular grooming, and perhaps a field cut before the season, are necessary around the ears, tail, and feet.

Trainability

Cockers are highly trainable, as evidenced by the fact that they also find many uses and have excellent results in the agility and obedience tests. Their smaller stature requires a softer hand, but their eager attitude, affinity for people, and natural hunting instinct (in hunting lines) should keep formal training to a minimum. Basic obedience must be taught to keep the dog a good citizen around the home and controllable in the field; specialized training is needed for other tests.

Strengths/Weaknesses

Perhaps the biggest weakness for the upland hunter considering a cocker spaniel, in addition to its smaller size that may limit some of the cover it can go through, is finding a sound hunting line of cocker spaniels. The American Spaniel Club is a great place to start, though; they even have hunt tests and trials open only to cocker spaniels. The hunting cocker can be an excellent flushing dog. With training, it can be a dependable retriever, too, although it is limited to the uplands.

Health concerns of the cocker spaniel are those that all dog owners encounter — from hip and elbow dysplasia to inherited eye problems, or joint and arthritis in the very active dog. Also, grooming may be more time-consuming with this breed.

Other Uses

In addition to being a flushing dog for the upland hunter and a dedicated family dog, cockers also find use — and are gaining in popularity — in the agility testing world. Their athleticism and desire to please their owner make them obedient and animated, two requisites for agility work. But the calm, obedient, well-trained cocker spaniel also makes an excellent candidate for therapy work, cheering up the sick or shut-in.

However, it is the show ring where most cockers are destined, and their appearance, while changing dramatically from its original ancestors, will turn many heads in conformation shows. The show ring cocker will not show many characteristics that would make it a good hunting dog, specifically its coat.

The Show Ring

Here the cocker spaniel finds its home, as this is where most cocker spaniels see their action — other than playing in the house. Their long, lustrous coats, rounded heads, long ears, and deep, sad eyes make for a beautiful dog to see trotting around the conformation ring. The show cocker does not have much in common with the hunting cocker; you can imagine what that near floor-length coat would look like after five minutes in a briar patch!

ENGLISH COCKER SPANIEL

In the U.S., this breed is referred to as the "English cocker spaniel," and their American cousins are simply "cocker spaniels." On every other continent and in every other country, it's the other way around – the English cocker is simply "cocker spaniel," compared to an "American cocker spaniel." In any case, the English cocker spaniel is a sound flushing dog, very different in appearance than its show ring brother, and a wonderful family animal.

- **Area & Date of Origin:** England, 1800s
- **Function:** Bird flushing & retrieving, gun dog, field trials
- **Height & Weight:** 16-17", 28-34 lbs (male); 15-16", 26-32 lbs (female)
- **Colors:** Solid black, liver, or red, black and tan, liver and tan, and any of these colors on a white background either parti-colored, ticked, or roan
- **Coat:** Short and fine on head, medium length on body; silky in texture, flat or slightly wavy; well-feathered but not a hindrance in the field
- **Standards:** Solid and compact, giving the impression of strength; deep chest; short, strong back; softly contoured head, with soft expression; slightly oval, dark brown eyes; low-set ears; topline slopes slightly to rear; docked tail carried horizontally and in constant motion while dog is working; firm, round, cat-like feet
- **Life Span:** 12-14 years

■ Appearance and Temperament

The English cocker spaniel may be confused most often with the cocker spaniel (American cocker), but the English cocker is usually taller (about 17 inches at the shoulder) and with a thinner coat. Additionally, the typical buff color seen in the American cocker is absent in the English cocker. The English springer spaniel, another dog that may be confused with the English cocker, is quite a bit larger.

The English cocker is a compact, sturdy dog weighing on average about 30 pounds. Their coat is silky and slightly wavy, and it may come in a variety of colors, among them blue roan (black spots on a white background with black flecking throughout the white), solid black or shades of red, and various mixtures of black, liver, tan, red, and white. This coat is well-feathered about the long ears, short legs, and docked tail; it requires some maintenance to keep in working order.

There has been a divergence in appearances of the show ring and field-bred English cockers, very similar to the divergence seen in the English springer spaniel. Typically, field-bred English cockers will have the coat clipped much closer to be more practical in the field. They have deep chests, which help in endurance in the field, and are low to the ground to break through thick cover. They may look very similar to a small English springer spaniel, and not so much like the show ring English cockers with the long coats, rounded skulls, and large, deep eyes.

They are an affectionate breed, loyal and loving to their family, but they are usually shy around strangers. Once they have become attached or used to new people, however, they are most often energetic and even protective. The breed may have undergone some dilution of the hunting instinct — with a large following in the show ring — but the dog finds a special niche as a family dog. And a field-bred English cocker will serve doubly as a fine hunter, too.

History

The English cocker spaniel was recognized as a separate breed (from just "cocker spaniel") in 1946. It is believed that around the time of the fine-tuning of the English springer spaniel (late 1800s and early 1900s) in England, smaller dogs in the same litter were used to hunt woodcock and were therefore called "cockers"; the larger dogs were used to flush, or "spring" game from cover. Hence the "cocker" and the "springer" we see today. Of course, this could all be simply doggy folklore.

We can safely assume that the development of the English cocker took place about the same time as the other spaniel breeds, fulfilling a need of hunters for a dog to quarter in front within gun range, flush game from thick cover, and then retrieve it to hand. Their inherent beauty carried them into the show ring, and with it, an exaggeration of the physical features that made the dog so practical in the field.

In the Field

The English cocker spaniel is a flushing dog, first bred to go through or under the English countryside's heavy cover. It is also a sound retriever, able to fetch downed game on both land and water. Its coat — if kept at any great length — will most likely be the biggest hindrance to a hunting English cocker; but if given a good field clipping, it should perform its duty on par with an English springer spaniel. However, the shorter English cocker may have a tougher time seeing above the cover to locate the hunter.

Another disadvantage to the hunting English cocker spaniel is the depletion of the hunting instinct due to the fact that these animals make excellent house pets — many more English cockers will never see the uplands than those that will. You will have to research hunting English cocker bloodlines carefully to find a reputable breeder. Many people have sought out hunting bloodlines in England.

Trainability

English cockers are fairly intelligent and energetic, making training fun yet difficult at times. They can occasionally be a bit absent-minded, so firm training may be necessary. They have superb noses, however, and basic obedience may be all that's needed to make sure the dog follows its commands and stays within gun range. Basic obedience will also help the dog learn manners for its other useful — and best — role: as a house dog.

Strengths/Weaknesses

Though the English cocker spaniel is a legitimate choice for the upland hunter desiring a flushing dog, it may be difficult to find a strain of hunting English cockers to choose from. Their smaller size may be a hindrance in some cover types, although an asset in others. While the dog does swim well, it is only suited to warmer-weather waterfowling. It has a good nose and a great desire to chase game and put it in the air in front of the gun.

There is not much written about the health of the breed, but it can be safely assumed that the hunting dogs will suffer from the same ailments typical of all our canine athletes. But because of the selective breeding of the field-bred English cocker — and careful observation by certain breed clubs — some genetic hip, eye, or elbow disorders may be kept to a minimum.

Other Uses

While finding its ultimate niche in the house as a family pet, English cockers have been taking part in tracking and agility testing for some time. And English cocker spaniel fanciers are finding that it's a lot of fun — the dog's good nose is helping them compete in the tracking tests, and the agility testing is just enjoyable to begin with. English cockers that have been bred for the family may also find use as therapy dogs and companion dogs for those in need.

The Show Ring

Most English cocker spaniel enthusiasts have as their primary goal the show ring. The coat on these dogs can be grown to great lengths and groomed to a beautiful finish, and the more rounded head of the show dogs, accentuated by the typical large, sad eyes of the cocker spaniel, have made them excellent show ring competitors. If searching for a field dog, be sure to seek out those parents with a history of hunting; you'll find many more destined for the show ring.

ENGLISH SPRINGER SPANIEL

The English springer spaniel is perhaps the most recognizable and popular of all the flushing spaniels. Its parent club, the English Springer Spaniel Field Trial Association, was founded in 1924, and the breed has endured as both a competitive show ring dog and a dedicated hunter; however, there has been a divergence in appearance and strains between those two uses. The English springer spaniel – or just "springer" – is considered the premier flushing dog.

- **Area & Date of Origin:** England, 1800s
- **Function:** Bird flushing & retrieving, gun dog, field trials
- **Height & Weight:** 20", ~50 lbs. (male); 19", ~40 lbs (female)
- **Colors:** Black or liver with white, black, or liver roan, or tricolored (black or liver and white with tan markings); also white with black or liver markings
- **Coat:** Outercoat is medium length, flat or wavy; undercoat is soft and dense; feathering on the ears, chest, legs, and belly
- **Standards:** Strong, compact body with deep chest; topline slopes gently to rear; oval eyes of medium size; long ears; docked tail carried horizontally or slightly elevated; compact feet are well-feathered between the toes
- **Life Span:** 10 -14 years

■ Appearance and Temperament

In contrast to the more white-and-red Welsh springer spaniel, the English springer spaniel has black or liver-colored spots on a white background. There is also the possibility of a blue or liver roan coloration — much like the English cocker spaniel in which there is extensive flecking of the liver or blue color on the white parts — and a tricolor, where tan is mixed in with the facial coloration with the black or liver. The coat can be flat or wavy, and there is nice feathering along the legs, ears, and docked tail.

The springer is a sturdy, compact, medium-sized dog, weighing on average about 50 pounds, with a height of about 20 inches at the shoulder. The springer also has slightly longer ears than its Welsh cousin.

The field-bred English springer spaniel is typically on the small side, and their ears and feathering along the legs may be shorter. However, they are strong dogs, fitting their history of being hunting dogs that were meant to bust through heavy cover.

The English springer spaniel is happiest when around its family, though it is probably not the best guard dog. It serves a good role as a watchdog, but the barking may be more in anticipation of meeting someone new than fending off a stranger! Though they may be hyper at times and need training to learn some manners, they are family dogs, through and through; hunting with their family will fulfill the life of any springer.

■ History

The AKC recognized the breed in 1902, but the English springer spaniel's history dates back much further, making it one of the oldest known hunting breeds. According to the breed's parent club, "The Spaniel is thought to have originated in Spain and was perhaps introduced to ancient Britons by the Roman legions. The Spaniel was known in pre-Christian Britain, and is mentioned by name in an ancient law of Wales as early as 300 A.D." Whether that was an English or Welsh springer spaniel was not noted, but it's clear that the role served by spaniels has been around for quite some time.

It is thought that English springer spaniels were used for flushing game birds and furred animals as early as the 1500s and 1600s. At this time, the game was caught by hawks, hounds, or nets. Since then, the dog has been a regular around the English countryside, and its role has been honed into what we see today — a tough, scrappy hunting dog able to bust through heavy cover or swim through most any water conditions to flush and fetch game.

North America's English springer spaniels got their start in 1913, and the divergence between show and field-bred springers is thought to have begun in the early 1940s when the springer's last Dual Championship — a dog with a title in both show and field competitions — was achieved.

In the Field
English springer spaniels currently find a large following among dedicated upland hunters, specifically pheasant hunters, and waterfowlers use them to a degree, though late-season or cold-weather waterfowling may be hard on these smaller dogs. But in the uplands, a springer is a tough dog to match in terms of stamina, nose, retrieving ability (with some training), quartering ability, and dedication to putting birds in the air. It has been agreed upon and stated by many knowledgeable writers and hunters that if they only hunted pheasants, day after day, they would get a springer.

Be conscious of the difference in field and show-bred English springers, and buy a puppy from a breeding that shows strong hunting instincts in the parents. Though they may be bold and inquisitive, they should also be even-tempered around the house, making them an ideal family and hunting companion.

Trainability
The English springer spaniel's willingness to please necessitates a compassionate yet firm training regime. They have natural tendencies to run and chase game, so some training will be necessary to keep the dog within shotgun range and to chase only the game the hunter desires. Some breaking of chasing such things as deer or rabbits may be necessary.

Take advantage of the dog's natural quartering and retrieving instincts, and mold those into a form that suits your hunting needs. You'll find that the English springer spaniel will readily learn lessons and retain them throughout its hunting career.

Strengths/Weaknesses
The English springer spaniel may not be the best retriever to choose from, but it does a fine job — particularly on upland game. But it should be confined to the earlier, warmer part of the waterfowl season. And though it is not necessarily a weakness, the dog's thick, feathery coat will attract many burrs and debris picked up from the cover it hunts, making grooming a ritual — and a pre-season field clipping a necessity.

The breed is relatively healthy, but some springers may suffer from ear infections (as almost all long-haired dogs do, especially those that spend any time in the water), or from aggressive or mild temperament disorders. Canine hip dysplasia occurs in English springer spaniels, so it is important to buy only from parents that have been certified by the Orthopedic Foundation for Animals or PennHIP; inherited eye disorders are also known to occur. Look for certification in a puppy's parents and grandparents from the Canine Eye Registry Foundation (CERF).

Other Uses
Most of the other uses for English springer spaniels — if not in the field or show ring — are around the house as a loving family pet. There are spaniel-specific field trials, and some dogs may compete in agility or tracking tests. But for the most part, the role of the English springer spaniel falls into three categories: hunting, show, or family. However, it's always a family dog.

The Show Ring
The competitive English springer spaniel is a beautiful animal, usually slightly bigger than its hunting brother. The ears are typically longer, and the feathering is groomed to an extensive degree and allowed to grow to great lengths. While the show ring springer may eventually find its way into the hunting field, that coat necessary for it to be competitive in the ring will soon be mangled due to the cover it goes through.

FIELD SPANIEL

Yet another flushing spaniel to consider is the field spaniel, a springer-like dog that is almost always a solid liver color. Field spaniels are not as popular as the English springer spaniel, but they perform many of the same functions, from hunting and show competitions to tracking and agility testing. They, too, are always a family dog.

- **Area & Date of Origin:** England, 1800s
- **Function:** Bird flushing & retrieving, gun dog, field trials, some tracking
- **Height & Weight:** ~18" (male); ~17" (female); 35-50 lbs
- **Colors:** Black, liver, golden liver or shades of each; any of these with tan points; white on throat and chest may be clear, ticked or roan
- **Coat:** Single coat, flat or slightly wavy, moderately long, glossy, dense, water-repellent; moderate feathering on chest, underbody, backs of legs, and buttocks
- **Standards:** Well-balanced, somewhat longer than tall; solidly-built; almond-shaped, medium-sized, dark brown to dark hazel eyes; low-set ears, long and wide; docked or natural tail slants downward when at rest; large, round, webbed feet
- **Life Span:** 12 -14 years

■ Appearance and Temperament

Field spaniels are very similar to English cocker spaniels and English springer spaniels; in fact, they fall between the two in size. Field spaniels are on average 18 inches tall at the shoulder and weigh around 50 pounds; during the breed's early days, the main difference between English cockers and field spaniels was size.

The field spaniel has a coat typical of the other spaniel breeds — slightly wavy and thick, meant to protect the dog while hunting, and feathery along the ears, legs, chest, and docked tail. Colors range from solid black or liver, to a black or liver roan, much like the English cocker. Field spaniels love to be around people and are great with children, but they may be timid or shy, especially around new people. Once comfortable, however, field spaniels are independent, inquisitive, and always desire to be around people.

History

The field spaniel owes most of its history to the show ring competitors. Early competitors wanted an all-black spaniel, and various crossbreedings attempted to achieve that color. A result of the breedings was, eventually, the field spaniel, though its black or dark-liver color was anything but appealing to the sportsmen of late 19th century England — the dogs simply did not show up in the cover. These crossbreedings also made the field spaniel somewhat short and elongated and not very practical for busting through cover, like its English springer spaniel ancestor.

But in America, the hunting field spaniel was saved by outcrosses to English springer spaniels, and taller, sturdier dogs began to emerge. However, a fire at a prominent field spaniel kennel in 1909 wiped out the breed almost entirely; it wasn't until the late 1960s that field spaniels began to regain a following. From this point on, breedings of field spaniels have led to the predominantly liver-colored hunting spaniel we see today.

In the Field

Field spaniels course the uplands in the same manner as the other spaniels, quartering in front of the hunter within shotgun range, flushing game, and then retrieving to hand. Field spaniels may have more of an affinity to water than some of the other flushing dogs, and therefore may be used extensively on waterfowl, though not in too-harsh conditions. They possess excellent noses, and many field spaniels compete in spaniel field trials and hunt tests.

Trainability

Because of their inherent docility, positive reinforcement will be the best training methods with field spaniels. They are intelligent animals that can pick up a variety of lessons and commands, which leads them to be used in a variety of ways. Basic obedience training will teach a field spaniel some manners so its natural tendency to explore will not get it into trouble.

Strengths/Weaknesses

The field spaniel is fairly versatile in being able to perform many different functions, learn numerous lessons, and be a great family dog all the while. They are a breed experiencing little in the way of health problems, except some cases of hip dysplasia and thyroid disease, but careful breeding and monitoring will help to keep those to a minimum. Regardless, field spaniels are not that popular, and therefore it may be hard to find a field spaniel for your particular desires.

Other Uses

Because of their easy trainability, field spaniels currently find activity in hunting, field trials, obedience, tracking (to which they excel because of their good noses), agility tests, and the show ring. Their easy-going, people-loving nature also leads them to be excellent candidates for therapy dogs, visiting people in hospitals or nursing homes.

The Show Ring

Perhaps the greatest use of field spaniels today is in the show ring, where today's show dogs don't have much in common with those of the late 1800s, early 1900s. Today's show ring competitors are built more like their hunting brethren, and this is apparent in that field spaniel enthusiasts have stressed the versatility of the breed. Therefore, the proper field spaniel should look like it could perform any of its functions.

SUSSEX SPANIEL

The Sussex spaniel is much like the Clumber spaniel, both in looks and functionality. The breed has not achieved much popularity in the U.S. as a hunting dog, which is attributed to the dog's slow-moving pace in the field. But the dog does well as a family animal and is gaining popularity in the realm of companion and therapy work. And if you desire a slower-moving hunting dog, the Sussex spaniel has an excellent nose and will bust through heavy cover with ease. You may need to work to find some hunting lines though.

- **Area & Date of Origin:** Sussex County, England, 1800s

- **Function:** Bird flushing & retrieving, gun dog

- **Height & Weight:** 13-15", 35 - 45 lbs (male & female)

- **Colors:** Rich golden liver

- **Coat:** Abundant body coat is flat or slightly wavy; legs are moderately well-feathered; soft wavy hair on ears; distinctive long feather between the toes, which should be long enough to cover the toenails (coat requires a fair amount of grooming)

- **Standards:** Massive build; low and long body with a level topline; round, deep chest; muscular back and loin; moderately-long skull with a full stop; heavy brows; somewhat pendulous lips; eyes soft and languishing, fairly large, hazel colored; large, thick, low-set ears; tail docked from 5 to 7" and set low; large round feet, with long feathering

- **Life Span:** 12 -14 years

■ Appearance and Temperament

The Sussex spaniel looks like a small, dark Clumber spaniel. It is a short (13 to 15 inches at the shoulder), compact dog with an overall rectangular appearance, more long than tall. They are usually a solid 35 to 45 pounds, but their characteristic feature is their golden liver-colored coat. The coat is thick and flat or slightly wavy, with feathering along the chest, legs, ears, buttocks, and docked tail, characteristic of all the spaniels. Sussex spaniels have the large, sad eyes of the cocker spaniel.

Behind those sad eyes, however, is an energetic dog with an enthusiastic temperament, always anxious to be around people, and quite protective of its family. They are not hyper; in fact they are rather calm. They can naturally keep their energy and enthusiasm in check, but you know it's always there. They are true people dogs, and are excellent around children. Their people-loving nature has also made well-trained Sussex spaniels excellent candidates for therapy dog work.

■ History

A man known in the literature as "Mr. Fuller" is credited with developing the breed in his home of Rosehill, Sussex, England, in the early 1800s, though the dog was being used earlier for hunting purposes. Little has changed in the way of appearance or function since then, and the breed's popularity was such that it was one of the first ten breeds recognized by the AKC. Careful breeding throughout history has maintained the characteristic liver color. But its popularity waned in the U.S. in the late 1800s and early 1900s when most hunting dogs were brought to this country, attributable mostly to the dog's slow gait in the field.

In the Field

The similarity with Clumber spaniels not only applies to general looks but also to hunting ability and procedure. The compact, sturdy Sussex spaniel moves methodically through very thick brush with a nose to the ground; this makes the dog easy to follow on foot, but it may move too slowly for some hunter's desires. But once on game, they are determined to put the bird to wing, usually howling once scent is picked up — the only spaniel to do this. They quarter naturally and can be trained to be reliable retrievers, which they may show some innate tendencies to do, but will perform better with a sound training regime. Though most Sussex spaniels in the U.S. are kept as family or show dogs, the breed still enjoys some hunting popularity in England, its home turf.

Trainability

Sussex spaniels may not be the easiest to train and are often stubborn, but they are enthusiastic. With firm yet compassionate training methods, you should be able to mold that eager-to-please attitude into whatever you desire from the dog. They will need basic obedience training to do well in the house.

Hunters will find that Sussex spaniels naturally quarter the field in search of game, and their slow pace makes ranging not too much of a problem. However, they have excellent noses and are tenacious once on game and might need to learn some boundaries. While they do retrieve, they will require some training to do it reliably.

Strengths/Weaknesses

The Sussex spaniel's slower pace may dissuade some hunters from choosing this flushing breed, and its darker color and short stature may make it harder to see in the brush. But the breed has an excellent nose and can be a natural hunter, provided litters with hunting backgrounds are found. They are a breed that delights in being around people, and they make an all-around hunting and companion dog.

Other Uses

With training, Sussex spaniels can be taught to do anything and are able to compete in most forms of hunting, obedience, and show tests. Some Sussex spaniels also put their affinity for people to work as therapy dogs, visiting people at hospitals and nursing homes. However, most Sussex spaniels find their primary use as a family dog and house pet, charming their owners with clownish behavior and growing protective of their owners.

The Show Ring

Sussex spaniels continue to find some use in the show ring, and their unique, rich, golden liver color makes them a sight to see in the ring, particularly when they are well-groomed.

WELSH SPRINGER SPANIEL

Though its cousin, the English springer spaniel, may receive more attention and notoriety, the Welsh springer spaniel enjoys a fine reputation as a sound hunter, though it is a rare breed. According to its parent breed club, only about 300 Welsh springer spaniels are registered per year, so if you decide to research the possibilities of getting a Welsh springer spaniel to hunt with, you'll have your work cut out for you.

- **Area & Date of Origin:** Wales, 1600s
- **Function:** Bird flushing & retrieving, gun dog
- **Height & Weight:** 18-19" (male); 17-18" (female); 35-55 lbs
- **Colors:** Rich red and white, in any pattern
- **Coat:** Flat, straight, and soft to the touch; chest, underside, and parts of legs moderately-feathered; ears and tail lightly-feathered
- **Standards:** Muscular chest with well-developed forechest; level topline; medium-length skull with clearly defined stop; brown, oval eyes; low-set, somewhat short ears; generally tail docked, carried near horizontal; round feet with thick pads
- **Life Span:** 12 -15 years

■ Appearance and Temperament

Most often confused with the English springer spaniel, the Welsh springer spaniel can be distinguished in comparison by its slightly smaller size (though there are variations) of between 35 and 55 pounds, and its reddish markings on a white background compared to the English springer spaniel's black or liver-colored markings on a white background.

They are a shorter dog, approximately 17 to 19 inches tall at the shoulder, and their flat yet feathery coat (like the other spaniels) has a natural undercoat for protection against the water and heavy cover it was bred to bust through. Occasional grooming around the ears, legs, buttocks, and feet will help the dog in its function. Its tail is docked, also like the other spaniels, and this practice is thought to have originated to spare the tail injury caused by the dog whipping it through the heavy cover. Also in contrast to the English springer spaniel, the Welshie appears more streamlined and not as stocky, and it has shorter, more well-proportioned ears.

Like its spaniel cousin, the Welshie is blessed with an affectionate temperament, making it a valued house dog and family animal, good with children. They can be hyper — as most hunting dogs are prone to be — and will need a regular exercise regime. They are friendly dogs, not bashful, and though they may not be the best guard dogs in the world, they are very loyal to the family.

■ History

Of all the spaniels, the Welsh springer spaniel has perhaps the longest history in western England and, of course, Wales, a lineage of hunting dating back hundreds of years to the mid 1500s. As with most other breeds, it was around the late 1800s and early 1900s that the breed became recognized, earning the registry of the AKC in 1906. The Williams family of Glamorganshire is credited with spearheading the breeding, beginning around 1900, that has led to today's Welsh springer spaniels.

Since then, however, this spaniel has seen its potential hunting use monopolized by the English springer spaniel. It wasn't until 1955 that the first Welshie earned an AKC championship in the U.S., and by 1960, the number of registered Welshies had dropped to around 100. This was a vast improvement, however, over the years of 1926 through 1948, when there weren't any registered Welshies.

The Welsh Springer Spaniel Club of America formed in 1961 to help save and perpetuate the breed; the result has been a sound, legitimate choice — albeit rare — for hunters to contemplate if considering a spaniel for their hunting needs.

■ In the Field

Typical of the other spaniel breeds, the Welsh springer spaniel is used primarily as a flushing dog, quartering in front of the hunter within shotgun range, finding and flushing birds, and then retrieving downed game. Their thick coat, while attracting burrs and other debris, protects them against the heavy cover and water they were meant to hunt through. In English terms, the Welshie is a "rough shooting dog."

The well-trained Welshie should stay within shotgun range so that birds flushed will be able to be taken on the wing. But Welshie's also serve a role as a retriever, able to fetch both downed upland game from any type of cover and waterfowl in most water conditions. While a dedicated retriever might be best for the avid waterfowler, the Welshie finds a welcome place in the home of the upland and part-time waterfowl hunter, and its smaller size may make it more tolerable around the house and family.

When looking for a hunting Welshie, you won't have many to choose from. And you may want to look for puppies of titled dogs, particularly those with some sort of AKC hunting title (JH, SH, MH).

■ Trainability

The Welsh springer spaniel is a very intelligent dog, and lessons are picked up easily. Because of their affinity for people and fun, lots of praise works best in training this breed. But firmness will be necessary to reign in the dog's mild hyperactivity to make a flushing dog that stays within shotgun range. The hyperactivity is not so much a product of the breed itself as it is a product of the hunting desire that runs through it — as it does with any of the hunting breeds. The Welsh springer spaniel can truly be trained to do just about anything — hunting, show ring, or even tracking and agility tests.

■ Strengths/Weaknesses

The well-trained Welsh springer spaniel can compete with any spaniel in the hunting field, but if used solely as a retriever, it will be outdone by any of the specific retrieving breeds. For an upland hunter who desires a flushing dog, however, the Welsh springer spaniel should be considered right alongside an English springer spaniel.

Because of the rarity of the breed, some of the health problems have been kept to a minimum. Some individuals suffer from idiopathic (unknown cause) epilepsy and hip dysplasia, as well as the other ailments befalling hunting breeds. Because of the longer, feathery ears, the Welshie may experience ear infections.

■ Other Uses

Tracking tests and show ring competition highlight the active Welshie (other than hunting), but perhaps the breed's greatest function when not quartering in front of the hunter is as a family pet. Watch to be sure that if you are choosing a Welshie for hunting that you find one with hunting in its background and not purely a family pet; conversely, if you're looking for the family Welshie, don't neglect the dog's inherent need to run and chase things.

■ The Show Ring

Though the English springer spaniel has diverged into two almost distinct lines of show ring dogs and field dogs, the typical Welsh springer spaniel can see action in both the show ring and hunting field. For that reason, the breed standard follows closely those features that make the dog an excellent hunter, both in terms of bone and muscle structure and coat.

One of the most thrilling sites in bird hunting: a pointing dog on staunch point.

CHAPTER 9

THE POINTING DOGS

by Ben O. Williams

OF ALL THE CANINES, the pointing breeds are the most interesting to me. I have had many pointing dogs over the years and each time I get a new pup it's a learning experience. No person can learn all the complexities or behavioral characteristics of a particular dog, and every dog's personality is unique. To me, when a dog locks up on point it's magical.

Many factors go into the selection of a gun dog. Acquiring a pointing dog involves a good deal of commitment. The place you live, how much time you're willing to spend, and the devotion to a daily routine is important in choosing the right breed of pointer to fit your lifestyle. Also you must consider the principal game you plan to hunt, physical characteristics of the terrain and the climate in which you live.

You probably have already been influenced by several outside factors that are not necessarily helpful in choosing a dog. For instance, popularity of the breed, eye appeal, or a dog you had as child is not the correct systematic approach in choosing the right breed. Your initial concern should involve what you expect the dog to do in the field. Bear in mind that

each breed hunts a little differently. Some breeds are big-running dogs, others are close-working. Some breeds take more time than others to train. I've had some great bird dogs and when everything goes right, training is easy. But I also know that things don't always go that way, and more hours of training are needed for some individual dogs.

Not everyone is exactly sure of what to expect of a pointing dog or what their activity should be in the field. There are two philosophies of what a pointer should do. The "classic" pointing dog searches out gamebirds, solidly stops, and points far enough away to hold the birds. The dog stands rock solid until the hunter arrives, then the hunter walks past the dog, flushes the birds and shoots the game. The hunter then commands the dog to retrieve. This is the most impressive pointer to watch and makes the biggest impression on those who witness the performance of a finished dog. This is a field trial dog, a bobwhite quail dog, or a woodcock dog; although this is not always what an average bird hunter wants in a pointing dog.

Wirehair

On the other hand, the "shooting dog," the dog that's going to hunt many species of gamebirds over its lifespan is a little different. The shooting dog searches out gamebirds, solidly points, and hold the birds until the hunter arrives. Some hunters flush the birds; some hunters walk in with the dog and flush the birds. These dogs are not steady to wing and shot, but are in a better position to fetch birds or catch cripples that might otherwise escape. Take your pick; it's up to you how to train your dog; all the pointing breeds will respond to either method.

Keeping a hunting dog healthy is important, and one of the best ways to safeguard a pointing dog's health is to get them plenty of daily exercise. Keep in mind hunting dogs work hard so be on the lookout for physical and behavior changes at all times. Generally all of the pointing breeds are healthy, but like almost all breeds, working dogs have some kind of joint discomfort as they age because they are so active in the field. Hip dysplasia is one of the most severe and painful ailments, but is less common in most of the pointing breeds, even though it does occur in almost all breeds of large and giant dogs.

The most basic and important decision is choosing the right breed of pointing dog for your needs. This book provides valuable information and helpful tips in determining that choice. Now for some particulars.

It is an innate tendency in all *canids* to chase game, for all *canids* are predators. Some breeds, such as the ones in this book, have been evolved to be better at performing this task, and some of these breeds have filled specific niches in the hunting environment: retrieving, pointing, flushing, and tracking.

But all the dogs have one trait in common: like all predators, just before they launch an attack on a prey animal, they pause to gather themselves. It is this pause that has been fashioned into the point of a pointing dog. Those dogs that showed a natural tendency to hold that pause longer before pouncing were bred. The longer pause was thus fixed as a genetic trait, enhanced through training, and passed on to succeeding generations as a full-fledged point, in which the dog stands his game when scent is detected and, properly, waits for a command from the hunter to either resume hunting or retrieve a downed bird if the shot is successful.

The pointing breeds are used almost exclusively for hunting upland birds. Some of the pointing breeds, known as "versatile" breeds, besides pointing upland birds, may also course the field for furred game, retrieve waterfowl like a retriever, and track much like a hound. But where a pointing dog exhibits the characteristic point is on birds. This behavior actually became quite valuable to hunters prior to the advent of gunpowder, when nets were thrown over the cover to capture game. The dog that could stop at scent, indicating where the game was, was a valuable tool; nets could be properly cast over the cover and the game captured and killed. With gunpowder, the pointing behavior helped the hunter get very close to the game so as to put himself within the killing effectiveness of his weapon — provided, that is, the dog didn't rush in on the game and flush it away before the hunter could get there. Dogs that did this well were valuable and, as stated above, were bred in a sort of "unnatural selection" process. Certainly traits and color and so forth became part of the breeding equation, resulting in the various breeds of pointing dogs, and bloodlines within the breeds.

This is a roundabout way of saying that a seven-week old pointing dog puppy freezing at the sight of a wing on a string is a matter of genetics. Something is telling this dog that it should pause slightly before pouncing on the desired object. A retriever or a spaniel may also pause, perhaps creeping forward slowly and low to the ground, but it is the pointing dogs that will be easier to train to hold that point. (In actuality, pointing a wing on a string is nothing more than a cute trick; it might be better to seek out that pointing dog puppy that is enthusiastic and relentless after the wing, as this dog may show more of a drive toward finding game.)

There is some debate among pointing dog enthusiasts about what the responsibilities of a pointing dog are. Some feel that finding the game by quartering a field in front of the hunter — either at extreme ranges or within shotgun range — and then pointing is the main objective; after the hunter is in position, the goal is then simply getting the bird.

But by and large, pointing dogs are expected to hold the point with intensity — known as *staunchness* — and allow the hunter to walk in front of it, flush the game, and shoot the bird, all while the dog holds the point. This is known as steady to wing (flush) and shot. This, in the eyes of the majority of pointing dog enthusiasts, is the epitome of training and pointing dog skills; it is the pinnacle of a dog's learning.

Most feel that the steady to wing and shot behavior is a way for the dog to mark the falling bird in order to retrieve it better. Putting it all together, then, the dog would be steady to wing, shot, and fall. If trained to retrieve — which some pointing dogs, especially the versatile breeds, do extremely well; others need proper training — this *marking* of the bird will greatly aid in recovery.

The matter of range is often discussed when pointing dogs are the topic, and here there are misconceptions. Many foot hunters want their dogs to be well within sight, often within shotgun range (40 yards) or close to it. This is usually the result of a failure on the dog's part to hold his birds. The dog may creep too close or use the wind wrong, and the birds may flush prematurely; the hunter wants to be in range for a shot should this happen. In short, the hunter doesn't trust his dog to hold a point but still wants to shoot the bird.

In opposition to this, the proper way for a dog to hunt is to hunt the places that his experience tells him will have the birds — the pockets of cover. This is called *hunting the objectives*. When the dog locates birds and establishes a point, the hunter should be able to quickly but without rushing get to the spot and flush the birds himself, with the dog remaining staunch.

One command, "whoa," is taught early on to help the pup in his training, to teach him that he is to stop and remain when he detects the presence of game other than a waft of vagrant scent. (An article in this book outlines the teaching of that all-important skill.)

The pointing dog often hunts with one or more other dogs at the same time (two dogs are called a *brace*), and there is a practical piece of decorum for this event as well. Dogs should *honor* or *back* each other. When one dog goes on point, the other dog also establishes point. This is more than mere good manners or tradition. Often, because of thick cover conditions, the dog that is actually on point cannot be seen, but the honoring dog can. In effect, the honoring dog is pointing the dog that is pointing the bird.

There are many nuances to dog training, and there are many highly-skilled professionals and amateurs who have devoted their lives to the betterment of the various breeds. But at bottom, dogs — and pointing dogs are no exception — are wolves, and the training consists of channeling their natural hunting instincts into a form that is compatible with the shooting sports as they exist in the 21st century. ■

AMERICAN BRITTANY

The American Brittany, just called Brittany in the United States, is among the most popular pointing breeds in America. There are many reasons for the dog's growing popularity, among them its skills as a hunter and its delightful temperament, making it a valued family member. The Brittany has proven to be an outstanding pointing breed that has rivaled the long-established traditional pointers and setters. The breed is suitable for both the avid and the occasional bird hunter.

- **Area & Date of Origin:** France, 1800s
- **Function:** Gun dog, setter, pointer, retriever, versatile hunting dog, field trials
- **Height & Weight:** ~ 17-20", 30-45 lbs (male & female)
- **Colors:** Orange and white, liver and white, or tricolored
- **Coat:** Flat or wavy (never curly) and dense; legs have some feathering
- **Standards:** Short, straight back; medium-length rounded skull; nose some shade of brown or pink; short, triangular ears, set high; tailless to about 4 inches long (natural or docked)
- **Life Span:** 12 -13 years
- **Also called:** Brittany spaniel (officially changed to "Brittany" in 1982)

■ Appearance and Temperament

The Brittany is a compact, medium-sized, leggy dog having a deep chest which contributes to its great agility in covering lots of ground. The male Brittany ranges in weight from 30 to 45 pounds (average 35 pounds); the female is slightly smaller. The official standard height of the Brittany is 17½ to 20½ inches measured from the ground at the highest point of the shoulders.

The breed's colors are white and rich orange or white and liver. Both color combinations can be patched or a roan pattern, and some ticking is desirable. Tricolor Brittanys are allowed but not preferred by the American Brittany Club, a member breed of the American Kennel Club. Its coat is fine, flat and a little wavy with sparse feathering on the legs. The stubby tail may be natural or docked, but no longer than four inches in length.

The Brittany may resemble and be the size of a spaniel, but they are classic pointers and strong rivals of the traditional pointers and setters. They are excellent house pets, friendly, well-mannered, playful and exceptionally fond of their owner and family. They are protective of young children in the household and by nature are wary of strangers.

The Brittany that hunts is the happiest of all. It's a high-energy dog that needs time and space to exercise. Brittanys should be walked vigorously several times each day or have a fenced-in yard in which to roam.

■ History

The Brittany gets its name from the French province where it originated. One of the older sporting breeds, there are paintings and other records dating back to the 17th century that show the exact characteristics of the Brittany as being different than other breeds. The Brittany is one of the only known sporting breeds to be developed by a class of people — the peasant class inhabiting and farming the land — rather than by an individual or a small group of breeders. It is thought that the breed was used for hunting on royal lands — illegally — and so its appearance was disguised by the breeding and the docked tail so that it would not resemble the pointers and setters used by the noble classes. But because few records were kept, the true genesis of the breed is not known.

The Brittany's history in America began shortly after the turn of the twentieth century. The first known pair of Brittanys were imported into the United States in 1912, and thus began the genetic trail to the Brittany of America.

■ In the Field

The Brittany is easy to train, intelligent, and responsive with a willingness to please, making it a fine choice for a first-time pointing dog owner. The Brittany takes direction well, checks in frequently, and adjusts its range to the cover — working closely in the grouse woods, ranging wide and covering ground on the prairies. The dog's color, with a majority of the surface area white or lightly ticked, makes it a good choice for a thick-cover hunting dog because of its visibility.

The Brittany's point is intense, its scenting ability is of the highest order, it can easily be trained to honor or it honors naturally, and it is a natural retriever. The dog's scenting ability is one of its outstanding assets. Some strains of Brittanys, depending upon the breeding, are more wide-ranging than others, and the buyer is well-advised to hunt with or watch the pup's parents in the field before selecting puppy.

■ Trainability

Perhaps more than any other pointing breed, Brittanys are capable of being "self-trained," meaning they require a minimum of formal training to achieve the necessary skills required by upland hunters — pointing, backing, and retrieving. Their willingness to please makes them eager pupils, and their precocity often results in a fine hunting dog the very first season. Brittanys retain their training and their learned and developed skills from season to season, requiring little re-training between seasons. They do require a great deal of exercise and love to be in the field.

■ Strengths/Weaknesses

The Brittany has many strengths and few weaknesses. They are intelligent and loyal, and when hunting have a strong prey — hunting — drive. They learn and "train up" quickly, often able to hunt independently and well at a very early age in comparison with other breeds that mature more slowly. Their lifespan is not curtailed by their early maturation, with many dogs living and hunting until they are 13 or 14 years old.

However, these are high-energy dogs that require constant exercise and they don't do well as apartment-dwellers or in families of non-hunters. Because of their popularity, finding a breeder and a litter of well-bred dogs is usually not a problem.

■ Other Uses

Brittanys are hunting dogs first and always, primarily for upland birds, but they also get some occasional use as waterfowl retrievers. Aside from its use as a pet, the breed is not used much for non-related hunting activities.

■ The Show Ring

Unlike a number of other sporting breeds, particularly the pointing breeds, there has not been a "split" between the show-bred dogs and the field dogs. The American Brittany Club has always intended that show dogs and hunting dogs be one in the same, although the main use of the breed is hunting.

ENGLISH SETTER

The aristocrat of pointing dogs, the English setter is a good-natured dog, long a favorite as an upland gamebird hunter for North American sportsmen. As the name indicates, the dog was once one of the breeds that "set," or pointed its game. What the pointer is to the bobwhite hunter, the English setter is to the woodcock and ruffed grouse hunter. It is not only an efficient pointer, but a mild-mannered, excellent family pet. English setters are gentle and friendly, and may well be the best of the several breeds of setters when it comes to finding birds.

- **Area & Date of Origin:** England, 1300s
- **Function:** Gun dog, setter, pointer, field trials
- **Height & Weight:** ~25", 55-65 lbs. (male); ~24", 45-55 lbs (female)
- **Colors:** Orange, liver, lemon, or black ("blue") flecks over a white ground color (belton markings); also a combination of black and tan flecks on white ("tricolor"); liver and lemon colors are rarely seen today
- **Coat:** Flat with feathering on the ears, underside, backs of legs, underside of thighs, and tail
- **Standards:** Head long and lean with a well-defined stop; dark brown, large eyes, nearly round; low-set ears; topline level or sloping slightly to rear; feathered tail carried straight and level with topline, tapering to a fine point
- **Life Span:** 10-14 years

■ Appearance and Temperament

Due to the number of lines and strains that have developed over the years, such as Ryman and Llewellin and Old Hemlock setters, the modern English setter comes in a variety of sizes. Small dogs can be as little as 35 pounds, while larger ones can weigh as much as 70 pounds. The average size gun dog generally is about 45 pounds. Their height is between 21 to 25 inches at the withers.

The English setter is distinctive in appearance with a long, lean body and long, often "feathered" tail. The coat is among the longest of the pointing breeds, although most hunters keep their dogs trimmed short during the shooting season. The preferred colors for the English setter are white and black, white and lemon, white and orange, white and chestnut, or tricolor (white, rust, and black). Dogs that are marked lightly with either orange on white or black on white are called "belton" in coloration — orange beltons or blue (black) beltons.

The setter's disposition is gentle and good-natured, and as a pet they are wonderful with young children. But for the dog to be truly happy, it's essential that it gets daily exercise. Even though an English setter makes a good housedog, he is a hard running hunting dog first. The ideal situation for a setter is to be a house dog that has a large fenced-in area in which to run. They love being with people and are not necessarily a good kennel dog.

History

The English setter is one of four breeds of setters. Perfected in England and Wales, it is difficult to accurately place the time and origin of the breed. Some breeders have said the setter is the result of over 400 years of crosses between pointers, springer spaniels, and water spaniels. Others, including Edward Laverack of England, claimed the setter was an improved spaniel and arrived on the scene after the Spanish pointer 200 years ago.

Laverack was the pioneer of the modern English setter. In 1825 he attained a good male and female, bred them, then bred their offspring together and then back to the original two. Using linebreeding, he developed his own strain of setter and it became the preferred standard at that time.

Fifty years later, R. L. Purcell Llewellin of Pembrokeshire, South Wales, bought some of Laverack's best dogs. These he outcrossed with setters from northern England and the offspring became the leading field trial dog of that time. His bloodlines produced the smaller type setter. Both strains of setters, large and small, were introduced into the United States, but the Llewellin setter was primarily the American bird hunter's choice, whereas the Laverack lines, although good hunters, were predominantly the bench show stock.

To this day, there are a few people who still claim to have the true bloodlines of the Llewellin setter, but this is unlikely.

In the Field

The primary work of the English setter is to find and point gamebirds, and in this enterprise, the breed is unmatched in beauty, in the eyes of many. Strong natural instincts with an exceptional nose and a good memory for lessons learned during training are the reasons the breed is a favorite among American sportsmen. It is a fast, active dog that can run in most any type of terrain, although it does not have the endurance of a Brittany or pointer. Once considered only a woodland bird dog, it is just as happy hunting wide open country. Today, any upland gamebird is fair game for the modern English setter.

In range and pace, setters can vary from close-working dogs to big-running, wide hunters, depending on the breeder. All the dogs are capable of matching their speed and ground coverage to the cover and the hunter's pace.

Trainability

There is an old belief among dog trainers that the longhaired breeds mature and learn slowly, but remember what they've learned longer; conversely, the shorter-haired dogs come into their own faster, but need more pre-season refreshers. If any part of this is true, it's in regard to the English setter.

With a bare minimum of between-season training — just normal conditioning — the average setter picks up right where he left off the previous year.

Setters have exquisite noses and are eager to please. They have a strong pointing instinct, but many are not good retrievers and must be force-broke to this skill. Like so many other breeds, they also benefit from early obedience training.

Strengths/Weaknesses

The English setter is a loyal and protective family dog — affectionate but not fawning. They are too friendly to be guard dogs, but like most hunting breeds, they are alert to unusual sounds about the house. They mature rather slowly, many not hitting their hunting stride until the third or fourth season. They are, however, relatively long-lived, many still hunting at 14 years old.

The long coat, while beautiful to look at, requires a lot of post-hunt grooming and brushing, even when cropped short for the season.

One plus for the breed is that there are a large number of reputable breeders producing fine dogs, so getting a pup is relatively easy.

Other Uses

The English setter is a hunting dog first, and a show dog second. Both types make fine pets.

The Show Ring

The American Kennel Club and other registries that hold conformation competitions find a number of English setters at each event. When the coat is allowed to grow long, the show-stock animals are breathtaking. There is a price paid for this beauty, however, and it is, like with some other breeds, the hunting drive. The show dogs simply have had the "hunt" bred right out of them. While the AKC registers a number of English setters (684 in 2000), the hunting strains are generally registered with *The Field Dog Stud Book*.

FRENCH BRITTANY

Native to France, the *epagneul breton* is that country's most popular breed of hunting dog; in the United States, they are called the French Brittany. Technically speaking, all Brittanys came from France, where the breed developed, but there are now two distinct breeds, the American Brittany and the French Brittany. The two differ in both appearance and hunting styles, the Frenchman being a closer hunter than his American counterpart, and each has its enthusiastic supporters. The original Brittany was a close-working dog, and on both sides of the Atlantic Ocean, they are still a "walking man's gun dog."

- **Area & Date of Origin:** France, 1800s
- **Function:** Gun dog, game flushing and retrieving
- **Height & Weight:** 18-20"; 28-40 lbs
- **Colors:** Black/white, liver/white, white, orange/white, tri-color, or roan of any of these colors.
- **Coat:** Fine, lying flat or very slightly wavy; some feathering
- **Standards:** Finely-chiselled head with moderate stop; dark eyes in harmony with the coat; high-set, triangular ears, slightly rounded at the tip; short, straight, firm back; very short or no tail; when present, tail is set high, carried horizontally or slightly lowered; round feet (the French Brittany has dark nose and amber or brown eyes compared to light nose and eyes on American Brittany; also, the French Brittany can be black/white)
- **Life Span:** 12-14 years
- **Also called:** Epagneul Breton

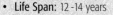
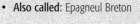

■ Appearance and Temperament

In general terms, the French Brittany is one of the smaller hunting breeds. Males are 18 to 20 inches in height and weigh 30 to 35 pounds; females are smaller overall, as is the way of canines.

A French Brittany's acceptable coloration patterns are white and orange, white and liver, white and black, tricolor, roan, or some combination of these. The coloration standards are more forgiving than are those for the American Brittany, and the inclusion of all these colors, according to French Brittany breeders, allows for a genetically more hardy stock since these were the breeds' original colors centuries ago.

The dog's coat is flat, or slightly wavy with feathering on the legs. The ears are set high, and are rather short. The color of the eyes is from light to dark brown, depending on the color of the coat. Many have a naturally stubby tail, or if not, it is docked to less then four inches.

The French Brittany is affectionate, friendly, and very devoted to its owner. Though an excellent house pet, they can be timid and standoffish with strangers.

History

This ancient breed of dog has its origin in the French province of Brittany. Though there were no records kept (or if there were, they have been lost to time), the oral history of the breed gives more than one version of the breed's history.

One story says that an Englishman, spending time hunting in northern France, left a pair of his setters behind with a local gamekeeper to be used the following year. The gamekeeper entrusted with these dogs also raised small black and white French spaniels. The accidental or purposeful crossbreeding resulted in a dog with both pointing and retrieving instincts, and the French Brittany was born.

What records do exist are in the form of works of art, and these indicate that the dog was a product of the working class. Like the dog we now call the American Brittany, the French Brittany was most likely developed by the peasant or working class. I speculate the French peasants developed the Brittany primarily for hunting and all sorts of crossbreeding took place. I also believe they had some idea of how to produce the best offspring. If not, it would never have become a separate breed. Whether inbred or out-bred, this dog's function was to put food on the table in the form of upland gamebirds, shorebirds, waterfowl, and small animals. Not only did they create an excellent pointer and retriever, but a devoted and animated family pet.

In the Field

The French Brittany is a close-working gun-range dog, with its scenting ability one of its outstanding assets. It's hard-working and tends to be a one-man dog devoted to hunting only in front of its owner. They are intelligent gun dogs, easy to train, mature into hunters at an early age, and most will point, back and retrieve instinctively.

Most French Brittanys have a close range for hunting woodlands and small agricultural farms, but will run wider in open country. A versatile hunting dog, the French Brittany is well adapted to both land and water.

Trainability

The breed's high intelligence makes training relatively easy. They are also natural or semi-natural backers and retrievers. Possessed of a good nose, they hunt to objectives well, remembering through experience what the birdy-looking spots are like and seeking out their quarry there.

They develop hunting instincts at a very early age, so they need to be taken into the field often when young. The best French Brittanys are self-trained and a joy to watch.

Strengths/Weaknesses

The French Brittany is intelligent and loyal, makes a fine companion, and adapts quickly to family life. Their small size makes them the perfect "apartment dweller's gun dog," though, like all the hunting breeds, they need regular, vigorous exercise. They are long-lived, often living to 15 years.

On the negative side, some strains are too small to easily retrieve such large birds as ringneck pheasants. Some individuals tend to be hyperactive, especially when not regularly exercised. The number of French Brittany breeders, and therefore the number of pups available at any given time, is small, and one may have to wait some time for a pup.

Other Uses

In their homeland, they are still a practical dog used for a variety of hunting situations, including for birds and small animals. Other than being a great companion, the breed is not used much for other purposes.

The Show Ring

In France, field trial competition has always been done while walking. Most of the fall field trials are shoot to kill, and the dogs are required to make flawless retrieves. The only distinction between a trial dog and other dogs is that the field trial dog has been campaigned and the others have not.

The French Brittany standards and the American breed standards are quite different even though both have the same aim to improve the breeds as hunting dogs.

GERMAN LONGHAIRED POINTER

There are three kinds of German pointers: the German short-haired pointer, the German longhaired pointer, and the German wirehaired pointer. The German longhaired pointer is believed to be the oldest of the three, but this breed has never gained much fame or notoriety outside its homeland. The German longhaired pointer historically has been the foundation of many other German breeds, such as the large and small Munsterlanders, which get their looks and gentle bearing from their longhaired pointing ancestor.

- **Area & Date of Origin:** Germany, 1800s
- **Function:** Gun dog, versatile hunting dog
- **Height & Weight:** 24-26"; 60-70 lbs
- **Colors:** Liver and white
- **Coat:** Long and dense; feathering on forelegs, ears, tail
- **Standards:** Long, lean head with sloping stop and straight muzzle; gentle-looking eyes set well apart; broad ears covered in long wavy hair; straight back; long, straight forelegs well-fringed with soft hair; tapered tail is profusely feathered; moderately round feet have thick hair between the toes
- **Life Span:** 12-14 years

■ Appearance and Temperament

The German longhaired pointer is a strong, muscular dog of 60 to 70 pounds, and 24 to 26 inches at the shoulders. The dog's color is generally solid chestnut or darker brown, but some are red and black, though this color scheme is not accepted for registration. The German longhaired pointer has a rectangular build, is tall-legged, and has a streamlined body with a noble-looking head. The breed has long ears that hang close to the head. The tail is sometimes slightly docked or left natural, and is highly feathered.

The German longhaired pointer's temperament is gentle and good-natured. They make excellent, obedient pets, and are happiest when hunting. In the field, their movements are active and energetic. The dog needs plenty of daily exercise and preferably a large fenced-in area to roam.

■ History

The history of the German longhaired pointer is not known, but their origin seems to have started from pointers and the extinct French water spaniel. The dog owes its looks and temperament to a variety of longhaired Continental bird dog breeds. There are several engravings and oil paintings from the 16th century that show dogs quite similar to the German longhaired pointer. Of the three different types of German pointers, the longhaired dog has a great deal more spaniel origin in its bloodlines.

By the 17th century, the German longhaired pointer developed into a large, sturdy, slow-working gun dog. But by 1850, crossbreeding with several different breeds of British setters, notably

the Gordon setter, made the breed once again a swift and agile, versatile hunting dog. In 1879, the German longhaired pointer standards were set, and today the breed remains much like it was then.

Because of the two World Wars and Cold War in eastern Europe, the German longhaired pointer almost became extinct several times. Even today, though a handsome, versatile gun dog, the breed has never had much of a following outside of Germany. In fact, many knowledgeable pointing dog enthusiasts have never seen one.

■ In the Field

The German longhaired pointer is well-known for its remarkably strong instincts and its exceptional scenting power for finding game. The dog is well-adapted to hunting any type of terrain, though it works best close-in, as in the woodlands for ruffed grouse. One of the best of the Continental breeds as a water dog, it can work hard all day and still withstand wet or cold weather.

■ Trainability

The German longhaired pointer is very obedient, easy to train, and has a close hunting connection with its master in the field. The dog matures into a hunting dog at an early age. Pointing and retrieving come naturally to the dog, which responds well to gentle handling. They are a breed that loves being in the field and never seem to tire.

■ Strengths/Weaknesses

The German longhaired pointer is calm, intelligent, affectionate, and a loyal family dog. In the field, they are steady hunters always searching for game. German longhaired pointers need daily exercise and are more suited to country living than urban life. The dog has long hair that should be combed and brushed after each outing in the field.

■ The Show Ring

In the dog's homeland, the longhaired pointer has been appreciated as a versatile pointer in both field trials and in the show ring. The North American Versatile Hunting Dog Association (NAHVDA) has long recognized and maintained the studbook for the German longhaired pointer.

GERMAN SHORTHAIRED POINTER

The German shorthaired pointer is probably the best known versatile hunting breed in America, and one of the four most popular pointing dog breeds (the others are the pointer, English setter, and American Brittany). Reasons for popularity are its handsome features and ability to be easily trained. It's a gentle dog, a good all-around hunter, and a wonderful companion or family dog for country and suburban life. One of the dog's most outstanding characteristics is its deeply ingrained, natural retrieving instinct.

- **Area & Date of Origin:** Germany, 1600s
- **Function:** Gun dog, pointer, versatile hunting dog, field trials
- **Height & Weight:** 23-25", 55-70 lbs (male); 21-23", 45-60 lbs (female)
- **Colors:** Solid liver or combinations of liver and white
- **Coat:** Short, thick, and tough to the touch
- **Standards:** Deep chest; short, strong, straight back; clean-cut head, with stop not as defined as in the Pointer; almond-shaped, dark brown eyes; large brown nose; broad, high-set, rounded ears; tail docked to 40 percent of length, carried down when relaxed or horizontally when moving
- **Life Span:** 12-14 years
- **Also called:** German pointer (shorthaired)

■ Appearance and Temperament

The German shorthaired pointer is a compact, medium-sized, long-legged dog that has a deep chest. It has great agility and speed. The "shorthair" (as it is called) ranges in weight from 45 to 70 pounds. The average male is 60 pounds with females slightly smaller. The dog's height is 22 to 25 inches at the withers.

The traditional shorthair has a rough, short, thick coat that takes minimal care. The dog's color may be solid liver or a combination of white and liver. Both colors can be patched, ticked, or a roan pattern. The tail is docked to 40 percent of its original length, in the Continental tradition.

Today, in the United States, there are two distinct types of German shorthaired pointers. One is the large-framed, solidly-built dogs that still look like the original German imports, and the other is the trim, lean, more streamlined shorthair that looks and runs much like the pointer. The modern German shorthaired pointers also have a much larger percentage of white on them than do the older, traditional dogs.

Shorthairs are excellent house pets. They are well-mannered and devoted to their owners and families. Even though the dog is fairly large, they adapt well to modest living quarters. In the home, they are ghosts, always nearby but never fawning or constantly begging for attention.

German shorthaired pointers are active dogs that need time and space to exercise. Although they can adapt to urban life, shorthairs need daily exercise and should be walked vigorously several times each day or have a fenced-in yard in which to run.

■ History

The origin of the German shorthaired pointer began roughly three centuries ago. The breed was developed to point, retrieve, and ground trail all types of game. The shorthair was developed from several descendants of

German hunting breeds, Spanish pointers, and a variety of scenting hounds, which to some extent accounts for its hound-like countenance, especially as a puppy.

The first German shorthaired pointers arrived in the United States in the 1920s. Having been used to hunt and trail all kinds of game, they were a close-working dog and not very practical for hunting upland birds in open country. Over the years, through selective breeding, the German shorthaired pointer became a rangier dog and its popularity increased.

■ In the Field

The German shorthaired pointer requires early obedience training. They tend to be a one-person dog, are intelligent, and love to work for their owner. As a versatile hunting dog, the breed has outstanding scenting, trailing, and retrieving instincts.

The new German shorthaired pointer's range and pace are ideal for both wooded areas and big open country. Most are mid-range hunters — close enough to their master to check in, and far enough to cover the country. As with many breeds, individual breeders have developed close-working dogs, while others have bred for open country to range farther.

■ Trainability

The German shorthaired pointer is a quick learner and matures into a hunting dog earlier than other breeds, such as the setters. They train easily, in the manner of the Brittanys, and as a result are often a hunter's first bird dog.

Unlike many pointing breeds, the German shorthaired pointer spends a good deal of time following ground scent, at which they excel. This makes them a popular dog among pheasant hunters, whose quarry would much rather run than fly. With their head down and nose low, they do not have a high head when running as do the pointer and the setters.

They have a remarkable memory for marking downed birds. The breed's supporters say they are on par with the average Labrador retriever (an opinion certain to start an argument). The best-trained shorthairs are the dogs that get in the field often. Though they may not have the style of the pointer or English setter, they give nothing away in intensity.

■ Strengths/Weaknesses

The German shorthaired pointer has many strengths and is possibly the best all-around versatile hunting dog today. They are highly intelligent, loyal, fearless, and aggressive when hunting. They have earned a great reputation and popularity among hunters because of this all-around hunting ability.

Because of the dog's dark color, they are difficult to see in wooded areas, although this is not true of those strains bred with large areas of white in the coat. Shorthairs do not adapt well to city or apartment life.

■ The Show Ring

The German shorthaired pointer is a versatile hunting dog and is very capable as a participant in the North American Versatile Hunting Dog Association (NAHVDA) programs. A popular show dog, hunting conformation and instincts have not been bred out of them for the ring as has happened with some other breeds.

GERMAN WIREHAIRED POINTER

The breeders' goal with the wirehair was to develop a pointer that could retrieve on land and water. The German hunter needed a rugged, close-working dog for hunting on foot, in dense-forest mountainous areas, and on small open farmland. The dog had to have a coat heavy enough to protect it in thick cover and during wet, cold weather. After several generations of careful crossbreeding, the result was a new versatile German dog, the German wirehaired pointer. Interestingly, those who have obtained dogs directly from Germany use the German designation – *drathaar* – while those dogs born in the New World are called by the English name.

- **Area & Date of Origin:** Germany, 1800s
- **Function:** Gun dog, pointer, versatile hunting dog, field trials
- **Height & Weight:** 24-26" (male); female is smaller than male, but not under 22", 45-75 lbs
- **Colors:** Liver and white, with ears and head solid liver, sometimes with a white blaze
- **Coat:** Straight, harsh, wiry, and flat-lying outercoat, about 1-2" long; undercoat is thick in winter for warmth but thin in summer; eyebrows, beard, and whiskers are of medium length
- **Standards:** Well-muscled; short, straight, strong back; moderately long head with medium stop; oval, brown eyes with medium length eyebrows; beard and whiskers of medium length; dark brown nose; tail docked to about two fifths of the original length, carried at or above horizontal; round, webbed feet
- **Life Span:** 12-14 years
- **Also called:** German pointer (wirehaired)

■ Appearance and Temperament

The wirehair is a compact, medium-sized dog, that is long-legged and has a deep chest. Even though the German shorthaired pointer and the German wirehaired pointer are about the same size and are both fine hunters, that's where the resemblance ends. The German wirehaired pointer is powerfully built; their weight can range from 50 to 70 pounds. The average male is 65 pounds with females slightly smaller. The dog's height is 24 to 26 inches from the withers.

As can be deduced from the name, the German wirehaired pointer has a distinctive outer coat that is straight, rough, and wiry, and an undercoat that thickens and thins with the seasons. The outer coat is water repellent and takes minimal care. The dog's colors can be solid liver, liver and white, liver and ticked, or a roan pattern. The dog has bushy eyebrows, beard, and whiskers. The tail is docked soon after birth. The breed has a distinctive white or light blaze between the eyes.

Wirehairs are good house pets and very devoted to their owner and family. But the breed's attitude toward strangers can range from aloof to unfriendly. They can be stubborn at times and need obedience training as pups. German wirehaired pointers can be protective of their home and aggressive toward other dogs. At times, their energy level is high and they should be given time and space to exercise. They are a country dog, not well-suited for urban life, and need a fenced-in yard in which to roam.

■ History

The development of the German wirehaired pointer was well planned. German breeders wanted a rugged, wiry, versatile dog that could point, retrieve, and ground-trail all types of game. The dog's origin started about 120 years ago by selectively crossing and combining the German shorthaired pointer, pudelpointer, griffon, Polish water dog, and several other Continental hunting breeds until the German breeders reached their goal.

The German wirehaired pointer has been a recognized breed in Germany since 1870, but was first brought to the United States in 1920, where it became quite popular in the Midwest. The *Deutsch Drahthaar* was officially recognized in 1959 by the American Kennel Club, and the name was changed to German wirehaired pointer. The word "Deutsch" means "German," "draht" means "wire," and "haar" translates into "hair." The AKC added "pointer" to clarify the dog's classification. The breed was recognized by the UKC in 1948.

In the Field

The German wirehaired pointer tends to be a one-man, one-family dog. They are intelligent and love to work hard for their master in the field. The best word to describe these dogs is "rugged," whether hunting in heavy cover, croplands, wooded areas, prairies, or mountainous terrain. The animal's coat was developed specifically to work the rugged terrain that other breeds are incapable of hunting.

The German wirehaired pointer is a mid-range to close hunter that works at a much slower pace than most other pointing breeds. As with many other pointing dogs, some individual breeders have developed strains as close-working hunters and others have bred a rangier dog. Wirehairs are used for upland birds and waterfowl, and are excellent at tracking other game as well.

Trainability

A favorite among hunters in Germany, the rugged German wirehaired pointer has a strong desire to please. They have an inbred ability in finding and tracking downed birds and other game, and like the German shorthaired pointer, the German wirehaired pointer also spends a good deal of time following ground scent. With their head down and nose low to the ground while running, they are superb ground trailers.

If given the chance, they develop their hunting skill early in life. They are energetic workers and an ideal dog for the hunter who likes to walk, hunting pheasants and other woodland game. The best trained German wirehaired pointer is the dog that spends many hours in the field. Though they lack the pointing style of the pointer or English setter, they make it up by finding downed game.

Strengths/Weaknesses

The strength of the German wirehaired pointer is it's a true versatile hunting dog. It's as good hunting ducks as it is hunting upland birds, and is arguably the best all-around versatile breed in the country. The German wirehaired pointer is intelligent, loyal, and aggressive

when hunting. They are great companions and adapt well to family life. In the United States, the dog has earned a reputation among many sportsmen.

They are active dogs and obedience training is recommended at an early age. They should also become accustomed to people when young, because they have a tendency to be unfriendly to strangers.

Their dark color coat is a disadvantage when hunting heavily wooded areas. The German wirehaired pointer is not well adapted to city or apartment life.

The Show Ring

The breed is a relatively popular show dog, but retains its hunting skills. In field trials as a versatile pointing breed, the German wirehaired pointer has done quite well. But it is at its best when participating in the North American Versatile Hunting Dog Association (NAHVDA) program events.

GORDON SETTER

Though an intelligent, efficient finder of game, the Gordon setter tends to be more calm and composed than the other setters while hunting, usually hunting at a slower, more methodical pace than the others. The dog has a good reputation for having an outstanding sense of smell, and makes a fine woodcock and ruffed grouse dog.

The Gordon setter is an affectionate, ideal family dog known for its gentleness with young children. If you are a casual bird hunter and want a good companion at home and in the field, the Gordon setter is a good choice.

- **Area & Date of Origin:** Great Britain (Scotland), 1600s

- **Function:** Gun dog, setter, pointer, field trials

- **Height & Weight:** 24-27", 55-80 lbs (male); 23-26", 45-70 lbs (female)

- **Colors:** Black with tan markings, either of rich chestnut or mahogany color

- **Coat:** Thicker than other setters; straight or slightly wavy, always soft and shiny; longer feathering on ears, underside, backs of legs, and tail

- **Standards:** Muscular and big-boned; body short from shoulder to hips; pronounced forechest; deep, rounded head with well-defined stop; dark brown, oval eyes; low-set ears, fairly large and thin; short tail carried near horizontal, tapering

- **Life Span:** 10-12 years

■ Appearance and Temperament

The Gordon setter is more muscular and not as streamlined as other setters. The breed's weight and size vary greatly according to the strain or line, weighing from 45 pound to as high as 80 pounds. The dog's range in height is 23 to 27 inches.

The Gordon setter has a strong-looking body. The coat of this handsome dog is soft, shiny, and sometimes wavy. The dog's legs, chest, and tail are feathered with long hair. The dog's colors are black with rich chestnut markings over the eyes, on the chest, muzzle, throat, inside the hind legs, under the tail, and on the feet (hence one of the breed's earlier names, the "black and tan" setter). A little white is acceptable on the chest.

Gordon setters are lovable, gentle, and affectionate, but can be reserved with strangers. They are excellent house dogs, but need to be walked or run daily. They are not good kennel dogs and need obedience training at an early age. The best owner for an Gordon setter is one who lives in the country.

History

The origin of the breed is the black-and-tan setting spaniel of Great Britain developed in the 1600s. It is certain that collie and bloodhound were mixed into the Gordon setter. The Gordon is the only gun dog developed in Scotland. Many noblemen in Scotland were breeding the black-and-tan setter for hunting, but it was the fourth Duke of Gordon who stabilized the breed between 1770 and 1820, and from whom the dog takes its name. He introduced collie blood into the breed and is generally given credit for the breed's genesis, although some sources indicate the duke did little more than lend his name to the breed. The duke's bloodlines are still the standards used today.

The recorded history of the Gordon setter in America begin in 1842 when Daniel Webster and George Blunt imported a pair of Gordon setters from the duke's kennels in Scotland. The first person to bring the Gordon setter to America is unknown, but by 1875, the American Kennel Club had over one hundred Gordons registered. For many years, the Gordon setter was one of the favorite dogs for the market hunter in the woods and fields of America.

In the Field

The Gordon setter's most outstanding characteristic is its high intelligence. The Gordon setter is a good hunter with natural instincts and good scenting powers. This dog is eager to please its master in the field. In range and pace, Gordon setters tends to be much slower then the other setter breeds, although some lines of smaller dogs are agile and quick.

Even though many breeders produce close-working dogs, there is a trend today to return to the smaller Gordon setter that runs moderate to wide in the field. The dog's hunting instincts have survived despite years of breeding only for the bench. If there are birds around, the Gordon setter will find them, and when he does, he will make a good retrieve. For the person who wants a gentle, loyal hunting and family dog, the Gordon setter fits the bill.

Trainability

The Gordon setter is a great companion in the field with a strong natural pointing instinct. They show a great desire to please and are easy to train. Obedience training should begin at an an early age and be reinforced regularly. They are not as stylish at pointing as the English setter, typically pointing with a low (level) tail in the manner of dogs from the UK, but their scenting ability is as good or better. They respond well to training, but patient and gentle handling in the field is recommended. With lots of days in the field, they will develop good hunting skills.

Strengths/Weaknesses

The Gordon setter is a happy, mild-mannered dog. In the field, they are sturdy pointers. While they may be suitable for city life, this active dog deserves to be run or walked daily. The Gordon setter is slow in developing their hunting skills, and on-going obedience training is the rule. The dog's beautiful coat needs to be combed and brushed after each outing in the field.

The Show Ring

In 1924, the Gordon Setter Club of America was founded, and if it hadn't been for this group, the breed may have died out. The problem today is too many breeders raise show dogs and not field dogs, which are typically smaller and less massive. But there are still breeders who raise Gordon setters for hunting and many have excellent stock.

HUNGARIAN VIZSLA

The Hungarian Vizsla is one of the oldest pointing breeds in the world, but it is relatively new to North America. Like other versatile hunting breeds, the Vizsla is a good natural retriever and is excellent at tracking. But unlike the other versatile dogs, this handsome Hungarian is more of an upland bird hunting specialist than an all-purpose dog. The Vizsla relies on finding birds from body and ground scent and rarely misses any game. The Vizsla is a close-working deliberate hunter, best described as a walking man's dog.

- **Area & Date of Origin:** Hungary, middle ages
- **Function:** Gun dog, pointer, versatile hunting dog, field trials
- **Height & Weight:** 22-24″ (male); 21-23″ (female); 45-65 lbs
- **Colors:** Solid golden rust in different shadings
- **Coat:** Short, smooth, dense, and close-lying
- **Standards:** Strong, well-proportioned body with short back; moderately broad and deep chest; lean head with moderate stop; brown nose; eye color blends with coat color; low-set, thin, silky, long ears; tapered tail docked one third off, carried near horizontal; round, compact, cat-like feet
- **Life Span:** 10 -14 years
- **Also called:** Vizsla, Hungarian pointer

■ Appearance and Temperament

The Vizsla is a long-legged, stylish dog and one of the smallest of the versatile breeds. The standard calls for the males height to be between 22 and 24 inches at the withers and a female between 21 and 23 inches. Males weigh from 45 to 65 pounds and females are usually less.

The Vizsla has a short, smooth coat that lies flat and close to the body. The color of a Vizsla is quite distinctive, occurring in several shades from cinnamon to reddish gold. The face is hound-like, even reminiscent of a Labrador retriever's. The ears are long and lie close to the cheeks. The color of the eyes blends with the color of the coat. The tail is docked by a third.

The Vizsla is a well-mannered, excellent house pet and also a good watch dog. They are very devoted, loving, and like being included as a family member. Their size enables them to adapt well to modest living quarters.

Like all hunting breeds, a Vizsla needs more than just a walk each day. The Vizsla is a highly active dog that needs to be exercised daily. Having a fenced yard is helpful; even better is being in the field hunting with their master, running free.

■ History

Like most of the old pointing breeds, few records were kept of the Vizsla's heritage, so much of their history is based on a few ancient records, some artwork, and stories handed down from generation to generation.

The Vizsla's origin may have come from the Magyar tribesmen from central Asia, who in the eighth century invaded and settled the territory that is now Hungary. Stone etching done by the Magyars suggest there was a dog very similar to the present-day Vizsla breed.

The Magyar conquerors and the settlers of the country brought several ancient breeds of dogs with them to their new home. The development of the Vizsla bloodlines probably evolved from descendants of the conquerors and the new settler's dogs.

Many years later, the conquerors became the Hungarian nobility and hunters of the land. There was a great need for good hunting dogs because the settlers developed agricultural croplands and game became plentiful. At the time, the Vizsla was the most outstanding hunting dog in Hungary, and they became the nobility's choice. Today's Vizslas started being developed at this time.

Somewhere around 1820, the modern breed's history began and a Vizsla Stud Book was established for the breed. Records were kept of each dog's pedigree. After two World Wars and the USSR invasion of Hungary, however, most of the records and dogs were lost. Several hundred refugees managed to escape the invasion of the USSR, and some dogs fled with them to other countries in Europe. Thus the breed was saved, and over the years the numbers have increased.

North America saw its first Vizsla in the 1950s, and by the 1960s, the American Kennel Club accepted the breed. In competition, this late-comer has done extremely well and, like its ancestors, excels more as an upland gamebird specialist than other versatile breeds.

■ In the Field

Vizslas are close-working dogs whose pace is slower than most pointing breeds. The dogs' scenting ability is outstanding, and they tend to be a one-man dog. The dog has a deliberate pattern to work all of the cover. Most Vizslas have an ideal range for hunting woodlands, small agricultural fields, and small parcels of grassland, making them a good choice for the hunter who pursues pheasants, woodcock, and ruffed grouse. The Vizsla is a versatile hunting dog, well-adapted to land and water too, provided the temperatures are moderate because of their light coat.

■ Trainability

The Vizsla is an intelligent gun dog, which often makes training easy. They are extremely alert and learn their lessons quickly. A Vizsla responds to training best with praise and affection. They are a dog that cannot take hard discipline or a loud voice.

When hunting, their goal is to please their master, and pointing and retrieving come to them naturally. The Vizsla requires a great deal of exercise and the more field experience the dog can get, the better hunter it becomes. As a pointing breed, they develop hunting instincts early and have a remarkable memory, learning early on to hunt the birdy places.

■ Strengths/Weaknesses

The Vizsla is a loyal, hard-working dog in the field. They adapt well to all types of hunting conditions and are a great dog for the man or woman who belongs to a hunting preserve. In the dog's homeland, they are still the best choice for a practical hunter and are used for a variety of hunting situations. Vizsla as a pointing breed mature early and start pointing and retrieving before their first year.

The Vizsla is an excellent companion, but can become highly protective as a house dog. They are a better house pet than a kennel dog and should not be kept outdoors for long periods of time in a cold climate.

■ The Show Ring

The official sponsor of the breed in the United States is the Vizsla Club of America, a member club of the American Kennel Club, where they are regular competitors in the show ring. Some Vizslas are also registered in the American Field Publishing Company's *Field Dog Stud Book*. Many Vizslas participate in the North American Versatile Hunting Dog Association (NAHVDA) testing program.

ITALIAN SPINONE

If you like a large pointing dog with a look of distinction, the Italian spinone may be the breed for you. Known in the United States as the Spinone or the Italian Griffon, this rugged, close-working bird dog has just recently found popularity outside of the country of its origin. One of the Continental versatile breeds, the spinone is a great, affectionate, sociable animal that adjusts well to family life whether you reside in the city or in the country.

- **Area & Date of Origin:** Italy, 1200s
- **Function:** Gun dog, pointer, retriever
- **Height & Weight:** 23-27", 70-85 lbs (male); 22-25", 60-75 lbs (female)
- **Colors:** Solid white, white with orange, or white with chestnut markings
- **Coat:** Dense & wiry; generally single, consisting of rough, dry, thick hair about 1.5 to 2.5" in length; eyebrows, mustache, and tufted beard of longer, stiff hair
- **Standards:** Muscular, with powerful bone structure; broad, deep, well-rounded chest; long head with long, square muzzle; large, well-opened, ochre-colored eyes; triangular ears, large and dropped; tail carried down or horizontal, docked to 5.5 to 8"; large rounded feet covered with short, dense hair
- **Life Span:** 12-14 years
- **Also called:** Spinone Italiano; Italian coarsehaired pointer

■ Appearance and Temperament

A spinone can weigh up to 85 pounds, but most fall between 60 and 80 pounds, making them one of the larger hunting dogs of any type. They range in height from 22 to 27 inches at the shoulders. The spinone is a solid, strong, well-muscled dog with a deep chest. The dog has several distinguishing characteristics. One is its *spino* coat (meaning thick brambles) for which the dog is named. The other features are its bushy eyebrows, long mustache, and beard. Overall, the dog's coat is rough, wiry, and slightly wavy.

The spinone's colors are white, white with patches of yellow, white with patches of brown, white roan, yellow roan, and brown roan. The breed is highly intelligent and affectionate. Italian spinones are very popular throughout Europe because they are used for all kinds of hunting and because they are also great companions. The breed is easy to train because of its high intelligence and willingness to learn.

History

The Italian spinone has a long history. But like other ancient European breeds, few records were kept and the dog's history is based on fragments of fact and stories. Though the roots of the breed are lost, a dog similar to the Italian spinone is featured in a painting done in the fifteenth century by Mantegna.

It is believed the origin of the breed dates to the 1600s during the Italian renaissance, and is a descendent of griffon stock. The breed became popular as an all-around hunting dog with both the nobility and the working class.

After the French Revolution, the breed declined and it was not until after the Second World War that the spinone started to make a comeback. Today, the spinone is again a popular hunting breed and family dog in many countries. In the United States, it is just starting to gain some popularity as a versatile hunting dog. Many experienced dog people have never seen one of these handsome dogs in person. The breed is also referred to as the Italian coarsehaired pointer.

In the Field

The spinone has excelled as a versatile hunting dog for centuries. Even today, it's used for all types of hunting. It excels as a retriever for upland game and waterfowl. The dog's heavy coat allows it to hunt in wet and cold, freezing conditions. The spinone is an enthusiastic, hard-hunting dog. They have exceptionally strong natural pointing instincts and are considered one of the better pointing versatile dogs for finding birds.

The spinone's style is to work at close range when hunting. They move slower than most other pointing dogs but are also more methodical, never missing any area that is likely to hold game. The dog is well-suited for riparian habitat and woodland cover. The dog has exceptional endurance and is excellent at ground-tracking game. The breed is known for its great memory when locating downed birds. After the hunting season is over, they fit quite easily into family life.

Trainability

The spinone has a great capacity at a young age to learn, and seldom needs retraining. They are naturally obedient and do well in training sessions. Though somewhat independent, their nature is to become intensely interested in whatever you are doing. Although they learn fast, they do have a mind of their own and can be stubborn at times.

Strengths/Weaknesses

For a hunting breed, the Italian spinone adapts well to urban or rural life. They are affectionate, patient, and just as happy at home as in the field hunting. They love children and get along extremely well with other pets. In the field, they are enthusiastic, though methodical. They need exercise daily but are quite content in a small yard. The dog's wiry hair should be combed and brushed a few time each week. The spinone is a family dog and does not belong in a kennel.

Other Uses

The dog can become a good watchdog if trained. Being extremely intelligent, spinones can be used for search and rescue and other tracking activities.

The Show Ring

Although not common in the United States, there is a Spinone Club of America. The breed's numbers are few compared to other pointing breeds, however. The North American Versatile Hunting Dog Association (NAHVDA) is open for the dog to compete in the Natural Ability tests. As a show dog, they are becoming more numerous.

POINTER

First, a little discussion of proper nomenclature: There is no breed named "English pointer," and no other pointing breed is formally called a "pointer." Some devotees of the German shorthaired pointer refer to these dogs as "pointers," but that is incorrect.

A pointer is a lean, mean, bird-hunting machine, the king of the bird dogs. In terms of field trial wins alone, these canine athletes are the world's best. Though some strains, notably the Elhew dogs, are friendly and personable dogs, these animals do not need the level of human contact some of the other breeds require, although they do better with contact. A pointer loves to hunt more than anything else. The breed is well-suited for warm weather and by tradition is the Southlands' plantation dog as well as the dog most widely used in the brush country of Texas.

- **Area & Date of Origin:** England, 1600s
- **Function:** Gun dog, pointer, field trials
- **Height & Weight:** 25-28", 55-75 lbs. (male); 23-26", 45-65 lbs (female)
- **Colors:** Liver, lemon, black, orange, either solid or mixed with white
- **Coat:** Short, dense, smooth
- **Standards:** Strong, solid back; square, deep muzzle, nose slightly higher at tip than at stop; long head with pronounced stop; rounded dark eyes; thin, soft, hanging ears, somewhat pointed at tip; tail tapering, straight; oval feet
- **Life Span:** 12 -15 years

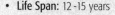

■ Appearance and Temperament

A pointer's muscles ripple under a taut skin. Deep chested and built for speed, these dogs look the part of athlete. The sculpted head and large eyes show intelligence. There is a fairly wide variation in size among pointer strains; males range in size from 45 to 75 pounds and are 25 to 28 inches tall at the withers. Females are smaller both in weight and height. Pointers have a short, dense, smooth coat, primarily white, either patched and/or ticked and mixed with liver, lemon, black, or orange.

The breed requires a lot of space and extensive daily exercise. They are even-tempered dogs, hard-driving, and will hunt with anyone who takes them out. Although sometimes stubborn, they do respond well to firm field training. They can become a good house dog if started young. They tend to bark more than other hunting breeds, and should not be left to run freely. Pointers are reserved by instinct and are not resentful of children or other animals, which they tend to ignore.

■ History

According to most historians, the pointer origin started in Spain centuries ago. Although its exact origins are unclear, it is believed at some stage the pointer bloodlines from England were developed from the Spanish pointer, Italian pointer, bloodhound, greyhound, setter, and perhaps the bulldog; what its true roots are will probably never be known, as with so many of our sporting breeds.

The pointer is believed to have evolved after the Middle Ages. The English noblemen wanted a speedier dog, so the principal development and first big improvement of the breed took place in England. Like the setter, the pointers became a nobleman's hunting dog for game birds and hares.

The pointer came to North America before the Civil War and was used mostly by Southern gentlemen for hunting bobwhite quail. In the post Civil War era, when Northern industrialists bought up and took over old Southern plantations, they carried on and expanded the gentlemanly "quail culture," and the pointer became the breed of choice. The modern pointer has changed little over the last hundred years. The dog today has a biddable disposition and a laid-back temperament.

In the Field

There is no prettier sight than a pointer running full speed in a big open field and slamming into a high-tailed point. They are the showiest of the pointing breeds and the classiest of the sporting breeds. The pointer is hard-driving, has great stamina, and is a bird-finding machine. Once considered dogs for hunting only "covey birds," today they are just as apt to be hunting a woodlot pointing ruffed grouse and woodcock, or running the big open country of the West working a flock of sharptails or prairie chickens.

The pointer is good at what it does. As a hunting dog, the breed very possibly has the best nose of any of the pointing dogs. Their hunting instincts become evident early in life and they usually develop their hunting skills at a young age. Many pointers reach their peak performance within two years and, once learned, retain those hunting skill for a lifetime.

Trainability

There are many affable pointers that need little field training, wanting to cooperate at every opportunity. There are others, though, because of their boldness and independence, that call for sterner discipline than other pointing breeds. Although these dogs are generally eager to work, they can be stubborn, and benefit greatly from field discipline and obedience training.

The pointer has been called "aloof," "not warm in manner," "a dog with a far-off look," or just "not friendly," but I don't think this is true of the pointer today. Pointers, like all hunting dogs, need love, affection, and time with their master outside of hunting. When given the opportunity, they become reliable companions and devoted friends in the field.

Strengths/Weaknesses

The pointer is intelligent, bold, and aggressive when hunting, but at home is mild-mannered and a good family companion. They also adjust quite well to a kennel life as long as they are exercised daily in a secured area.

Even though the pointer is capable of learning hunting skills at a young age, obedience training is also strongly recommended early in life. As a sporting dog, they require a great deal of frequent, rigorous exercise and should be hunted or worked in the field often. They live to hunt and that is exactly what they were bred to do, but caution should be taken if running the dog on a very cold day for long

periods of time; the dog's coat is among the canine world's lightest and thinnest. After being in the field, they need little grooming; a quick brushing over their short coat usually takes care of any burrs. The pointer is a country dog and not well-suited for city or apartment living.

A large number of breeders are currently producing top-quality pups, so one can be had fairly easily. But the really top breedings can be quite expensive.

Other Uses

Pointers are hunting dogs first. Their main purpose is pointing upland gamebirds. Other than being a great companion, the breed is not much used for non-related hunting activities, with the exception of conformation shows.

The Show Ring

The pointer's conformation is a matter of proportion and balance. The pointer is a great show dog and is considered one of the flashiest in the show ring. They are sleek and confident.

LARGE MUNSTERLANDER

If you are looking for an unusual, beautiful, obedient family pet that thrives on companionship and is an enthusiastic all-round hunting dog, you may consider the large Munsterlander. It is a breed that almost lost its identity, but as the German longhaired pointer declined, a breed club was formed that saved the large Munsterlander. The two breeds of Munsterlander are quite different from other German breeds, as they draw their looks and temperament from other longhaired pointing dogs.

- **Area & Date of Origin:** Germany, 1800s
- **Function:** Gun dog, tracking, pointing, retrieving, versatile hunting dog
- **Height & Weight:** 23-24"; 55-70 lbs
- **Colors:** Black and white; solid patches, ticked, or roan regions
- **Coat:** Long and thick; featherings on forelegs, chest, tail, ears
- **Standards:** Broad, slightly rounded head with moderate stop; broad, round-tipped, feathered ears hang close to head; straight forelegs; fully-feathered tail is held in line with back, tapers to a tip; firm, strong feet with ample hair between toes
- **Life Span:** 12-13 years

■ Appearance and Temperament

The large Munsterlander weighs from 55 to 70 pounds, with the average weight about 60 pounds. They range in height from 23 to 25 inches at the shoulders.

The breed has an elongated head, strong neck, and a lean muzzle with round-tipped ears that hang close to the head.

Their long, dense, silky hair is not coarse or curly, and is of medium length. The tail, front and back legs are well-feathered. The standard color is a combination of black and white with patches or speckling. The large Munsterlander is happy, good-natured, gentle, and an excellent family pet. To keep them cheerful, it's essential for them to be used as hunting dogs. Even though the large Munsterlander makes a great house dog, they need a large fenced-in area and plenty of outdoor exercise.

History

The large Munsterlander's origin began in the early 1900s in the town of Munster, Germany. The breed's offspring most likely came from the black and white color variation of the old German longhaired pointer. These were crossbred with imported spaniels and the breed became known as the grosser Munsterlander. Twenty years later, a breed club was formed and the large Munsterlander not only became a popular breed in Germany, but also throughout Europe. During the Great Depression in the late 1920s, and then in the Second World War, the breed declined rapidly and almost vanished. But after the war, a few dedicated German breeders reorganized the German Large Munsterlander Club and saved the breed. Today in the United States, the Munsterlander Club of North America serves both the small and large Munsterlander and controls the standards.

In the Field

The large Munsterlander is considered by many Germans to be the best all-around gun dog among the pointing breeds, as it points, retrieves, and tracks with aplomb. The dog's strong natural instincts, along with its exceptional scenting power and good memory are the reasons the breed is so popular.

The large Munsterlander is well-adapted to hunting any type of terrain. Not only is it a good hunter in the open field and wooded country, but is an outstanding and versatile water dog. The dog has exceptional endurance, can run for hours, and can withstand wet or cold weather. The large Munsterlander is noted for unerringly finding downed birds, and for its sureness of retrieves on land and water. The breed goes about hunting, tracking, and retrieving with intense desire.

Trainability

The large Munsterlander's desire to learn along with its devoted companionship is one key to the breed's success. The dog has a strong, natural pointing instinct, and is an animated, happy hunter with a keen nose. Highly trainable, the large Munsterlander learns hunting skills at a very young age, but needs gentle handling.

Strengths/Weaknesses

Both breeds of Munsterlander pointers are mild-mannered, intelligent, loyal, affectionate family dogs. In the field, they are hard hunters and have a great desire to please. The large Munsterlander needs an enormous amount of exercise and is not suited for urban living. The dog's long hair needs to be combed and brushed after every outing in the field. Due to the breed's relative rarity, and the fact that breeding is tightly controlled by a governing body (see below), there is often more demand for pups than there is supply.

The Show Ring

The Large Munsterlander Club in Germany has numerous members and has brought this great, versatile pointing and retrieving dog to where it once was. The North American Munsterlander Club has a breeding program for both large and small Munsterlanders, and requires each dog be tested in the North American Versatile Hunting Dog Association (NAHVDA) program. To be able to breed, a dog must win a Prize I in the Natural Ability test before two years old. The club then approves the breeding if the standards are met. By doing this, they maintain the high standards and instincts of the breed.

PUDELPOINTER

This versatile gun dog may be the answer for today's new hunters who are hunting on smaller and smaller parcels of land, and many of whom live in apartments or small houses with small yards that cannot house a kennel of dogs for all the diversified hunting activities. As a result, many hunters today are looking for a gun dog that can do it all. There are a number of breeds of versatile gun dogs that have been developed in Europe for the exact sort of conditions North Americans now face. The pudelpointer, one of the lesser-known versatiles, fits the bill perfectly and is worth a serious look.

- **Area & Date of Origin:** Germany, 1800s
- **Function:** Gun dog, tracking, pointing, retrieving
- **Height & Weight:** 21-26"; 45-65 lbs
- **Colors:** Solid liver, chestnut, or black
- **Coat:** Short, rough, waterproof, and tight-fitting
- **Standards:** Sturdily built; eyebrows, mustache, and beard of bushy, coarse hair; dark eyes; large, black nose has wide nostrils; sturdy and substantial forelegs; strong loins on powerful, straight hind legs; docked tail; insulating hair grows between toes
- **Life Span:** 12 -14 years

■ Appearance and Temperament

The pudelpointer ranges from 45 to 65 pounds, with the average weight about 55 pounds. Their height is from 21 to 26 inches at the shoulder. The dog is bred only for hunting, so there is no set conformation standard. In weight and height, there is great variation. The pudelpointer has a heavily built, muscular body. The dog's head is medium in length, has thick eyebrows, and a full beard above and below the mouth. One third of the tail is docked after birth. The ears are tight to the head and the neck is thin and muscular.

The dog's hair is coarse, thick, and tight to the body. The tail, front and back legs have no feathering. The standard color is chestnut or a rich dark brown, though some are black.

The dog's disposition is good-natured and gentle. These dogs are extremely intelligent and fast learners. Pudelpointers are excellent family pets and wonderful companions at home and in the field. They are athletic dogs and it's essential for them to be used for hunting. Although a great house pet that can live in a small place, they need plenty of exercise.

■ History

The origin of the pudelpointer's first breeding dates back to 1870. This dog was developed by crossing a precursor of the standard poodle, called a *pudel* (*pudel* comes from the German and means *to splash*), with a pointer. This standard poodle was a German breed rather than a French breed (see standard poodle in the retriever section of this book).

The pudelpointer was a planned breed by German sportsmen who sought a versatile dog that was both a water-loving retriever and an instinctive pointer. After several years of breeding and crossbreeding, the pudelpointer bloodlines were established and the result was outstanding. It just so happened that it inherited the best hunting qualities and characteristics from both breeds.

In 1881, the first German Pudelpointer Club was established. The first pudelpointer to arrive in North America was in Canada in 1956. Today, the pudelpointer is not registered by any kennel club in America because the breed's owners claim the show bench will destroy the dog's versatile hunting quality. Over the past few years, the pudelpointer has become a star as a versatile dog in the North American Versatile Hunting Dog Association (NAVHDA).

In the Field

In both Europe and North America, the pudelpointer is considered an up-and-coming breed as a versatile hunting dog. Some breeders claim (with good reason) that there is no such thing as a poor pudelpointer. You may get a dog that does not have all great versatile hunting instincts, but you will never get a pudelpointer with no hunting instincts.

The pudelpointer is not as big-running as some of the field trial pointing dogs, but in open country, it will hold its own with any breed finding game. Not only is it a good hunter in the open field and wooded country, but also an outstanding versatile retriever on land and water. The dog has exceptional endurance and, thanks to its unique coat, can withstand wet and cold weather.

Trainability

The pudelpointer has a great desire to please and is a devoted companion. In the field, pudelpointers have keen noses and are enthusiastic, energetic, and extremely obedient. They are a dog that is happiest when it is hunting. In the dog's native land, it is used for hunting game birds, waterfowl, marsh birds, rabbits, and fox.

The breed develops its natural hunting skills at an early age. Pointing, retrieving, and tracking come to them naturally. The dog is easy to train, but needs gentle handling. Like most hunting breeds, the more a pudelpointer is worked in the field, the better the dog responds.

Strengths/Weaknesses

As already described, the pudelpointer strengths are many. Intelligent, loyal, and affectionate as a pet, the breed is also outstanding in the field. They are hardy whether hunting a cold day in a duck blind or working a flock of sharptails in open grasslands. They are hard-driving dogs that can also relax and be mellow after a hunt. The pudelpointer adjusts well to city living but needs to be exercised daily. The dog has a mellow disposition and is good with children.

The breed has few weaknesses. Because of the dog's color, it can be difficult to see when hunting in wooded areas. The pudelpointer is not a good kennel dog; instead, one belongs in the home with a yard of its own. Because the breeding is tightly controlled by the Pudelpointer Club of North America, finding a pup can be a problem as the supply is always very small.

The Show Ring

The German Pudelpointer Club and the Pudelpointer Club of North America's main interest is in developing versatile hunting dogs, not show dogs. In North America, club members participate in the North American Versatile Hunting Dog Association (NAHVDA) program.

RED SETTER (IRISH SETTER)

To many observers, the red or Irish setter is the most beautiful of all the pointing breeds. In the United States, the breed has split into two varieties: a smaller, lighter dog from hunting and field trial stock, and a larger, darker show dog with the hunting drive virtually extinguished. Both varieties are good-natured, friendly, and make excellent family pets. But today the smaller red setter has not only made a comeback as a good pointing dog, but there is also an effort being made to return the breed to a middle-sized dog with a renewed hunting drive.

- **Area & Date of Origin:** Ireland, 1700s
- **Function:** Gun dog, setter, pointer, field trials
- **Height & Weight:** 24-27", 35-70 lbs
- **Colors:** Mahogany or rich chestnut red
- **Coat:** Short and fine on head and forelegs; elsewhere flat, straight, and of moderate length; feathering on ears, backs of legs, belly, chest, and tail
- **Standards:** Long, lean head with distinct stop, muzzle moderately deep; medium-size, almond-shaped brown eyes; low-set, thin ears; topline slopes to rear; tail carried straight or slightly curving upward, nearly level with the back; small, very firm feet
- **Life Span:** 12 -14 years

■ Appearance and Temperament

The modern red setter comes in a variety of sizes. The smaller dogs can weigh as little as 35 pounds and the larger dogs more than 70 pounds. The dogs range in height from 24 to 27 inches. In both weight and height, the male is overall larger than the female.

The red setter gets its name from its coat, which is moderately long and wavy but not curly. The dog's legs, chest, and tail are feathered with long hair. The dog's colors are rich mahogany to a chestnut-red. A small white patch on the throat is acceptable.

The red setter's temperament is much like his English cousin's: gentle and loving, yet not fawning or overly affectionate, making them excellent family dogs, including for households with children and other pets. They do, as is true of all the hunting breeds, need plenty of daily exercise.

The red setter is truly a breed that needs a special owner, one who has time to train and exercise this fun-loving hunting dog. Perfect for a red setter is being part of an outdoor sporting family that lives in the country.

■ History

The Irish setter or red setter is one of four breeds of setters. Known in Gaelic as the "modder rhu" (red dog), the red setter is probably older than the English setter, but shares the same common ancestors. The red setter is believed to be the result of many crosses between spaniels and local Irish hunting stock.

The true history of the breed is not known, but originally most of the Irish setters were red and white. The hunter preferred the two-colored dogs because they were more visible against the red heather. They were used only for hunting and not bred for show or conformation. When they began to be bred for show, most breeders selectively bred only the red dogs for the show ring. As with other such splits in the breedings, the hunting instincts were bred out of the dog as well.

In the 1950s, some breeders started to selectively breed the Irish setter for field trials, while others who loved the breed as a hunting dog started outcrossing the Irish setter to English setters in order to bring back the dog's hunting instincts. *The Field Dog Stud Book* was opened to all who wanted to bring the breed back to what it once was, and the red dog again became a hunter.

Soon after, a group of breeders got together and formed the National Red Setter Field Trial Club. As a result, the Irish setter is now known as the red setter, and has become successful in the Open Stakes against all pointing breeds. It is again a fine pointing dog. Today, the red setter's ancestor, the true red-and-white Irish setter, is also making a comeback as a hunting breed.

■ In the Field

The red setter's primary work in the field is to find gamebirds and point them for the gun. The red dog is again becoming a great field dog with natural instincts and good scenting power. The red setter responds well to training and is gaining a reputation as an outstanding pointer among bird-hunting sportsmen.

The red setter is a fast dog suitable for use in any type of terrain and on any species of upland gamebird in America. They make good walking man's dogs but are also wide-ranging enough to be hunted from horseback, depending upon the strain or breeding.

■ Trainability

The red setter is a good companion and a reliable

hunter for its owner, with strong natural pointing instincts. Some, but not all, are capable retrievers. They are spirited hunters and show a great desire to please. The dog's obedience training should begin at an early age. They respond well to training but like their English cousin, respond best to a gentle hand; patient handling in the field is recommended. If given time in the field, they develop good bird hunting skills and will pay you back with many a bird in the hand.

■ Strengths/Weaknesses

The red setter's strengths are its fine hunting instincts and abilities. It is a hard-working, mild-mannered breed. In the field, they are staunch pointers. The red dog requires an enormous amount of exercise, so country life is far more suitable than city life.

One weakness of the breed is the red setter develops its hunting instincts slower than some of the other pointing breeds. An additional drawback is the lack of available puppies, since this breed is still on the comeback trail.

■ Other Uses

Many red setters are still show dogs, but these strains are of show-dog breeding and not considered for the field. Today, more of these handsome pointers are out hunting and running in the field. The breed also possesses good qualities as family pet and companion.

■ The Show Ring

The red setter is still a good bench show dog, clean looking and aristocratic. But it's the members of the National Red Setter Field Trial Club that have brought this fine red dog back to where it belongs in the field, and it's once again becoming the classy hunter it used to be.

RED-AND-WHITE SETTER

At one time, the true, pure Irishmen's hunting dog may have been the best bird finder of any setter. The working or hunting Irish setter was originally a red-and-white or a dark chestnut-colored dog. But breeders began to select-breed for only red dogs and the red-and-white setter almost became extinct. Both the red setter and the red-and-white setter have the same origin, but today, the red-and-white setter comes the closest to the true Irish setter. Only recently has the big, magnificent red-and-white setter undergone a revival to renew the breed's hunting desire.

- **Area & Date of Origin:** Ireland, 1700s
- **Function:** Gun dog, setter, retriever
- **Height & Weight:** 25.5-27" (male); 23.5-25" (female); 60-70 lbs
- **Colors:** Parti-colored; white base coat with red patches (red is deep chestnut red), flecking around face, feet, up forelegs and hindlegs
- **Coat:** Moderate length, flat, thick; feathering on legs, underside, chest, tail; short and fine hair on head, fronts of legs, and tips of ears
- **Standards:** Well-boned and muscular; powerful back; deep chest; well-chiseled head with defined stop; square muzzle; round, dark hazel to dark brown eyes; black or dark brown nose with well-opened nostrils; moderately-long, well-muscled neck; well-feathered, tapered tail set as natural extension of topline, carried straight or curving slightly upward, nearly level with back; round feet have some feathering between toes
- **Life Span:** 12-13 years
- **Also called:** Irish Red-and-White Setter, Parti-colored Setter

■ Appearance and Temperament

The modern red-and-white setter is a large dog with a deep chest; it typically weighs 60 to 70 pounds. The dogs range from 24 to 27 inches in height. The red-and-white setter has sloping shoulders with a long body. The ears are triangular and the coat of this handsome dog is dense, long, and wavy. The dog's legs, chest, and tail are feathered with long hair, which is white and chestnut red, but predominantly white.

The red-and-white setters' temperament is gentle and affectionate, but the dogs can be headstrong at times. They are an excellent family pet and good with children. The red-and-white setter is a smart, active animal that needs daily exercise.

History

Originally the Irish setter was all red or red and white, and dates back further than the English setter. This fine dog was the result of many crosses between spaniels and an Irish breed of dog that was from red-and-white hunting stock.

The true origin of the breed is not known but most of the dogs were red and white before the days of bench shows, and they were all hunting dogs with no standards for conformation. The hunter preferred the white and red dog because it was more visible against the red heather. As the dog moved into the show ring, breeders bred out the white and produced only red dogs. Along with the change in color came a loss of this great bird dog's hunting identity.

There were still a few breeders who bred for hunting instincts and the true old Irish setter hung on by a thread. Today, the red-and-white setter is on the upswing and at this point, the red setter and the red-and-white setter are classified as two different breeds in the United States.

In the Field

The red-and-white setter has again become a great hunter with good instincts and scenting power. The dog responds well to field training and is a breed being recognized again as a good pointing dog.

The red-and-white setter is an active and ideal dog for hunting woodlands and riparian habitat. Although it can hunt most any terrain, the breed is not well-suited to big open country as the dogs' range is fairly close. It has a moderate pace and covers ground thoroughly, making it a good walking man's dog.

Trainability

The red-and-white setter has strong natural instincts for pointing and retrieving. The dog responds well to learning, but gentle handling is recommended. Training should start at a young age because they need more time for obedience training than most other gun dogs. Once trained, however, they make reliable hunting companions. They are very enthusiastic and should be worked often in the field to develop good bird hunting skills.

Strengths/Weaknesses

The red-and-white setter is a lovable, good-natured breed. In the field, they have a refined sense of smell and are sturdy pointers. The red-and-white setter is very mild-mannered and requires patience when handling. They thrive on physical activity and need daily exercise. Country life is far more suitable for them than city life, and their love of people does not make them good kennel dogs. They develop their hunting skills slower than most other pointing breeds.

Other Uses

The red-and-white setter is a handsome pointer that belongs in the field as a hunter. When not hunting, it should be a family pet and companion.

The Show Ring

The red-and-white setter is a dog that can compete and win field trials. It has had a long climb back to becoming a good field dog, and is once again becoming an excellent hunter.

SMALL MUNSTERLANDER

Like the large Munsterlander, the small Munsterlander belongs to the versatile hunting breeds, which were once called the Continental breeds. This all-purpose gun dog is the youngest of the versatile hunting breeds. The smallest of all the German gun dogs, the small Munsterlander was bred as a working dog for all kinds of hunting. It is a rugged, swift dog that points and has an enthusiastic desire to retrieve. If you are looking for a good, small hunting companion that does just about everything on land and water, consider the small Munsterlander. It's a dog you can hunt with anywhere.

- **Area & Date of Origin:** Germany, middle ages/1900s

- **Function:** Gun dog, tracking, pointing, retrieving

- **Height & Weight:** 19-22"; 30-38 lbs

- **Colors:** Chestnut and white; solid patches, ticked, or roan regions

- **Coat:** Smooth, close-fitting, slight wave, dense undercoat; feathering on ears, forelegs, and tail

- **Standards:** Broad, slightly rounded head; muscular neck is slightly arched; lighter-colored hair on pointed ears, amply feathered; close shoulders; well-boned, straight legs; well-muscled thighs; ample tail feathering is longer than elsewhere on body; firm, strong feet

- **Life Span:** 13-14 years

■ Appearance and Temperament

The small Munsterlander weighs between 30 and 38 pounds. They range in height from 19 to 22 inches at the shoulders. The small Munsterlander is exceptionally solid, and has a deep chest and a long head and muzzle. The ears are round and hang close to the head, like the large Munsterlander, but are pointed at the tips. The neck is sturdy and slightly arched. One characteristic of the small Munsterlander is that the eyes are very dark brown and well set into the eye rims.

The small Munsterlander has a dense, sleek, wavy coat of medium length. The tail, front, and back legs are feathered. The standard color is chestnut and white with dark patches and speckling, or a roan pattern.

The dog is mild-mannered and good-natured. The reason the dog is so popular in Europe is it's outstanding at finding game, while also making a wonderful small family pet. They are happy dogs, but need lots of time in the field. The dog loves being outdoors and is better in the country than in the city.

History

The small Munsterlander's origin, like that of the large Munsterlander, began in the early 1900s in the town of Munster, Germany, by crossbreeding German longhaired pointers and spaniels. The dog became very popular in northern Germany with hunters who sold game for a living. The dog was a "meat dog" and not only had to be an outstanding pointer, but also reliable in tracking and finding dead or wounded game.

After the start of the Great Depression and during the war years, the breed declined rapidly. After the Second World War, however, the German Small Munsterlander Club was revived. Today, the Munsterlander Club of North America serves both small and large Munsterlander owners.

In the Field

In Germany, both the Munsterlander breeds are considered one of the premier breeds for the serious all-around hunter. The small Munsterlander has exceptionally strong natural pointing instincts and a great memory for locating downed birds, whether in the water or on land. One reason the breed has become so popular in Europe as a hunting dog is because of its ease in training.

The small Munsterlander is a medium range dog. It's happy and lively whether running the open plains for prairie game birds or hunting covers for ruffed grouse. The dog has exceptional endurance and can run for hours. The small

Munsterlander is an outstanding water dog and can withstand both wet and cold conditions. Like the large Munsterlander, the small Munsterlander is also noted for its non-slip retrieving skills on both land and water. The breed is not only a good pointer and retriever, but excellent at tracking.

Trainability

The small Munsterlander has a great desire to learn and a great desire to hunt. The dogs develop their skills at a young age and retain them well. They have strong, natural pointing and retrieving instincts. They are easy dogs to train because of their willingness to learn and their gentle temperament, but are not cut out for force training or a heavy hand.

Strengths/Weaknesses

Both breeds of Munsterlander pointers are mild-mannered, intelligent, loyal, affectionate family dogs. Today, this small, longhaired pointer in Europe and the United States gets high marks. They need exercise daily and are more suitable for country living. The dog's long hair needs to be combed and brushed after every outing.

The Show Ring

Today, the Small Munsterlander Club in Germany has over 4,000 members. The organization has worked hard to bring the dog back as a great versatile hunting dog. The North American Munsterlander Club has a breeding program that requires each dog to be tested by the standard of The North American Versatile Hunting Dog Association (NAHVDA). For the dog to be approved, it must win a Prize I in the Natural Ability test before it is two years old. By doing this, the Club maintains the breed's natural instincts and fine hunting and retrieving abilities.

WEIMARANER

The Weimaraner (*Vi'-mar-honor*) is a German breed favored in times past by that country's noble class. Originally the dog's main purpose was hunting wooded cover to track and find big game, such as wild boar, bear, and deer, although they were also good at pointing and retrieving. After the decline of big game in that region, the aristocrats used the dog more for hunting upland birds, waterfowl, and small animals. The Weimaraner was never intended to be a dog of the working class. By the time the breed arrived in the United States, that had changed, but even today the dogs are still considered to be a gentleman's hunting companion.

- **Area & Date of Origin:** Germany, 1800s
- **Function:** Gun dog, pointer, versatile hunting dog, field trials
- **Height & Weight:** 25-27″ (male); 23-25″ (female); 55-85 lbs
- **Colors:** Shades of mouse-gray to silver-gray
- **Coat:** Short, smooth, and sleek; unique gray color
- **Standards:** Strong back set in straight line, slopes slightly from the withers; deep, well-developed chest; moderately long head with skin drawn tightly; gray nose; eyes shaded light amber, gray, or blue-gray; high-set, long ears; tail docked to 6″; webbed feet
- **Life Span:** 10-14 years

■ Appearance and Temperament

The Weimaraner is a strong, medium-sized dog that has a deep chest. There is a fairly wide variation in size, depending upon strain, from 55 to 85 pounds in weight, and 23 to 27 inches at the shoulder. Females are a bit smaller than males.

The Weimaraner's coat is short, sleek, and smooth. The coat is various shades of gray, from which the dog's nickname — the "gray ghost" — comes. Some dogs have a small white patch on the chest, permissible in the breed's standard. The dog has unusually-colored eyes, some being bright amber, others range from gray to blue, which contribute to its "ghostly" qualities. The dog's ears are also quite noticeable; they are high-set, folded slightly, and are lighter than the body fur. The tail is docked, leaving about a third if its original length.

The "Weimie" is an excellent house pet, devoted to all the members of the family. Obedience training is important for a young dog's behavior. Even though they are an active dog, they do equally well living in the suburbs or a rural setting.

■ History

The story of the Weimaraner's origin is interesting, but much of it is not factual history. Some German breeders hypothesize that the dog was developed from bloodlines of the great Dane, German pointer, bloodhound, and German shorthaired pointer. All or part of this may be correct, but no one knows the true origin of the Weimaraner because the dog's historical records were lost or destroyed in Germany during the two World Wars. More than likely, the theory that the dog's origin began in Weimar, the capital of the province of Thuringis, by German noblemen is correct. A painting by Van Dyke in 1631 shows a dog with a portrait of Prince Rupprecht vonder Pfalz. The dog in the painting is steel-gray and resembles the Weimaraner of today.

By 1820, the breed was well-known in that region of Germany, and most of the noblemen who hunted had Weimar pointers; no doubt there were many outcrosses made during this long period of time.

By 1896, the Weimaraner Club of Germany was started, and the dog was recognized as a distinct breed, but only the upper class belonged to the club. Twenty years later, the Weimaraner had become well-known by the German gunning elite for its great ability and enchanting color.

In 1929, the first Weimaraner was brought to the United States by Howard Knight. For years, he kept these original imported bloodlines pure. He founded the first Weimaraner Club of America in 1941. In 1943, the breed was recognized by the American Kennel Club.

After World War II, the breed had its ups and downs because of the Weimaraner Club's long list of rigid restrictions. But since then, some restrictions placed on the breed have been dropped or changed, and for the last 20 years, the Weimaraner has done remarkably well as versatile hunting dog.

■ In the Field

The Weimaraner is close working, has an outstanding nose for finding birds, and is easy to handle in the field. It's a rather slow hunter compared to most versatile hunting dogs, but a sound hunter just the same. It is an excellent hunter in heavy cover. The dog makes a great ruffed grouse, woodcock, and shooting preserve hunter.

■ Trainability

The Weimaraner is an intelligent gun dog, extremely alert and a quick learner. Obedience and field training should start at a very early age and be ongoing for several seasons.

Most of the time, Weimies should be handled with praise and affection. They can be stubborn at times, and require a master to be calm yet firm (although a "little" firmness is usually enough).

When in the field, the Weimie checks in often and likes to know the whereabouts of its owner at all times. Although generally calm, the Weimaraner requires an enormous amount of daily exercise. The breed is precocial and will develop its hunting skill early in life when given the chance.

■ Strengths/Weaknesses

The Weimaraner is a friendly and energetic dog. As a field dog, they have stamina, a good sense of smell, and are excellent retrievers on land and water. Being a close-working dog, they are easily controlled. They are a loyal companion, enthusiastic when learning, excellent with children, and are obedient family pets. The Weimie is well-adapted to city or apartment life, but is still a hunting dog and needs to run daily. Because of the dog's solid gray-colored coat, when hunting a wooded area during low light, they can become difficult to see.

Unfortunately, because of their beauty, there are strains bred specifically for the show ring, with some strong indications that the "hunt" is being bred out of them. A hunter seeking a pup must look for hunting bloodlines.

■ The Show Ring

Today, the Weimaraner is also a show dog and, like some other pointing breeds, there is a split in thought as to how the dog should be used. Too often this results in "hunting" lines and "show" lines.

Many Weimaraners compete in the North American Versatile Hunting Dog Association (NAHVDA) programs.

WIREHAIRED POINTING GRIFFON

The wirehaired pointing griffon is one of the Continental versatile breeds. It has the reputation of being a supreme hunting dog, gentle and easily trained. The griffon is not only a wonderful hunting companion, but an ideal family dog. The dog's most outstanding characteristics are that it is known as an "all-game, all-terrain, all-weather, all-around family dog." If you are looking for an average-sized, strong hunting dog, the wirehaired pointing griffon is a good choice.

- **Area & Date of Origin:** France, 1800s
- **Function:** Gun dog, pointer, water retriever, versatile hunting dog, field trials
- **Height & Weight:** 22-24" (male); 20-22" (female); 50-65 lbs
- **Colors:** Steel gray with brown markings, chestnut brown, roan, white and brown; less desirable is solid brown, solid white, or white and orange
- **Coat:** Outercoat of medium length, straight and wiry, harsh texture; under coat fine, downy, and thick
- **Standards:** Medium-sized dog; strong, firm back slopes slightly to rear; from the side, the muzzle and head are square; abundant mustache and eyebrows; large and rounded eyes in all shades of yellow and brown; brown nose; high-set, medium-sized ears; tail docked to two-thirds to one-half length, carried straight or slightly raised; round webbed feet
- **Life Span:** 12 -14 years

■ Appearance and Temperament

A dog strikingly like the German wirehaired pointer, the wirehaired pointing griffon is a powerfully-built, medium-sized, leggy dog with a deep chest. Their weight is from 50 to 65 pounds. The average male is 60 pounds while females average 55. The breed's height is 20 to 24 inches at the withers.

The griffon's most striking characteristic is that the dog's outercoat is medium length, straight, but wiry.

The dog's undercoat is fine, thick, and almost down-like.

The dog's rough outercoat takes minimal care. Other distinguishing features include bushy eyebrows, a beard, and large, bright yellow-brown eyes. They typically do not have the light-colored blaze between the eyes as does the German wirehaired pointer.

The dog's color can be a combination of gray chestnut roan, steel gray with chestnut markings, a dirty white and chestnut, or chestnut and white. Most dog have some ticking or a roan pattern. The tail is docked at birth to 40 percent of original length.

They are excellent house pets, devoted to their owner and family. Wirehaired pointing griffons can be highly active and need time and space to exercise. This is a country dog and needs an enormous amount of daily exercise.

History

The origin of the breed far predates the wirehair's, going back to the middle 1550s. Some sources claim the true griffon's ancestors are from the ancient griffon hounds, pointers, setters, and several kinds of water retrievers. But the breed's ancestry, like that of so many others, is not entirely known.

The wirehaired pointing griffon was perfected between 1865 and 1885 in Germany, by a Dutchman named Eduard K. Korthals (1851-1896); it was because of him that the breed was first known as "Korthals Griffon." His goal was to create the ultimate all-game, close-working, walking-man's hunting dog that could hunt in all types of weather and terrain. He started his breedings in Germany and later in France. After several years, he achieved his goal and spread the word of this new breed throughout Europe. For the next 20 years, he continued to develop the Korthals Griffon.

In 1888, the International Griffon Club was formed, and in 1916, the official breed standard for wirehaired pointing griffons was established in the United States.

In the Field

The wirehaired pointing griffon was the first versatile European breed to be recognized as a general-purpose dog in the United States. The breed's followers claim it can be trained to hunt and handle any type of game, and retrieve from water or land. The dog has an excellent nose, handles easily, and works very close to its master.

The griffon is a rather slow hunter compared to other versatile dogs, but a solid performer nonetheless, especially in heavy cover where proximity to the gun is important, as in hunting ruffed grouse and woodcock. It is also a great hunting companion for shooting preserves and for hunting waterfowl.

Trainability

The wirehaired pointing griffon, as is characteristic of the versatile dogs, is possessed of a high intelligence with a great desire to learn. Somewhat "softer" than the wirehair, they need praise and encouragement. Since the breed seldom ranges far from the hunter, the dog is easily controlled by hand signals and voice commands. The dog is very eager to please, but can become sensitive to too much control. As a breed, like the other versatiles, the griffon is not a good kennel dog.

The griffon checks in often when hunting in the field. Although generally calm, the dog requires daily exercise. The dog matures quickly, and is not dissuaded by the harshest weather conditions.

Strengths/Weaknesses

The griffon's hunting range is very close and slow. In fact, it may be the slowest and the most methodical pointing dog in North America. But in some types of hunting, this is a strength, not a weakness.

The wirehaired pointing griffon is an all-around, general-purpose gun dog, an obedient family pet that is good with children, and usually easygoing with other dogs. It can be timid at times with strangers. When hunting a wooded area, the breed's dark coat blends with the background of the forest making the dog hard to see at times.

The Show Ring

Recognized by the AKC as a sporting breed, these dogs compete in conformation shows, but the hunting drive has not been sacrificed. Like some of the other versatile dogs, they can not compete in the traditional pointing dog field trials, but their popularity has been expanded by the North American Versatile Hunting Dog Association (NAHVDA) programs.

Beagles readying for winter rabbit hunting action.

CHAPTER 10

THE HOUNDS

by Vickie Lamb

QUIET AND STILL IS THE NIGHT. From his lofty perch on a grassy hill, the hunter watches as a barely perceptible shroud of mist twists among the dark sentinels of the wooded rural landscape below him; high above, a glowing crescent hangs in a cirrus-streaked sky glowing slightly against an inky, star-studded backdrop. Wild beauty permeates his senses.

There is a chill to the night air. The hunter adjusts the collar of his jacket as he listens intently. Somewhere in the distance, a yard dog yips about some vexing detail of his life. Suddenly, a wavering, wafting bawl emerges from the river bottom, a deep, resonant drawn-out bark that hovers in the darkness. Then, more voice, even longer and more resolute than the first. Soon, it is evident that the hound is working his track down river, with purpose.

Near Sandbar Bend, the mottled dog begins to give more tongue as he warms the track, and the hunter starts toward his hound. Soon, he hears the unforgettable three triple-locate chops — as his hound tells the world that he has treed his quarry — and he picks up his pace. As the hound settles in with a regular, musical tree chop, the man reaches the tall, spreading water oak.

He backs up from the tree and directs his light among the stout, plentiful branches of the impressive oak. Then, he circles around, shining a dim amber light. He backs up and squalls a few times. There! Two shiny orbs peer down from high in the tree as the wily ringtail reveals his presence. Now, the hunter collects his hound while praising him; they leave the raccoon where he sits and go in search of another track to run.

Hounds in General

The above scenario involved a coonhound from the scenthound group. There are two types of hounds: sighthounds and scenthounds. Most sighthounds pursue with the intent to catch their quarry, and these include the greyhound-type dogs. By comparison, most scenthounds work by scent and have a heavier, albeit athletic build. Also, certain hound breeds can perform admirably well by either sight or scent, and a few can even double as retrieving dogs on waterfowl and upland birds.

Bloodhound on scent.

The art, need, and sport of hunting with hounds enjoys a storied history that can be traced back to medieval times. Indeed, the powerful greyhounds of regal Egyptians were mummified and entombed with their masters. References to hunting with hounds can be found in ancient literary and art works that have survived through the ages.

Hounds have helped put food on the table and money in the pocket of their owners from sales of furs. They've been used for hunting deer, fox, bear, cougar, bobcat, jaguar, coyote, rabbit, raccoon, hog, squirrel, opossum, badger, and other large and small animals. Certain breeds have even been used to hunt upland game, even waterfowl.

Lore from this country traces references to hounds back to the days of DeSoto; they were reportedly used on Indians as well as game. Breeds enjoyed an upsurge during colonial days. Our country's first president, George Washington, kept a pack of foxhounds. General Custer also had a pack of hounds that traveled with him.

In the last century, hounds were an important part of rural America, as they enabled many families to obtain game for food and pelts for income. Most families owned some type of hound hunting dog back then.

There have been many evolutions of the hound hunting sport. Hunters have followed hounds while mounted on mules or horseback, and they've followed on foot. Hounds have been turned loose after game during daylight and nighttime hours. For the latter, oil lamps have given way to carbide lights, flashlights, and eventually the high-powered battery pack-operated lights of today.

Accessory gear has changed greatly, as well. For example, the modern raccoon or big-game hunter has everything from a hunting rig, special dog box, training and tracking collars, hip boots, a high-tech light, and GPS directional equipment. As hunting habitat continues to change, so do hunting methods.

From Sea to Shining Sea

Foxhunting carries much tradition; the sport has not changed over the last few hundred years, excepting improvements in methods and ethics. This type of hunting still flourishes in North America, and the number of hunts continues to grow. Packs of hounds are used in organized, prestigious hunts with horses, a master huntsman, the hunter's horn, color, and circumstance; these hunts are strictly self-regulated. In this country, the thrill of the hunt is the chase, as opposed to England, where the hunt generally ends with a kill.

Big-game hunting can be found from the Southwest to the Northwest with many different methods of hunting various species of game. A variety of breeds are used, as well, usually in small packs numbering two to four. Mountain lion or cougar hunting is legal in several Western states. Bear hunting, another form of big-game hunting, can be found nationwide.

In several Midwestern states, coyote and rabbit hunting have become a big industry. With continually changing habitat and the coyote's uncanny ability to adapt to all changes, his presence throughout the country has expanded coyote hunting as well.

Although little known, hog hunting and deer hunting are still legal in various Southern states; many of those states allow hunting in certain counties only. These sports are steeped in tradition in the areas where they still abound.

Raccoon hunting continues to grow in appreciable percentage every year. This is due in part to the wholesome exercise that the pleasure hunting aspect of the sport provides, but possibly more due to the explosion of the competition hunting events. Few other sports have enjoyed such notoriety as that afforded by the timeless film *Where the Red Fern Grows,* or as much mystique. In today's competition hunts — depending on choice of registry — prestigious titles can be earned as well as large purses of money. It should be noted that never in any competition event are raccoons harvested. The hounds are simply scored on their ability — or lack thereof — to strike, run, and tree ringtails.

Another interesting tree dog event that has rapidly grown from its pleasure hunting counterpart is the squirrel dog competition. Here, too, attractive purses of money may be won by talented, savvy squirrel dogs and their owners. To many, the attraction of squirrel dogs and accompanying squirrel dog events is the marked decrease in hunting territory and habitat needed to pursue and tree squirrels. There is also appreciably less physical exertion required of the handler.

Men and women who love to follow hounds usually have a fondness for beagles and rabbit hunting as well. There is an unmistakable thrill in hearing a pack of beagles in full cry on a rabbit. In addition, several different registries and types of competition have evolved for this breed; competitive events, usually run in braces (two), have become very popular.

Bobcat hunting is usually done during the winter months by experienced hunters, an offshoot of the bigger cougar hunting, which also takes place over winter months.

Hound hunting is not for the faint of heart. Even with today's improvements in transportation and methods, the average hunter must be in good physical shape to pursue his love of hounds and the hound hunting sports.

Summary

In the past, use of hounds was a necessity to aid in providing sustenance for the family. Today, although the necessity is gone for many people, it still exists for some. In addition, necessity has evolved to a new height and translation as many men and women derive their livelihoods from the training, breeding, selling, and competition of these hounds.

Use of trained dogs in pursuit of game lends an added dimension to the sport of hunting. However, it should be recognized that the thrill of creating a union with the wild outdoors is as much a draw, a definition, as any other variable of the sport. There are many more times spent hunting where no game is struck than when game is trailed; thus, there are intangible rewards derived from communion with the outdoor presence. Also, much more game eludes the hounds than the game that is treed or bayed. Finally, many modern-day hunters of all persuasions run and tree their game, then leave it, unharmed, for seed and another day.

The advent of successful competitive events has helped foster additional interest in a multi-faceted sport with many colorful histories and traditions. Many of these events and organizations sponsor benefit hunts for many worthwhile causes, such as the Shriner's Hospital and St. Jude's Hospital, to support and give back to communities and the youth of this country. Life today is based on give-and-take, just as it always has been, but accentuating and recognizing that fact has never been more important. Preservation of sports such as hunting with hounds requires education of non-hunters as well as the practice of good morals and ethics demonstrated by the average modern-day hunter, and the art of "giving" back to those in need.

There is a certain thrill to being out in wild country and turning a hound loose after game. Whether one chooses to hunt solo with one dog or many — or whether several hunters go together — there is an inexplicable rush when a hound opens deep in the timber as he makes game, and smells a trail worthy of following. Whether that trail is cold, warm, or hot, and how he handles his obstacles en route is a constant source of amazement for the avid hound hunter. Then, his ability or lack thereof, to accurately tree his game is another measurement for the hunter, one that never goes unrecognized.

And, once again, many such excursions produce nothing more than a trip out with the dogs, as the wild outdoors and its inhabitants don't always keep the same schedules and appointments as its visiting hunters and hounds. Good hunters realize and recognize this fact and still have an enjoyable time because of the many rewarding factors involved.

Today's hunter is evolving for the better. After a period of apathy, the modern hunter shows concern for his surroundings, just like his forefathers did. He develops knowledge for the way of the wild, as well as for the peculiarities of the game he pursues. And he knows and has an intuitive sense about his dogs. There is an overall sense of respect for Mother Nature, wild animals, and those wonderful, lovable hound dogs. ■

AMERICAN BLACK AND TAN COON HOUND

Recognized in 1945 by the American Kennel Club as a hound breed, the black and tan was first admitted into United Kennel Club's registry back in 1900. These graceful hounds are very adaptable and have a big following throughout the country. The very presence of the black and tan says "coonhound."

- **Area & Date of Origin:** United States, 1700s
- **Function:** Scenthound, trailing and treeing raccoons (also deer, bear, big game), night hunts
- **Height & Weight:** 25-27" (male); 23-25" (female); 65-100 lbs
- **Colors:** Coal black with rich tan markings
- **Coat:** Short and dense
- **Standards:** Deep chest; long, strong limbs; muscular neck; well-developed flews; skin devoid of folds; hazel to dark brown eyes, almost round; large, black hound nose; low-set, long ears hanging in folds; strong tail carried high, nearly perpendicular to back when working
- **Life Span:** 10-12 years

■ Appearance and Temperament

These hounds have an aristocratic look about them as they go about their business, be it work or play. Just as the breed name sounds, these hounds are black and tan in color, with the tan ranging from light tan to a deeper mahogany shade. The tan should cover no more than 15 percent of the body. There should be a slight bit of tan over each eye. In addition, a small amount of white is permissible on the chest but none is allowed elsewhere.

The carriage of the black and tan depicts grace and power. This begins with a noble, broad head carried high and complemented by long, rolling, rounded velvety ears. A smooth, dense, rich black coat with points of tan covers a slightly arched and well-muscled back. The black and tan has good, strong straight legs.

Black and tans are very agreeable hounds and are a pleasure to have around. These dogs enjoy popularity among both families and seasoned competition coon hunters because of their affable demeanor. The black and tan can double as a good family dog as well, but should never be left alone — which applies to most hounds — because the temptation of scent could draw them away from home.

■ History

Legend has it that these hounds descended from crosses between bloodhounds and foxhounds in medieval England. Early descendants made their way to North America back in colonial days. Inspection of pedigrees of today's hounds goes back to the foxhounds prevalent at that time. Most folks believe that bloodhound stock was used on this side of the Atlantic during the development of this breed. There are many factors that contribute to this belief, including the black and tan's cold nose, its characteristic houndy ears, and of course, its color. Also, the black and tan tends to sport heavier bone than some of the other coonhound breeds.

While the United Kennel Club first registered black and tans as the American Black and Tan Fox and Coonhound, and later amended the name without "Fox," the American Kennel Club did not accept the black and tan as a breed until 1945. Still, this was an accomplishment. Until recent times and the advent of the AKC's competition coonhound program, this breed was the only representative of coonhounds included with AKC. Indeed, to this day it remains the only coonhound in the scent hound grouping for bench show purposes.

In the Field

Many of today's black and tans possess great speed and can perform admirably in pursuit of big game. They are used primarily for raccoon hunting, however. Their short, tough coat enables them to withstand the rigors of thick cover as well as cold swamps.

Black and tan breeders strive to keep the deep, melodious bawl mouth that is a famous trademark to this breed when running a track. These hounds are bred to be open trailers on track, and hard, pressure tree dogs. As pups, the open trailing tendency can cause them to open, or bark, a little too much to suit some, but the dog usually outgrows this as it matures.

They are also quick, accurate tree dogs and seem to resist the temptation to pull to other running hounds once they end their track. These hounds are easy-going and handle well during hunting; they boast a large following of fanciers throughout the country.

Trainability

With the introduction of more and more speed on track, the black and tan has become a little more prone to interest in off-game at an early age. When this occurs, the hounds must be broke off "trash" and they can be a little obstinate about this. However, this is characteristic of many hounds that are "gamey" and like to pursue their quarry.

Generally the black and tan becomes a good handling dog because of its inherent willingness to please its owner or trainer. Many representatives of this breed display strong natural tendencies, wherein the core of training simply becomes trips to the woods, which is a pleasure to hunters.

Strengths/Weaknesses

This hound is generally clean of health problems, other than the occasional ear infection due to their very long, droopy ears. As with any droop-eared dog, preventive maintenance performed on a regular schedule can prevent most potential ear problems.

Bloat — and resulting torsion — is a threat because of the large size and deep chest of this hound. Thus, feed and exercise schedules should be sharply observed so that these hounds are not worked on a full stomach.

Occasionally, allergies plague these dogs, particularly to certain grasses, but overall black and tans are robust and healthy.

Other Uses

The black and tan is one of a growing number of hound breeds that are being used in search and rescue endeavors, as well as for drug detection, because of their superior noses. Both of these fields are relatively new for this breed. However, because of the friendly nature of these hounds as well as their strong prey drive, the potential in these areas will likely continue to grow.

The Show Ring

Because of the regal air possessed by these hounds they are a popular favorite in the show ring. Black and tans have won many coveted titles over the years. There are more and more breeders that promote these beautiful animals strictly for the show ring.

Performance black and tans can and do still compete successfully against their show ring counterparts, but care should be taken when looking for the hunting dog to be certain to select balanced hunting bloodlines. Too much show stock in the pedigree has been the ruination of many a worthy sporting breed.

AMERICAN BLUE GASCON HOUND

For the hound fancier who prefers the old-fashioned hound in type and mouth, the American Blue Gascon Hound fits the bill. This dog can be an affectionate family dog while performing many worthwhile functions, such as big game hunting and search and rescue. Overall, the distinctive "houndy" look that is characteristic of the blue Gascon attracts many folks to this breed, from the United States to Canada, Mexico and Central America.

- **Area & Date of Origin:** France, middle ages
- **Function:** Scenthound, gun dog, wild boar, deer, fox, hare hunting
- **Height & Weight:** 25.5-27.5" (male); 23.5-25.5" (female); 75-100 lbs
- **Colors:** White background speckled with black and irregularly-shaped black patches (the black speckling gives the "blue" appearance)
- **Coat:** Smooth, profuse, not too short or fine
- **Standards:** Long, broad, deep chest; strong, elongated head with loose skin; black nose; dark brown eyes have visible eyelids; distinctive ears are attached very low, are thin and well-twisted inward, tapering to a point (an identifying feature of the breed); thick, long tail carried sickle fashion; long, oval, wolf-like feet
- **Life Span:** 12-14 years
- **Also called:** Grand Bleu de Gascogne

■ Appearance and Temperament

With minimum height requirements of 27 inches at the shoulder for the male and 25 inches for the female, and minimum weight requirements of 90 pounds for the male and 75 pounds for the female, there is no question that these are large hounds. The Gascon's large, broad head sports characteristic long, narrow ears that hang with a rolled appearance. The muzzle is long and heavy with deep, square flews and well-developed black nostrils. This head shape gives the breed its classic hound appearance.

Puppies of this breed are born white, excepting permanent black markings, and underlying blue pigment begins to show as early as a few hours after birth, gradually darkening to adult color by puberty. Adult colors include bluetick, roan mottled steelblue, blueblack, bluebrindle, and grizzle. A blue blaze is preferred on the muzzle area.

The coat should be short, thick, and dense, capable of withstanding rough hunting conditions. A medium-length neck that is strong and muscular, along with a deep, wide chest and well-sprung ribs, combine with a strong back and muscular, broad loins to produce a powerful animal.

This dog possesses stamina and endurance for the long haul. In addition, dark brown or black eyes reflect intelligence and a certain gentleness that contribute to the reference "gentle giant." While these dogs can withstand the rigors of difficult terrain, they are equally at home with family and children. They also get along well with other dogs.

■ History

The American Blue Gascon Association cites evidence of blue-mottled Stag or Boar hounds dating back as far as 1200 A.D. These dogs were used in packs to hunt wild boar before and during the Napoleonic age. In addition, records of Gascony boar hounds from French origin exist. Today's blues and Gascons — indeed, strains of most hounds — are descendants of the *Grand Bleu de Gascogne* hounds that date back hundreds of years.

Shakespeare sports a quote on hounds that fanciers of blues and Gascons believe referred to their hounds: *My hounds are bred out of the Spartan breed, so Flewed, so Sanded and their heads are hung with ears that sweep away the morning dew. Slow in pursuit, but match in mouth like bells. A cry more tuneable was never hallo'd to, nor cheered by horn.*

In the early 1900s the breed was registered as bluetick and recognized as the third hound breed by the United Kennel Club. However, the breed became standardized and the larger Gascons were left out; a parting of the ways occurred in the early 1970s. At this time, fanciers of the old-fashioned blueticks met to form the present-day American Blue Gascon Association, and chose the name from the Grand bleu de Gascogne hounds of France, Americanizing the word "Gascogne" to Gascon. Thus, the American blue Gascon became a separate entity.

In the Field

These hounds have demonstrated ability in pursuing all types of big game. Although speed is not a strong suit, these animals will persevere until the game is treed or bayed, and will continue their task under the most extreme conditions. Physical type allows for stamina and endurance wherein these dogs excel.

Gascons are at home in the high country, such as the mountains of Idaho, as well as in the Midwest and in Southern swamps. They can track and trail animals under a variety of conditions and environments.

Trainability

Gascons possess an intelligence that makes them easy to train on certain tasks, and an affable demeanor that makes them a pleasure to hunt and handle. They have a tenacity to finish jobs that they start with accuracy.

Strengths/Weaknesses

Superior scenting ability puts these dogs at the top of their group. Gascons are capable of scenting very old tracks on uncompromising terrain that has poor scent retention. Generations of breeding for this trait have resulted in an excellent nose. While many folks might assume that this large breed is slow on track, the reverse is generally true. However, this breed is noted for having the tendency to check a tree before settling on it; in the case of coonhound competition hunts, this could cost some well-earned points on the scorecard.

Gascons are also noted for their beautiful, deep bawl mouths, the kind of "hound music" that old-timers and literature alike extol. Fanciers of the breed today are proud of this type of mouth that has been preserved through different breeding generations. This characteristic voice is representative of the breed.

Due to the blue Gascon's size, certain health problems exist. The most notable threat is hip dysplasia. In addition, there can be some shoulder problems. Also, because of the deep chest and size of this animal, there is a propensity toward bloat and torsion. None of these problems are widespread, however. The standard for the American blue Gascon provides for strength in conformation that will help ward off the physical problems that do exist.

This animal, while physically appealing, has not succumbed to some side-effects of heavy show ring popularity in that overall, most desirable hunting traits remain intact for representatives of this breed.

Other Uses

The blue Gascon's biggest calling is for use in many types of big game hunting, although they are also used for hunting smaller game such as the raccoon. The perseverance of the blue Gascon continues to make it a popular choice in certain areas of the country by houndsmen.

In addition, because of this breed's superior nose, it is becoming more popular as a search and rescue prospect. Of note is the fact that this dog can follow scent over tough terrain and in difficult conditions, which is lending to its growing popularity with this faction.

Hollywood has also noticed this breed and has included it in various movies and television commercials, along with its close cousin, the bluetick. These dogs are personable, even comical sometimes, and are generally a pleasure to have around.

The Show Ring

Few breeds can boast that their show ring prospects possess the same physical traits as their hunting counterparts, but this is generally true for the American blue Gascon. Partly because the numbers of this breed remain fairly low and partly due to the fact that breeders conscientiously keep necessary traits at the forefront of their programs, the American blue Gascon remains true to its standard.

AMERICAN FOX HOUND

A considerable amount of history surrounds the American foxhound. Its popularity abounds in many areas of the country to this day; thanks to organized field trials and fox pens found everywhere from the East to the South and up to the Midwest. This breed also is included in the colorful foxhunts that began centuries ago and still take place in the United States.

- **Area & Date of Origin:** United States, early 1700s
- **Function:** Scenthound, trailing fox
- **Height & Weight:** 22-25" (male); 21-24" (female); 21-24 lbs
- **Colors:** Any true hound color
- **Coat:** Close, hard, medium length
- **Standards:** Head fairly long with broad backskull; large brown or hazel eyes set well apart; fairly low-set, broad ears; moderately long back, muscular and strong; rather narrow chest; loins broad and slightly arched; tail carried gaily, but not over the back, with slight curve and very slight brush
- **Life Span:** 10-13 years

■ Appearance and Temperament

The American foxhound is comprised of three major strains — Walker, Trigg, and Goodman — and therefore can be of any color with a short, glossy coat. Generally, foxhounds will be of medium-large size and will be built for speed and agility. According to the standard, ears — when stretched toward the tip of the muzzle — should nearly touch the nose, lending to the hound look.

Accordingly, these hounds should possess an air of intelligence with wide-set, gentle hound-like eyes of dark brown or hazel color. A long muscular back should slope to a tail carried gaily, but never curling over the back. Shoulders should be clean and sloping, but not ponderous, to facilitate speed, and the chest should be deep but narrower in proportion to depth than this breed's English counterpart.

Legs should be straight and strong with fox-like feet that possess full, hard pads capable of withstanding long days of running and pushing fox. Good feet should be complemented by strong toenails, which will aid the chase.

These hounds are smart and wily, out of necessity, to find and jump both gray and red fox. They are pack animals and do much better in the company of many. It is not a good idea to keep just one foxhound as it may become bored in short order. When boredom sets in, hyperactive and neurotic behavior can result.

■ History

The traditional foxhunt with horses and hounds came across the ocean with the colonists in the 1600s; this sport enjoys a healthy following to this day. Original dogs were of English descent, with some French blood imported about a century later. This combination of English and French bloodlines evolved into the American foxhounds used in pursuit of the red fox over horseback.

In yet the next century, an interesting tale unfolds. American foxhound fanciers like to talk about "Tennessee Lead," and the highway marker later erected as a tribute to this hound. Says the marker, found on Tennessee Highway 42 at the bridge over Obey River, just south of Albany, Kentucky: "Near here in November 1852, a Black and Tan hound was stolen out of a deer chase by a horse trader, taken to Madison County, Kentucky, sold to George Washington Maupin. There as Tennessee Lead, he became the foundation sire for all Walker, Trigg, and Goodman fox hounds."

It is further told that gray fox abounded in Kentucky back in the 1800s, but in the 1850s red fox began to infiltrate the countryside. These wide running red fox proved too much for the local gray fox hounds and deer hounds. So, what happened next? Tennessee Lead jumped a red fox and proceeded to run him into the ground, apparently the only hound in Kentucky capable of accomplishing all aspects of jumping, running, and putting to ground a red fox.

Females from around the country were brought to Tennessee Lead. Later in the 1850s, more foundation blood came from English imports. However, as the breed progressed, the American foxhound became a separate entity from the English foxhound.

■ In the Field

There have evolved many uses in the field for the American foxhound. The aforementioned traditional foxhunt still enjoys a healthy following in this country. It's quite a sight, particularly in the autumn months, when scarlet-coated riders on horseback follow packs of melodious foxhounds over hill and dale in pursuit of the red fox.

In addition, there are organized field trials and fox pens located throughout the country. These sports enjoy a huge following and continue to grow in popularity and in numbers.

American foxhounds hunt and compete well because of their efficient build and their excellent noses. They possess uncanny speed in pursuing their quarry and have impressive stamina.

■ Trainability

Intense desire to pursue game remains at the forefront of this hound's makeup and will affect all training efforts. This being said, these hounds are quite intelligent and have a willingness to please overall. Listening skills diminish as pack behavior increases with regard to chase and bay drive.

These dogs do possess some strength of will that can be interpreted as stubbornness, but this is not always the case. Taking the time to teach these dogs what is expected can eliminate a lot of training time.

It should be noted that while these dogs get along well with other canines — being pack-oriented animals — they do not necessarily coexist with other animal or pets.

Foxhounds can be somewhat "trashy" and run game other than fox. In certain areas of the country, foxhounds are used to chase coyotes, but otherwise most "off" game is considered "trash," with deer being the number one offender. Because of the high desire to chase possessed by these hounds, the trash-breaking procedure can be time-consuming and difficult.

■ Strengths/Weaknesses

Among the foxhounds strengths are an affectionate nature and a good temperament around the house. Foxhounds can be either friendly or protective when it comes to strangers, however, with many being quite aggressive.

One weakness of the breed is its high activity level. The foxhound needs an incredible amount of exercise and should not be confined to a small pen area without access to adequate run time. Also, this dog does not fare well as a solo animal and can actually become destructive when kept apart from other dogs.

The American foxhound is exceptionally healthy, and although on the large side, does not have a propensity toward the genetic orthopedic problems. The distinctive short, hard coat requires little care.

■ Other Uses/The Show Ring

Because of this breed's friendly nature toward people, it has enjoyed a surge in popularity as a family pet. Its attractive appearance has given it increased attention in the show ring, and breeding for certain show qualities may have toned down some of the foxhound's hyperactivity.

When looking for hunting prospects, pups should be obtained from field lines.

BASSET HOUND

This strange and distorted-looking fellow wins the hearts of dog people in many different walks of life, but the basset's very build evolved for reasons specific to his needs. The basset, of the scent hound group, is very versatile and is one of only a few breeds that actively competes in all four canine sports, and also ranks toward the top as a popular pet. But his hunting ability puts him in a class of his own, with a nose so accurate that he is second only to the bloodhound.

- **Area & Date of Origin:** France, 1500s
- **Function:** Scenthound, trailing rabbits and hare, field trials
- **Height & Weight:** Preferably not over 15"; 40-60 lbs
- **Colors:** Any recognized hound color
- **Coat:** Thick, tight, hard, smooth, and short; skin is loose and elastic
- **Standards:** Skull domed with prominent occiput; pendulous lips with hanging flews; soft, sad, brown eyes, showing prominent haw; loose skin falling in distinct wrinkles over the brow when the head is lowered; extremely long, low-set ears; straight topline; tail slightly curved and carried gaily; short, powerful forelegs with wrinkled skin; massive, round feet
- **Life Span:** 8-12 years

■ Appearance and Temperament

While the basset's strange shape and proportion make it appear gangly and awkward, this animal is agile and deliberate; he also possesses great endurance afield. With very short legs and a long body, his maximum height at the shoulder is only 15 inches, a figure quite surprising in relation to his build. Thus, his weight can come as a surprise, ranging from as little as 25 pounds to as much as 75 pounds.

The head of the basset is well domed with loose folds of skin that wrinkle over the brow when the head is lowered. The muzzle is deep and heavy; the dewlap is quite pronounced. Eyes — which give this hound his characteristic look in relation to his dewlap and loose skin — are dark in pigment and sunken, with a sad expression. Add to this the basset's extremely long ears and you have quite an individual.

The build of the basset is powerful, not noticed by the casual observer. Heavy bone and huge paws with tough pads blend with strong shoulders and hindquarters. He carries his head low with his nose near the ground and moves in a graceful, effortless gait which belies his size and shape.

A typical hard, dense, short hound coat affords the basset the capability of functioning in all types of weather. As with some other hounds, color is not important; any recognized hound color is permissible. However, the most common colors are tri-color, red and white, and lemon and white.

Bassets are extremely affectionate and loyal in temperament and make great companions as well as hunting dogs. They are friendly around all types of animals and are overall quite gentle.

■ History

According to basset lore, this breed evolved hundreds of years ago in Europe from the French bloodhound and the St. Hubert hounds, and was popular in many European countries before first being shown in England in the late 1800s. Indeed, the basset hound is mentioned in a book by Fouilloux, dating back to 1585, as skilled in badger hunting.

It is said that friars from the French Abbey of St. Hubert (the patron sain of hunters) bred for traits that incorporated the low-slung body of today's basset to facilitate a slower hound that could be followed afoot. It didn't take long for this animal to gain in popularity.

The first recorded registry of this breed by the American Kennel Club was in 1885. The breed enjoyed increased numbers in the States. Then, a picture of a basset puppy graced the cover of *Time* magazine in its February 27, 1928, issue. His hunting prowess and gentle, easygoing personality earned him much respect in sporting circles and competition arenas alike.

■ In the Field

In keeping with form and function, the basset's heavy bone structure make him sturdy, and his large feet give him assured steadiness and purpose. His ease of movement is a marvel to those who follow him.

While used primarily on rabbits, this breed can also hunt other small game and gamebirds such as pheasants. The basset hound works by following ground scent and bruised foliage. In keeping with his form and function, the basset's long ears are meant to stir up scent for his sensitive, powerful nose to smell. The characteristic loose skin under the chin, called the *dewlap*, functions to "trap" or hold the scent while the basset works.

In days of yesteryear, like many hounds, bassets were hunted in packs, but nowadays Bassets work in braces (pairs); they are also hunted alone. Bred to handle all types of terrain and heavy cover — which provide typical haunts for rabbits and game birds — they also have the stamina to work all day.

■ Trainability

Because of their mild and gentle disposition, bassets adapt wonderfully to virtually all types and methods of training. However, they can be somewhat obstinate at times. Perhaps this comes from their "hound" background; hounds have been known for a propensity toward stubbornness.

■ Strengths/Weaknesses

With an incredibly sensitive nose, the basset enjoys a ranking in scenting ability second only to the bloodhound. Add to this his laid-back temperament and versatile abilities, and you come up with a surprisingly good all-around dog that is a pleasure to have around.

The basset sports few health maladies. However, there are a few problems that are worthy of mention. With regard to eyes, glaucoma is a concern. Some bassets are prone to allergies. Also, elbow-related lameness can occur during growth; it is often *paneosteitis*, an orthopedic disease that is only recently being recognized and understood. Most dogs with this problem eventually outgrow the accompanying lameness, but it can be difficult to diagnose.

In addition, *von Willebrand's* disease — a disorder that causes bleeding — plagues bassets, although conscientious breeders have reduced the incidence of this strange problem through careful screening and appropriate testing procedures.

Because of this hound's pendulous lips with accompanying loose, hanging flews, bassets can slobber. A lot. In addition, by virtue of this physical makeup, they can be messy drinkers. So, bassets tend to "drool" more than one might expect.

Finally, the Basset can't swim well and has difficulty with natural breeding. These are things to keep in mind. Also, this dog shouldn't be left alone without confinement as it is prone to wander off in search of scent or because of it.

■ Other Uses

In addition to being popular as a hunter, this dog can compete in all four of the recognized dog sports competitions. The basset performs well in field trials, tracking, obedience, and conformation events. Quite a feat for such a "clumsy" fellow. And, the basset ranks high on the list as a best friend and quality pet.

■ The Show Ring

For all its hunting ability, the basset has enjoyed enormous popularity in the show ring, with its first entrance at a British conformation show dating back to 1875, and its first exhibition at famed Westminister in the States took place in 1884.

Show dogs seem to be a bit more ponderous than their field counterparts; when in search of a hunting companion, it's probably wise to stick to field bloodlines.

BEAGLE

Quite a fellow, the beagle. He's the smallest of the scent hunting hounds, and comes in two sizes, those being the 13-inch and the 15-inch varieties. His presence in literature dates back to the 1400s. And, he's been in the top ten in popular breeds of both the UKC and the AKC registries for most of the past 30 years. What makes the beagle so popular?

- **Area & Date of Origin:** England, 1300s
- **Function:** Scenthound, trailing rabbits, field trials, contraband detection
- **Height & Weight:** 13" variety & 15" variety; 18-30 lbs
- **Colors:** Any true hound color
- **Coat:** Close, hard coat of medium length
- **Standards:** Broad and full cranium; square muzzle; stop moderately defined; large brown or hazel eyes set well apart; rounded ears; short back; slightly curved tail with brush, carried gaily but not over back; round, firm feet, pads full and hard
- **Life Span:** 12 -15 years

■ Appearance and Temperament

The beagle is a handsome, compact package with a happy demeanor. He is bold and brave and merry. He is determined, possesses remarkable endurance, and remains extremely businesslike during his work. Neither shy nor aggressive, he is very alert to his environment and is outwardly friendly. The beagle is an energetic bundle of action.

Indeed, the beagle looks like a miniature foxhound or Walker hound. His straight sturdy legs match a tight, muscular body with a strong tail, carried high but not curled over the back. He has a pleasing head and dark, friendly eyes.

It is true that the beagle is extremely outgoing and can be quite stubborn. This breed has its own way of doing things and has a dominant, strong hound temperament; surprising to be found in housing of such small dimensions.

Colors for the beagle can be any recognized hound color except liver. The most popular versions are tri-color, red and white, lemon and white, and the occasional black and white, with ticking or freckling permissible in any color variety.

■ History

The background of this tiny package of dynamite is actually little known for centuries. References to small hounds are made as far back as 400 B.C., 200 A.D. and 1066 A.D. It is generally accepted that beagles were present in Britain, France, Greece, and Italy during the 1400s.

Around the 1700s, the beagle emerged as a good rabbit hound, while foxhounds became more popular for foxhunting. Two Englishmen, Reverend Phillip Honeywood and Thomas Johnson, were responsible for active beagle breeding in the 1800s that produced the forerunners of today's dogs.

According to record, the first beagles came to the States in 1876 and were recognized by the American Kennel Club in 1884. The year 1888 marked the formation of the National Beagle Club; in addition, the first organized field trial was held. Popularity of beagle competition has spawned numerous organizations, registries, and events for evaluating the many qualities that comprise the good rabbit hound. In this country, their value as keen rabbit dogs goes uncontested; superior breeding practices of hunting beagles continue to produce better quality animals.

■ In the Field

Beagles can excel as pack animals and in braces. There are several different types of field trialing events available today with just as many registries. In addition, rabbit hunting remains one of the most popular small game pursuits in most states where the sport exists.

Beagles have enjoyed a remarkable surge in popularity as the availability of suitable hunting ground for their larger coonhound cousins continues to dwindle. Many hunters who love the sound of hound music, yet cannot hunt their coonhounds as often as they like due to restrictions of hunting area, turn to beagles as a means of continuing their love affair with hounds.

■ Trainability

Although small, the beagle has one of the most dominant and headstrong personalities of all the hound breeds. While this is true, they do not respond well to pressure and should receive patient teaching with emphasis on consistency of method.

Beagles tend to tune out their owners when running with a pack, and thus become prone to distractions such as running deer. This can be quite a problem and often requires more sophisticated training methods to cure, such as the use of remote training aids. These can be used very successfully when implemented properly.

Because beagles are so exuberant about life, it usually takes a longer period of time to accomplish any given training task. However, don't let these dogs fool you, as they are smart and savvy.

■ Strengths/Weaknesses

Because beagle pups are so cute, the breed is a popular choice of puppy mills. Generally, these establishments should be avoided. Take care to buy a beagle puppy from a reputable breeder who specializes in field lines with sound health guarantees. There are many health ailments and problems that plague the beagle.

Beagles are prone to many eye diseases. For some reason, "cherry eye," or the swelling of the gland in the third eyelid, is quite common. Often this has to be surgically corrected. In addition, beagles could harbor glaucoma or cataracts, as well as progressive retinal atrophy (PRA) or retinal dysplasia.

Epilepsy is quite common in the beagle. Low thyroid is another pretty common problem that results in weight problems, reproductive problems, and poor hair coat. There are potential palate deformities. Either *monorchidism* or *cryptorchidism* can occur, where one or both testicles, respectively, do not descend from the abdomen into the scrotum. In addition there are potential heart defects, the possibility of kidney failure, and bladder problems. Although this list seems formidable, many, if not all of these problems can be avoided by buying responsibly.

The beagle is so outgoing and persistent in his work and play that he wins the hearts of prospective dog owners everywhere. While he is ideally-suited to the active hunter, or even the pet owner who leads an active lifestyle that will be shared with the dog, he shouldn't be resigned to the role of sedentary pet.

■ Other Uses

The beagle's main popularities continue to be centered on rabbit hunting and the varied field trial activities that are available today. However, beagles are quite popular as pets and can be excellent companions for children.

The beagle has enjoyed some notoriety on the silver screen as well, with the release of *Shiloh*, a story about a beagle with an irresponsible owner who is befriended by a young boy. The beagle that "plays" Shiloh does an excellent job and is representative of the breed. Through the course of the storyline, the boy is forced to grow up and learn some serious lessons about life. *Shiloh* now has a sequel, as well.

■ The Show Ring

Beagles have been represented in the show ring ever since the breed was recognized by the American Kennel Club. This breed's strong personality traits remain truer in the show ring than many of its hound counterparts, but care should be taken to buy any pup from a reputable field breeder.

BLOODHOUND

A superior nose is this mammoth hound's most prominent claim to fame. The bloodhound's scenting ability is second to none. This hound takes its name from being "blooded," through painstaking centuries of breeding, which lends to his aristocracy. He has demonstrated such remarkable prowess in search-and-rescue and law enforcement endeavors that it is amazing to see this hound still utilized for hunting purposes.

- **Area & Date of Origin:** Belgium, England, middle ages
- **Function:** Scenthound, trailing, search and rescue
- **Height & Weight:** 25-27", 90-110 lbs (male); 23-25", 80-100 lbs (female)
- **Colors:** Black and tan, liver and tan, red
- **Coat:** Dense and short
- **Standards:** Proportionally long, narrow head; pendant folds of loose skin around neck and head; deep hanging flews; sunken diamond-shaped hazel to yellow eyes; low-set, thin, extremely long ears that are soft to the touch; long tapering tail, carried high
- **Life Span:** 7-10 years
- **Also called:** St. Hubert's hound, Chien St. Hubert

■ Appearance and Temperament

Probably no other breed today is as instantly recognizable as the bloodhound. His massive size, powerful head, loose skin, and incredibly long, drooping ears simply shout his name. The bloodhound looks at the world with an imposing air of solemnity and reserved dignity that defies reproach. When you add a size consisting in height up to 27 inches and weight soaring as high as 110 pounds, you have a lot of canine in one package.

The bloodhound comes in three colors. Black and tan, liver and tan, and red, or red and tawny, are all prevalent colors. Many folks think of the deep red bloodhound when this breed's name is mentioned, but in fact all three colors are popular.

This hound is so incredibly gentle that it could almost be called a fault. Some bloodhounds, despite their size and strength, are actually quite shy, even timid in nature. These dogs are incredibly good with children and are well-mannered around most animals and humans. However, they should never be left unattended as they have the propensity to take any scent trail and follow it to its end.

■ History

With ancient literature on the origins of this breed dating back over a thousand years, it is safe to say that this is one of the oldest recorded breeds in existence today. First known data goes back to central Europe, in Belgium and France, where St. Hubert and white Talbot hounds were crossed to produce the bloodhound. Eventually, the dogs were brought to Great Britain, then to the United States. This breed was superior in cold-trailing large and small game animals.

The first known use of the bloodhound in law enforcement dates back to 1805 when one was used in England by the Thrapthon Association for the Prevention of Felons to track criminals.

Bloodhounds have been used in the States for trailing of big-game animals, primarily in the Western states, and have become mainstays in law enforcement man-trailing cases in this country. Otherwise known as the *Chien de St. Hubert*, bloodhounds have been crossed with many breeds to improve their nose, including some recognized breeds of coonhounds, and bloodhound lineage can be found flowing in the veins of many big-game hounds.

■ In the Field

These massive dogs, although slow compared to other big-game hounds, have impressive endurance and deliberate movement. They do not know the word "quit" and will persevere until the game is treed, bayed, or put into sanctuary.

The heavy loose skin, lip, flews, and dewlap, as well as the neck of this hound trap scent and hold it close while he works. A bloodhound on a trail becomes oblivious to everything else around him, working entirely by scent, and has been known to run into things while tracking his target. The bloodhound is relentless and can start on a scent trail that is many days old.

■ Trainability

While the bloodhound is very affectionate and gentle, he is also stubborn and willful. It takes a firm hand to train the bloodhound and to keep him under control. Because of his intense scent drive, it is nearly impossible to teach this dog conventional obedience.

As far as general manners go, certain ground rules should be set while this dog is a puppy and they should be strictly adhered to; this dog will become very strong and quite large and he will be aware of his size and its subsequent intimidation. No one should acquire a bloodhound unless he or she is prepared to be firm with him from initial socialization on. This is not to say that one cannot have a good time with these dogs; they can be quite gentle and love to romp. But, certain rules will make life far more enjoyable for everyone involved and will become necessary.

These dogs love to track and take to the task naturally, improving in skill with each session and experience. Their ability is absolutely uncanny.

■ Strengths/Weaknesses

Of course, the merits of this hound's superior nose should be adequately extolled. The overall grand gentleness of most specimens of this breed is quite exceptional, considering the size and strength they possess. The willful, stubborn streak that many bloodhounds harbor is partially hidden by their lovable, awkward approach to life.

Bloodhounds have certain health concerns. Of course, because of their exceptional size, gastric torsion is a very real threat. Many experts and veterinarians recommend multiple small feedings per day to keep food volume to a minimum at all times.

This breed suffers from its share of hip dysplasia. Also, they can have entropion, an eyelid problem where the lids and lashes are turned inward, which can be corrected by surgery. Ear infections are a possibility because the long, droopy ears can harbor moisture necessary for bacterial growth.

Any large breed of dog can develop calluses on its joint points if allowed to sleep on a hard surface such as concrete or a tile floor. This is especially true of the bloodhound; he should be provided with an orthopedic bed or other soft surface on which to lay and sleep.

■ Other Uses

As mentioned, this dog, once a grand specimen for trailing game in the hunting environment, is still used as such in certain areas of the country. However, his usefulness has been eclipsed by man's need for scent detection in law enforcement and search and rescue.

Bloodhounds are so accurate on scent trails that evidence turned by a proven bloodhound trailer is admissible in all courts of law in this country. These hounds have been known to finish trails started at over 100 hours old. In addition, they can cover incredible distances to finish the job. Poor conditions such as concrete and dry land seem to pose no problem for these hounds.

■ The Show Ring

Many people learn to enjoy the company of this likeable, oversized brute of a canine, and in lots of cases there is no work available for these hounds. Enter the show ring. Some lines of bloodhounds have evolved strictly for show, as is the case in many canine breeds. This is not a fault, by any means, but a concern for the working dog enthusiast when inherent traits become less prevalent in exchange for bench show looks. However, bloodhound enthusiasts take great pride in the powerful scenting ability of their beloved mammoths. Perhaps this superior nose will remain for generations to come.

BLUETICK COONHOUND

Widely recognized by its distinctive coloring, the bluetick coonhound is a perennial favorite among dog fanciers in general, and has a huge following within hound circles. This breed has made a splash in Hollywood, appearing in many major network commercials for various products and also mugging it up in some movies. With two major breed registries that actively promote good breeding practices, there appears to be a strong future for the loveable bluetick.

- **Area & Date of Origin:** United States, 1900s

- **Function:** Scenthound, raccoon and big game hunting

- **Height & Weight:** 22-27″, 55-80 lbs (male); 21-25″, 45-65 lbs (female)

- **Colors:** Dark blue, thickly-mottled body spotted by various shaped black spots on back, ears, and sides; tan on head and feet

- **Coat:** Medium coarse, lies close to body, appears smooth and glossy

- **Standards:** Muscular back; slightly-domed skull, broad between the ears; prominent stop; rather large, round, dark brown eyes; thin ears with slight roll, taper toward a point; straight forelegs; long, muscular hindlegs; moderate-length, tapered tail, carried high with a forward curve; round, cat-like feet

- **Life Span:** 10-12 years

■ Appearance and Temperament

The color of this hound breed is described as blue — usually dark blue — with ticked, mottled coloring on the body; most dogs of this breed also have some black spots in various locations on the body and head. The dog should be predominantly blue. There should be tan "pumpkin seeds" over the eyes and tan markings on the cheeks. Also, there should be tan on the feet and lower legs, as well as on the chest and below the tail. However, it is permissible for the bluetick to be "all blue" — with no tan markings — at the discretion of the breeder. Coloring that resembles light ticking on white is not desired. The coat is short and hard with a dense tight undercoat that helps this hound withstand cold water and extreme winter temperatures.

The head of the bluetick should be carried high without appearing disproportionate to the body; the tail should be carried gaily and high without looping over the back. This hound should not be chunky and thick, but should show good muscle tone and athletic build. The eyes are alert but with a soft hound attention.

Bluetick coonhounds are noted for their overall agreeable temperament, but can be "hound stubborn" at times.

Puppies of this breed are born white, or nearly white, excepting permanent black coloring and spots; the distinctive mottled ticking gradually appears over a period of several weeks. By the time pups reach eight weeks of age, they have received most of their adult coloring.

■ History

This hound draws its early heritage from most of the other American breeds of coonhounds. In addition, the American blue Gascon was considered the same as this breed for many years; thus the bluetick shares some specific history with its larger "cousin." The two did not part ways until the mid-1970s.

It was 1946 before the bluetick was recognized as its own breed separate from the English fox & coonhound (later known simply as the English coonhound), in recognition of its unique bluetick coloration and traits.

The bluetick coonhound of today enjoys a strong support system with two breed organizations, BBOA — Bluetick Breeders of America, and BBCHA — Bluetick Breeders and Coon Hunters Association.

This hound has evolved over the years into a breed with distinctive traits all its own, and bluetick fanciers continue to improve the gene pool with selective breeding practices.

■ In the Field

The bluetick brings with him a certain stigma, not entirely undeserved. Most houndsmen and women are familiar with the phrase: "He's certainly blue-ticking that trail," as some of the older strains of blueticks were uncommonly slow and stubborn while on track. Many of these dogs just couldn't finish certain tracks, and when they couldn't, they refused to give up. So, they just went round and round the same area, trying to pick up more scent while opening frequently on the old scent.

In all fairness to this breed, those problems largely existed in yesteryear. The blueticks of today possess incredible speed on track; in fact, in certain lines their speed is considered a strong suit. Blueticks have good noses and take workable tracks of all ages and put game at the end.

Blueticks possess strength of voice and open on track with a characteristic bugle or bawl mouth that can change over to a chop on track as the scent warms. Most blueticks tree with a hard chop, although some just turn over to a shorter bawl on the tree. The average blue has lots of volume and fairly deep tone to his or her mouth.

■ Trainability

There is no question that the bluetick brings with him a certain degree of stubbornness. Trainers do well to recognize this characteristic early in any blue's life. Once this trait has been conquered, the bluetick can be a willing and able student.

The bluetick's ability to pursue most scent trails and his undying desire to stay with the track to the bitter end are reflected in his level of trainability. This hound can work trails under all types of conditions and in virtually every type of terrain.

■ Strengths/Weaknesses

Because of the bluetick's incredible improvement in so many different areas of trailing and treeing, he has become one of the breeds of choice for competition coon hunters. The bluetick has exhibited the characteristics necessary to win night hunts.

This breed is an excellent choice for the big-game hunter as well. The bluetick possesses a fierce tenacity to complete any track he starts, no matter his location. His strong, carrying voice and powerful build make him a favorite among many hunters.

There are few health problems that concern this breed. Relatively long ears are prone to infections, as with any long-eared breed, and as such should be inspected regularly. Some blueticks are prone to various allergies, but other than that, the breed is fairly disease-free.

■ Other Uses

Because of the bluetick's extremely sensitive nose, he has been used for many search and rescue efforts, and the bluetick is gaining more popularity in that field. Otherwise, the bluetick remains an excellent choice for any type of tree-game hunting. In addition, the breed's overall agreeable temperament makes it an excellent companion, keeping in mind that he was bred to hunt.

In addition, this breed has won recognition by Hollywood for being camera-savvy — due to its "houndy" appearance and distinctive coloring — and has starred in various food and apparel commercials on television, and has been included in numerous movies.

■ The Show Ring

In keeping with the English coonhound breed that he evolved from, the bluetick is a winner in the show ring and has won many major United Kennel Club bench show championships. As with those English counterparts, these hounds have been bred for performance, and most show dogs can actively compete as well out in the woods and swamps as they can on the bench.

DACHSHUND

Hot dog. Otherwise affectionately called "the weiner dog." This lively little breed is one of the few that is easily recognizable by its size and shape. It is this robust little dog's very build that lends to its field usage as a hunting dog. If you want to hunt your doxie, you'd best be prepared for an action-packed day afield.

- **Area & Date of Origin:** Germany, 1500s
- **Function:** Scenthound, flushing, earth dog trials, field trials (originally used to hunt badgers)
- **Height & Weight:** 8-9", ~16-32 lbs
- **Colors:** Solid red, sable, or cream; black and tan, chocolate and tan, wild boar and tan, gray and tan, or fawn and tan; single dapple (lighter color set on darker background, as in a merle); double dapple (white in addition to dapple); brindle
- **Coat:** Smooth Coat variety is short and shiny; Longhaired variety is sleek, sometimes slightly wavy; Wirehaired variety has tight, thick, hard hair with a finer undercoat, along with distinctive beard and eyebrows
- **Standards:** Long in body and short of leg; robust muscular development; breastbone strongly prominent; head tapers uniformly to the tip of nose; little perceptible stop; almond-shaped, very dark eyes; high-set, rounded ears; straight back; tail set as a continuation of the topline
- **Life Span:** 12-14 years

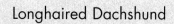

Longhaired Dachshund

■ Appearance and Temperament

There are two different sizes of this compact little dog, as well as three recognized hair coats. The miniature dachshund term applies to dogs that are 11 pounds or less at 12 months of age or older; larger dogs fall into the standard category.

This "hot dog" looking animal has a long body and very short legs. However, this dog is by no means clumsy or awkward; he moves with fluid grace and purpose. The dachshund radiates a boldness and confidence and has an alert expression in the face. He is intelligent and clever with a persevering attitude. In addition, there is good muscle tone to the structure of the dachshund.

Coat texture comes in smooth, wirehaired, or longhaired varieties. With the smooth dachshund, the coat should be smooth, hard, and short. Any color can prevail but most one-colored dogs are red — and may or may not have dark hairs immersed in the coat — or cream, with a small amount of white allowed on the chest. Two-colored dogs are black, chocolate, gray or blue, fawn (known as Isabella), and a color called "wild boar," with tan markings over the eyes and on the face in the jaw and lower muzzle area. Tan markings are also found on the edge of the ear, on the chest, on the inside and back of the front legs, on the paws, rear end, and underneath the tail and back legs. Odd colors such as dapple, double dapple (with white), and brindle are permitted. The dapple color permits blue, or wall, eyes, but with all other color schemes the eyes should be an intelligent dark brown. The tail is smooth with no feathering.

The wirehaired dachshund has a short, thick, rough outer coat with an undercoat found on most of the body. This coat version has a beard and distinctive eyebrows, with short, smooth hair on the ears. Also, the tail has an abundance of hair and tapers to a point at the tip. Colors remain the same as the smooth variety.

Finally, the longhaired dachshund has a sleek coat, sometimes with waves. The hair is longest on the underside of the body, the ears, behind the legs, and on the tail. Hair that is proportionately too long is not desired, as is hair that masks this breed's distinctive body type. Again, all colors are the same as previously mentioned.

■ History

This breed originated in Germany several hundred years ago for the express purpose of hunting badgers. Hence, the name of this breed, named for "dachs" or badger. There are varying theories as to which other breeds contributed to the gene pool that developed the dachshund, including a breed of terrier and even the bloodhound (for nose.) This breed has evolved into a very bold, focused hunter for earthwork; its build is ideal for burrowing into dens and beating through dense brush.

The first National Specialty for the dachshund in this country was held by an AKC parent club in 1895. In the early 1900s this breed advanced from 28th to sixth in popularity rank with registered dog breeds in AKC, and it has admirably maintained its popularity since 1940.

■ In the Field

This amazing breed has enjoyed a tremendous upsurge in popularity with hunters who enjoy pursuing rabbits and various other small animals. The confident perseverance and strong hunting drive of this dog make it adaptable and well-suited to many types of game.

In addition, there is a strong popularity for using this breed in conjunction with falconry, primarily for pursuit of rabbits. The dachshund has an iron will to finish what it starts and a commanding personality, coupled with an excellent nose.

■ Trainability

While dachshunds have superior intelligence, they can be a little stubborn and headstrong. As such, any owner or prospective owner of this breed should plan to get a handle on this dog at an early age. It is important to remain firm with these surprisingly willful little dogs. However, once the trainer has this dog's attention, it can learn quite easily.

■ Strengths/Weaknesses

The dachshund has few health problems but certain ones merit mention. This breed is prone to certain thyroid conditions.

Also, because of its build, this breed can suffer from canine intervertebral disk disease, which is similar to the human form of this condition. It is described as a neurological problem, although differences in anatomy between humans and dogs give distinctions between the two forms.

This breed's strongest suit is its pleasing, bold, friendly personality. Around children, a firm hand and guidelines may be required, but care with any dogs should be taken around toddlers.

■ Other Uses

From apartment buildings to country living, numbers of this breed abound. It is a popular choice as a pet and companion, sometimes does well in obedience, and is an excellent hunting choice for its specific forms of game.

■ The Show Ring

Dachshunds have seen tremendous popularity in the show ring. Due to their confident, alert, exuberant air, they can take the show ring by storm in spite of their unusual size and shape. Most dachshunds appear to really enjoy showing.

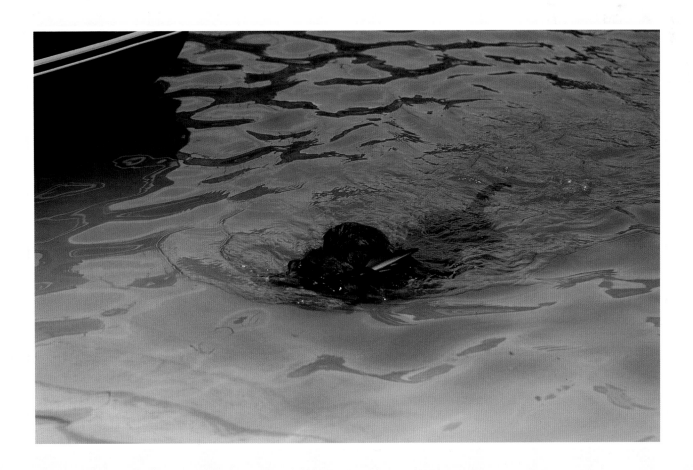

ENGLISH COONHOUND

The foundation for most of today's recognized coonhound breeds stems from the English coonhound, with the exception of the Plott hound. Many of this breed's prepotent sires are found in other breeds' pedigrees. This speaks volumes for the abilities and traits possessed by the English coonhound; in addition, the breed maintains popularity as one of the top coonhound breeds in the country.

- **Area & Date of Origin:** United States, 1800s

- **Function:** Scenthound, fox, raccoon, rabbit, big game hunting

- **Height & Weight:** 22-27" (male); 21-25" (female); weight proportional

- **Colors:** Redtick, bluetick, tricolor with ticks, white-red, white-black, or white-lemon

- **Coat:** Hard, medium length, dense

- **Standards:** Deep, broad chest; strong, slightly arched back; very-slightly domed skull; medium stop; square muzzle; large open nostrils; dark eyes set wide apart; ears hung a little low, with fine texture and soft feel; medium-length tail with slight brush, carried gaily; well-padded, compact feet

- **Life Span:** 11-12 years

- **Also called:** Redtick Coonhound

■ Appearance and Temperament

English coonhounds come in three color phases, but most prevalent is the distinctive "redtick" color, which is benchmark to the breed. Others include the "tri-color with ticks" and the "bluetick" color; the latter is often confused with the bluetick coonhound breed. There are a few white-red, white-black, and white-lemon varieties wherein the second color becomes the ticking on white, but these are not common. Too much red or black is not acceptable, and no brindle markings are allowed. The hard coat of short to medium length provides protection from the elements.

The broad head is pleasing in shape with the skull somewhat domed. Eyes are set wide apart and are dark in color; they express intelligence. Body and legs impart power.

Widely known for an agreeable temperament, this breed's standard actually specifies that extreme aggression or shyness is grounds for disqualification. English hounds tend to be affectionate around children and in the yard, but will be very focused once turned loose in pursuit of game trails.

■ History

As with most of America's coonhound breeds, the English coonhound traces its ancestry back to the foxhounds brought to this continent from Europe. Indeed, this breed was first known as the English fox & coonhound and was first registered in 1905 by the United Kennel Club.

Two breeds evolved from the registered English coonhound, those being the treeing walker and the bluetick. These breeds separated from the English breed and earned their own recognition much later, in 1945 and 1946, respectively.

While these hounds descended from American and English foxhounds, colonial Americans adapted these hounds to withstand much more rigorous terrain and climate, as well as developing the treeing instincts necessary for pursuit of raccoon and other small game, and mountain lion and bear.

This hound has become extremely popular with night hunters since the advent of competition hunts. The liberal color requirements allow for less strict breeding practices and give breeders better potential to continually infuse good traits in the breed.

Of note, the first major coon hunt, known as Leafy Oak, was won by an English hound named Bones; he was owned by Colonel Leon Robinson.

■ In the Field

The English coonhound possesses tremendous track drive and opens on first scent, then barks freely while trailing game. He has a tremendously effective nose and can work all types of tracks, including rather old trails; this makes him a favorite for big- and small-game hunters alike.

While on strike, the English will use a coarse bawl mouth; this hound's voice turns over to a hard chop at the tree. English coonhounds are known for their hard treeing ability; they sometimes lose the ability to pace themselves while treeing.

Although not unfriendly around the tree, English hounds will stand their ground once they have located a tree and believe that the game is there. These hounds have a tendency to hug the tree and display a minimum of tree faults, which is of note since they can be extremely hard tree dogs.

Because of the tenacity of this breed and their fast track ability, they are used successfully on both small and large game. They have the ability to really push big game and hold mountain lions and bears treed or bayed until the hunters arrive. Due to their speed and quick locating ability, English hounds are favored among hunters in the growing competition coon hunt sport.

■ Trainability

The English coonhound harbors a one-track mind at times. This can make training difficult under some circumstances, because this hound seems to tune everything out but the game he has been trained to chase and tree. However, when this tendency is conquered, this breed is willing and receptive to training.

It is notable that while this hound is so focused on his game, he is at home with children and can be very gentle. He can actually be trained by children to do small tasks and will respond to them with remarkable attention. However, one should always keep in mind that this hound is first and foremost a treeing hound.

■ Strengths/Weaknesses

Because this breed tends to lose any perspective once he trees, he could overheat during extremely hot weather while treeing. This hard treeing ability is regarded as an asset, but this factor should be kept foremost in mind when this breed is hunted during summer months. Hunters should position themselves whenever possible to get to the tree quickly when pursuing game in extreme conditions.

The English coonhound is a hardy breed that displays few health problems. The normal concerns for breeds of this size should apply to the English

coonhound, such as occasional hip dysplasia. It is an interesting note that few coon and big-game hounds are prone to hip dysplasia, however; this perhaps evolves because these dogs are heavily bred for performance and must be able to withstand grueling days and nights of hard hunting. The policy of "best to the best" applies, and dogs that cannot perform are not used for breeding purposes.

English coonhounds as a whole demonstrate excellent physical conformation. This is an interesting point since they are so strongly bred toward performance.

■ Other Uses

Widely regarded as a top choice by hound hunters of all types, this hound simply excels in virtually all types of conditions and in varying terrain. However, this breed has not been used much in other venues such as search and rescue or drug detection.

■ The Show Ring

The English coonhound is always a popular choice in the show ring because of its overall impeccable conformation. This beautiful hound shows well and its color variation brings added notice to the breed. English coonhounds have won many of the major United Kennel Club bench shows throughout the country. Most notable bench show English coonhounds are also good performers out in the timber.

ENGLISH FOXHOUND

There are many similarities between this breed and the American foxhound, but avid sportsmen of either breed beg to differ on that point. The English foxhound has been bred in the purest sense of the word, and is actually one of the rarest of the hound breeds. Much tradition lies behind this breed, which is beginning to regain popularity and increase in numbers.

- **Area & Date of Origin:** Great Britain, 1700s
- **Function:** Scenthound, trailing fox
- **Height & Weight:** 23-27", 55-75 lbs
- **Colors:** Any true hound color (black, tan, & white)
- **Coat:** Short, dense, hard, and glossy
- **Standards:** Larger in bone than American Foxhounds; pronounced brow; long nose; low-set ears, often "rounded" (1.5" cut off); level topline; forelegs strong and straight; tail has slight brush, carried gaily but not over back
- **Life Span:** 10-13 years

■ Appearance and Temperament

Above all, this hound has a classy look that is defined as quality by knowledgeable judges. Most English foxhounds are tri-colored or otherwise color combined in black, white, and tan, but any combinations of these colors or white and a shade of tan, called "pies," are admissible. The coat is healthy, short, hard, and dense.

A characteristic of the English foxhound is extremely straight, well-boned legs. These legs must depict strength. There should not be any noticeable tapering at the ankle; presence of bone in this area is quite important and should continue to round, catlike, powerful feet with pronounced strong toes.

Also, the head is striking in shape. It should be both broad and long while showing symmetry. Ears are rounded, and positioned low. The stop is noticeable but not abrupt with a fairly long nose and well-developed nostrils.

Shoulders, back, loins, and hindquarters should be well-muscled but not overly so, and should flow with a decided symmetry to aid in smooth, flowing movement. These dogs are built for endurance and should have a necessary classic, well-defined build.

This hound has an outgoing disposition, and gets along well with and desires the company of other dogs, stemming from its pack origin. He has an agreeable disposition overall.

■ History

By all available accounts, this breed first entered North America in the 1600s. One account credits Robert Brooke as bringing them into Maryland in June of 1650. Foxhunting soon became a sport of choice in the colonies, particularly in Virginia and Maryland. Prior to this, however, accounts say that the English foxhound originated from crosses between bloodhounds, greyhounds, and staghounds on the European continent.

The bulk of known history on these hounds from Colonial times is derived from writings by Thomas, Sixth Lord Fairfax of northern Virginia, who instituted the first known organized fox hunt for hunters, and from journals penned by our first President of the United States, George Washington, who was a dedicated fox hunter with his own pack of hounds.

Tradition evolved with the advancement of the sport. There are some multi-generational packs in existence today that originated back in the 1700s and 1800s. In 1907, the Masters of Foxhounds Association was formed to maintain high ethical standards to support the future of the sport, as well as to record areas for hunts, to keep the MFHA Foxhound Kennel Stud Book, and to facilitate improvement of the sport and the recognized breeds.

There are three breeds recognized by MFHA, those being English, American, and crossbred foxhounds, with English foxhounds numbering least of the three (except in Canada, where its numbers abound), yet steeped in tradition and quality.

In the year 2000, a strict Code of Ethics was adopted by MFHA to preserve the tradition, quality, and future of the sport, which continues to grow in modern times and now exists in 35 states and in Canada. Indeed, there are 171 organized fox hunt clubs in North America today.

■ In the Field

English foxhounds are notably run in a pack; it is a thrill to hear a pack in "full cry" on a chase. When run in an organized hunt, there is the hunter's horn that contributes to an air of excitement, as well as mounted horsemen coursing through the countryside over any and all encountered obstacles.

A fox hunt can involve pursuit of either the red or the grey fox, as well as the coyote and the bobcat. Because of the coyote's ability to adapt to modern habitat changes, they are found in large numbers in most areas of the country. Both species of fox are found throughout the eastern and southern parts of the country, but coyotes become more predominant the farther west one moves.

Emphasis in this country is primarily centered on the chase of the animal and not the kill, unless the host landowner specifies otherwise. In addition, there can be drag hunts, where only fox scent and not live quarry is used. There are also cub hunts, during which young hounds and horses receive training, and formal hunts, when all rules strictly apply to the hunt.

■ Trainability

The English foxhound receives an impressive amount of training before he reaches performance age at 12 to 18 months. He must learn how to stay with the other hounds, for it is vital to run as a pack and not scatter. Although the ultimate goal is to manage a pack while mounted on horseback, initial organized training begins on foot. Control is emphasized.

Therefore, this hound has been bred through generations to accent trainability in the highest degree, which contributes to its courageous yet ebullient personality. The foxhound must be trained off any "trash" and should never stray from pursuit of the designated quarry.

One of the five requirements of a successful pack foxhound is that he be "biddable," and that he must willingly take commands from the hunter's horn, by voice, and from the position of the huntsman and horse. In short, he must be under control and must take direction at all costs and in all situations.

■ Strengths/Weaknesses

It is safe to say that this hound is a hardy, tough, endurance animal. He does crave pack companionship and requires much exercise. Since many of these animals are kept in packs, strict guidelines have been presented to facilitate clean living conditions for good health.

The few English foxhounds that are kept for pet, companionship, and show reasons adapt well to such life but need attention and lots of space to run. Maintenance requirements in grooming and health are relatively low.

■ Other Uses

This breed has been shown successfully as a conformation animal, but numbers are significantly low. Indeed, the first English foxhound was registered with AKC in 1909, and just 31 were registered with this organization in 1995. Most English foxhounds are kept in the registry of the MFHA aforementioned Stud Book.

This hound does adapt as a pet and can be successfully obedience-trained because of its high degree of trainability.

■ The Show Ring

This pleasing breed of hound has seen eight show champions recognized by AKC in 1995, just down from identical numbers of 10 in the two previous years. It is classified as a rare breed by AKC.

GREYHOUND

When most people think of a greyhound, organized racing comes to mind. However, as a sight hound, the greyhound is very popular for use in pursuit of rabbits, hares, and coyotes in many areas of the country, from Texas to North Dakota. These large, fast dogs can run upward of 40 miles an hour for short distances, and can maintain 30 miles per hour for as much as a mile.

- **Area & Date of Origin:** Egypt, 2700 BC
- **Function:** Sighthound, coursing, racing
- **Height & Weight:** 27-30"; 65-70 lbs (male); 60-65 lbs (female)
- **Colors:** Immaterial (includes black, gray, red, fawn, either solid or brindled, either whole colored or spotted)
- **Coat:** Short, smooth, and firm
- **Standards:** Long, narrow head with scarcely perceptible stop; dark eyes; small, folded ears; well-arched loins; deep chest; long, fine, and tapering tail with a slight upward curve
- **Life Span:** 12-14 years

■ Appearance and Temperament

The greyhound has a very distinctive appearance. The long head and neck seem to blend together as there is very little stop between the muzzle and forehead, and the small ears are normally laid flat against the neck. When at attention, the ears may become erect; a name has been applied to this look is "rose ear."

This sight hound has a powerful, long back that arches over the loin area. In addition, the deep chest area — which narrows appreciably toward the abdomen — gives him a singular, characteristic graceful look. The greyhound stands on strong, long legs that have small feet with powerful, pronounced toes. A long, curved, graceful tail completes the unique look.

Males can attain heights at the shoulder up to 30 inches, although hunting and racing dogs are generally about an inch shorter than show dogs, and can weigh as much as 90 pounds. Greyhounds exude an air of strength, power, and speed.

The short, clean coat can come in many colors, including black, white, cream, fawn, red or rust, blue or grey, and different types of brindle; any of these colors including brindle can be found on white.

Most greyhounds belie their reputations and are in fact quite calm and docile. They are highly trainable and are extremely motivated to run and chase. Greyhounds have been bred as pack animals and usually get along well with other dogs, as well as most children.

■ History

The greyhound has an ancient past, as is proven by written word — in such sources as Homer, Shakespeare, and the Old Testament — as well as art throughout the ages. However, no one can agree as to how this breed was named. A popular version — and one that hunters choose to observe — is that a combination of the Old English word "grei," which meant dog, and "hundr," which meant hunter, produced the breed name.

Greyhounds have enjoyed a royal history as well, with ties going back to Alexander the Great. It is said that in England a law prohibited any "mean" people from owning the breed, and that retribution for such infraction was death. Greyhound-like dogs were mummified and buried alongside their owners in ancient Egypt, signifying their importance to society members of stature from that era. The first such reference goes back to the Tomb of Amten in the Valley of the Nile, in the time of the Pharaohs.

The tales of these type dogs, praised for their hunting abilities as well as their grace, can be found throughout history. Of note, General Custer held greyhounds in high esteem, keeping a large pack of greyhounds and other sight hounds with him in his travels.

It has been said by many sources that at some point, perhaps the 1700s, the breed was crossed with some bulldog blood, which produced the short, clean, glossy coat of today's greyhounds.

Greyhounds were used to pursue many animals, including deer, and were bred to outrun, or catch their quarry. As pack animals, they proved superior in this usage.

■ In the Field

Greyhounds are very popular in areas of the South, Southwest, Midwest, and West for sight pursuit of primarily coyotes and hares. These hounds are run in packs and surprisingly can withstand the heat of summer as well as unforgiving cold of winter.

Their strong feet have tough pads that can handle frozen grass and snow, rock, and most types of terrain. These dogs have an incredible drive to attempt to catch their prey, which is why they can attain such high speeds for short distances. It is possible that the greyhound is the fastest breed of dog known to man today.

■ Trainability

The average greyhound, contrary to popular belief, is quite docile and sensitive. He is very intelligent as well. He is pack-oriented and tends to view members of the family in the same way, as a "pack."

This sight hound, like others of this category, has a strong prey drive and as such will want to chase other animals, such as cats and neighborhood rabbits. It is possible to teach them parameters for daily living, but once out of their home element, they will probably feel that anything is fair "game" and should be handled accordingly.

This breed proves to be an adept student at virtually any form of training and can make a good companion as well.

■ Strengths/Weaknesses

Health concerns rate at the top of any weaknesses that this breed might harbor. First and foremost, because of the extremely deep chest, this hound is prone to bloat and torsion. In addition, the greyhound has an extremely low tolerance to anesthesia and many toxins. Extra care must be taken when surgery is necessary. Any flea or tick preventive methods must be chosen carefully.

Because of an extremely low body fat percentage and large body mass and bone density, greyhounds can develop calluses on the elbow area when housed on hard flooring. These calluses can sometimes progress further and develop fluid that sometimes requires veterinary care.

It seems that greyhounds are more prone to bone cancer than many other sporting breeds. They also have a tendency toward low thyroid levels, as do many other athletic breeds, which should be treated when present.

Greyhounds are extremely clean animals that require little grooming. They have a wonderful disposition, are a pleasure to have around, and can live for 12 to 14 years.

■ Other Uses

While the greyhound is extremely popular in sight forms of hunting previously mentioned, the breed is best known for its racing ability. Greyhound racing tracks are found throughout the country, which is a big industry.

Adoption centers have sprung up in most urban areas near racetracks and racing kennels to aid in finding homes for retired racing dogs. Most of these animals adapt well to the change of lifestyle that adoption brings, but suitable care should be taken in any adoption decisions.

Lure coursing is another form of recreational sport and competition for the greyhound breed. This form of dog performance has become very popular with sight hound breeds.

■ The Show Ring

Greyhounds are intensively bred for show as well. Most show greyhounds are slightly larger in body mass and height than racing and field dogs. They also tend to have a more graceful head and neck carriage than their more heavily-muscled performance counterparts.

The greyhound depicts considerable grace and power, and maintains an aura of regality that shines in the show ring.

HARRIER

A rare hound to consider is the harrier, often mistaken for a large beagle. Harriers are pack hounds and have a long history of use in England. It may be difficult to find a pure strain of hunting harriers these days, but with a little legwork, you may find some still chasing fur for their masters.

- **Area & Date of Origin:** Great Britain, 1200s

- **Function:** Scenthound, trailing hare and fox

- **Height & Weight:** 19-21", 50-60 lbs

- **Colors:** Any hound color

- **Coat:** Short, dense, hard, and glossy

- **Standards:** Sturdily built with large bones; head has moderately defined stop; brown, hazel to yellowish eyes are set well apart; low-set ears with round tips; nose must be wide with well-opened nostrils; level topline; long tail tapers to a brush, carried gaily but not curled over back; round, cat-like feet

- **Life Span:** 10 -12 years

■ Appearance and Temperament

Harriers are extremely similar in appearance to beagles, and sometimes discerning the differences is a challenge. In general, harriers are taller at the shoulder — around 20 inches — than beagles; they weigh more as well, averaging between 50 and 60 pounds. Harriers are solidly built and are a bit longer than they are tall; they have been likened to a small English foxhound. Coloration is a mixture of black, tan, and white.

Their coat is short, dense, and glossy, much like the other scenting hounds. In other contrasts to beagles, harriers almost never have rear dewclaws or blue eyes; these can be characteristics used to tell if the dog you're looking at is a harrier or beagle.

Harriers are good family animals, especially around children and other dogs or cats (because of their pack nature). As most hounds, they are persistent, and their strong desire to sniff out and trail game will need to be circumvented by a good fenced-in yard. And be watchful around that fence, too, as harriers may try to dig their way out to track game. They are good watchdogs, but not great guard dogs. Harriers are an all-around family dog, and they love to play. They are very vocal, almost "singing" when excited.

■ History

Harriers have a long history of hunting in packs for foxes and hares, dating back as early as Sir Elias de Midhope's Penistone pack in 1260. Harriers found employment in early colonial America, and remained a standard hunting hound right through the early 1900s; even General George S. Patton used harriers in hunting. They were an early breed of the AKC, admitted in 1885, but things have dropped off considerably since then — 1996 saw only six litters of harriers registered in the entire U.S., and the breed consistently ranks at the bottom of the AKC list of registered dogs. Harriers today are mostly housepets, though some are still used for rabbits and hares.

■ In the Field

Harriers are pack hounds, and as such work well with other dogs. But because of the rarity of the breed, they may not be a logical choice for the hunters of hares and rabbits. If interested, though, you may have a hard time locating a breeder, and then will probably have a long wait for a puppy.

Harriers are very determined, and will stay on the scent trail all day long if need be. Their sturdy, solid frame lets them bust through any cover, and it contributes to their stamina.

■ Trainability

Harrier are very intelligent, possess great scenting ability, and have the ability to trail game all day long. They can be taught basic obedience fairly easily, and you may be able to teach your harrier to keep vocals to a minimum. But you will most likely not be able to train a harrier to ignore a scent trail and stay in the yard; a fenced-in yard will be necessary to make sure your dog doesn't wander off in pursuit of game.

■ Strengths/Weaknesses

The biggest weakness comes from the rarity of the breed. However, that rarity also has kept genetic disorders to an extremely low level. Their biggest strength comes from their affectionate nature — they are people dogs. Their stamina also makes them a good choice for the rabbit hunter, provided a hunting harrier can be found.

■ Other Uses

Many harriers are currently competing in agility testing. Most harriers you see, however, will actually be crosses with beagles or other hound breeds. To find a hunting harrier, you'll need to seek out some pure strains; those left should be good hounds.

■ The Show Ring

There are some harriers competing in the show circuit, but the scarcity of the breed doesn't make them popular in show ring competition — or any other competition for that matter.

MAJESTIC TREE HOUND

Regal in appearance, this hound resembles its bloodhound ancestry. The majestic tree hound has been selectively bred to accentuate its exceptional big-game hunting qualities. Large in size, if not in numbers, this breed has an equally large heart, as do the sentiments of admirers of this remarkably talented dog.

- **Area & Date of Origin:** United States, 1900s
- **Function:** Scenthound, trailing, treeing big game
- **Height & Weight:** 26-30", 80-110 lbs (male); 24.5-30", 75-100 lbs (female)
- **Colors:** Any hound color
- **Coat:** Short, hard, glossy
- **Standards:** Powerfully built overall; head is narrow in proportion to its length, long in proportion to the body; sunken eyes; thin, extremely long, and low-set ears are soft to the touch; long neck; strong back and loins; deep and slightly arched thighs; strong, well-knuckled feet
- **Life Span:** 10-13 years

■ Appearance and Temperament

The majestic tree hound more closely resembles the bloodhound than any other breed, and derives much of his ancestry from the bloodhound. The majestic has an extremely "houndy" countenance due to large size, complemented by a powerful head with extra long ears.

There is excess of dewlap as well as considerable loose skin in the throat area. Eyes should be dark and reflect a wise countenance. The chest should blend well with the powerful shoulders and well-muscled body. Overall, this hound should not present a clumsy appearance, despite its size, but should depict coordination, strength, and stamina.

Any color or combination of colors is acceptable with this breed. The coat of the majestic tree hound is short, hard, and glossy with a tight dense undercoat, typical of many hound breeds.

This hound is known for its even temperament, which enables this large dog to take training well. They also do quite well with most children and other dogs.

History

The name Francois Hubert continually surfaces when one delves into much hound history. He was known as the Patron Saint of hunters and is known for the St. Hubert's hounds that provided foundation blood for most of today's hound breeds. Primarily, his efforts were centered on breeding and improving the qualities of excellent scenting hounds, which he did in southern France during the eighth century. Other religious men continued his breeding practices for generations after he passed away, particularly in present-day Italy, Belgium, and France. Eventually, another strain of large hound emerged from the St. Hubert's, known as the Talbot hound, as other types of hounds were crossed into the bloodline.

History shows that William the Conqueror brought these two strains of hounds to England to run deer in the 11th century. Over the years, these hounds were used on fox, then crossed with greyhounds to introduce more speed for this endeavor.

When these type hounds were brought to North America, additional strains of hounds were created and many different breeds were formed. During this process, some of the emerging breeds became predominantly skilled in handling trails on big game.

By all accounts, the majestic tree hound emerged as a breed through careful breeding and crosses intent upon furthering the best qualities of the bloodhound with the speed and tenacity of other hound breeds to produce the ultimate big-game hound. The Majestic Tree Hound Association was formed in the late 1970s through the efforts of Lee Newhart, Jr.; the breed was recognized by the National Kennel Club in 1980.

In the Field

This extremely large hound delights the eye with his speed and customary grace on track. He possesses an impressive endurance to stay with a difficult big-game trail for the long haul. Majestic tree hounds have been used successfully on bear and mountain lion as well as the difficult jaguar.

The majestic tree hound has a beautiful, deep, melodious hound voice that is pleasing to the ear and loud in volume. His sense of smell is sharp, as is that of his bloodhound predecessor, which makes him so effective on cold big-game trails. The combination of loose throat skin and dewlap assist him by holding scent as he works difficult scent to a more manageable trail.

Trainability

While the bloodhound is known for a stubborn streak, the majestic tree hound is more even-tempered and manageable. This breed possesses a willingness to please and to learn and takes training relatively well. The majestic is intelligent and keen.

However, this hound is bred with a strong desire to follow scent and this can override any situation. Majestic tree hounds should never be left unattended as they may wander off on a scent trail; with their characteristic determination, they could be gone for days.

Strengths/Weaknesses

Large breed maladies apply to this hound. Because of the large, deep chest, this breed is prone to bloat. Other concerns include hip dysplasia, eyelid problems, and ear infections.

This breed should be housed with some form of supportive laying surface to protect his joints and elbows. They can also drool sometimes.

The majestic tree hound possesses an excellent nose and impressive speed on track, coupled with a pleasing, deep hound voice. These qualities, as well as the tenacity necessary to bay or tree big game, makes this hound a good choice for serious big-game hunters.

Other Uses

The majestic tree hound would be a good candidate for search and rescue efforts and can make an excellent pet, as long as his scent-trailing drive is continually recognized by his owner.

PLOTT HOUND

The Plott hound traces its origin back to Germany, giving this hound the distinction of claiming an ancestry separate from most of the other reigning hound breeds. This breed functioned as an all-purpose dog in Colonial America and is probably best known as being the most popular big-game hound in existence today.

- **Area & Date of Origin:** Germany / United States, 1700s
- **Function:** Scenthound, coonhound, trailing big game
- **Height & Weight:** 20-25"; 50-60 lbs (male); 20-23", 40-55 lbs (female)
- **Colors:** Any shade of brindle (a streaked or striped pattern of dark hair on a lighter background), solid black, or brindle with a black saddle
- **Coat:** Smooth, fine, glossy; rarely, a dog will have a doublecoat
- **Standards:** Moderately boned, strong, agile; deep chest; well-muscled, strong, level back; head carried high; brown or hazel eyes; fairly broad ears set moderately-high; rather long tail, carried free and well-up, saber-like; tail is strongly tapered and sometimes has a slight brush
- **Life Span:** 10 -15 years

■ Appearance and Temperament

The Plott has a graceful and powerful appearance with high, appealing head carriage. The head is rather flat with no pronounced stop, and ears are set higher on the head than any of the other hound breeds. In addition, the ears have rounded tips and are of medium length. The muzzle should not be square; the eyes will be wide-set and of a deep brown or hazel color.

The coat of this hound is medium in length, and hard and glossy, laying flat and appearing sleek. The Plott should have a slightly arched back that complements his well-muscled shoulders and hindquarters and strong, straight legs.

Color is unique in the Plott hound with brindle being the predominant color. This coloration is described as darker hairs on a lighter background, or vice versa, that gives a streaked or striped effect. The National Plott Hound Association defines many brindle colors, including yellow brindle, red brindle, tan brindle, brown brindle, black brindle, grey brindle, and maltese — described as slate grey/blue brindle. The United Kennel Club doesn't recognize any solid colors for this breed; the Professional Kennel Club allows a solid fawn or buckskin color. Many staunch supporters of the Plott believe that the buckskin coloring occasionally appears as a reflection of the pure breeding in the Plott's ancestry. Finally, a small amount of white is permitted on the chest and feet.

This hound is extremely agreeable and well-mannered. He is affectionate and loyal, even protective, of his human family.

■ History

This brindle breed originated in Germany where it was developed for use in hunting game, particularly wild boar and stag. Two brothers of the Plott family departed for the shores of North America with some of these brindle hounds. One brother died en route, but Johannes Plott made it to the Colonial shores of this country, settling in North Carolina.

The family eventually moved to the Smoky Mountains, part of the Appalachians, and the breed was preserved and perfected for use in hunting bear. The Plott, by many accounts, was an all-purpose dog that served as a guardian, a night hunter of tree game, a big-game hunter and a companion.

The popularity of the breed grew as the breed continued to develop and was passed through to the hands of Henry Plott, then continually remained in the family to one of the last active hunting members of the Plott family, Vaughn Plott, who is now deceased. Actually, there were five Plott brothers at that time, including George, Sam, Ellis, Vaughn, and John. A son of John's, known as Little George, continued the hunting tradition, but sold his pack of Plotts to Henry "Hack" Smithdeal the night he set sail for duty in World War II, where he was killed in action.

From this point, two of the serious breed promoters were Hack Smithdeal and Dale Brandenberger, and today the breed has staunch supporters throughout the country. There are a few reports of possible outcrosses, which undoubtedly occurred, one dating back to the late 1700s and the other around 1900, possibly with regional big-game hounds. However, as a whole, the maintenance and breeding practices of this breed have been kept notably pure.

The Plott hound was accepted as a breed by the United Kennel Club in 1946.

■ In the Field

The Plott hound quickly developed a sterling reputation as a tough, fast, spirited big-game hound capable of finishing difficult tracks with success. He bravely approaches the adversity of his large opponent with tenacity and has the endurance to outlast his adversary.

This brindle hound has a fighting instinct with regard to his quarry and will not back down. He is cunning and confident. He runs a track by opening freely with a clear bawl or chop, and changes over to a hard tree dog at the end of the line. Primarily used on bear, he excels on other types of big game as well, including wild boar and mountain lion.

An extremely good water dog, this hound can handle any type of terrain and can withstand the toughest of elements. He has developed the qualities necessary to be an excellent coonhound as well.

■ Trainability

The Plott hound was required to be a member of the family back in North Carolina and in the Appalachians. As such, he became an extremely biddable hound, very agreeable and willing to learn. This hound can be trained to do virtually any task and is extremely versatile.

Because this hound has such an inherent affection toward his master, he wins friends easily. The Plott hound — to be such a formidable opponent to big game — is a surprise find as a companion as well.

■ Strengths/Weaknesses

This hound breed has many strong qualities, including its ability to handle all types of terrain, from rough swamps to difficult mountainous and rocky regions. Its voice is clear and carries well. He is fast and tough to beat on big game.

His even temperament and loyalty endear him to his followers. In addition, these qualities contribute to their particular ease of training.

This hound does not have any particular health problems other than the typical large breed and hound-related potential concerns. He is hardy and tough, and is generally considered a low maintenance dog and an easy keeper. He will live from 10 to 15 years.

■ Other Uses

The Plott hound remains predominantly a big game hound with recent major inroads into the sport of competition coon hunting over the last 50 years. Once again, he is versatile and excels as a companion and watchdog.

■ The Show Ring

This brindle bundle of grace is a beautiful animal by anyone's standards and has proven this by winning some major United Kennel Club bench shows. At any given event, the eye-catching Plott hound is a threat to other competitors.

REDBONE

Most avid sportsmen and animal lovers have seen the classic movie *Where the Red Fern Grows*. We lived and loved with the boy who starred in the movie – a boy who fell in love with his two redbone pups and trained them to become accomplished coonhounds – then became a man as he dealt with the rigors, decisions, and hard lessons that life dealt along the way. Yes, the redbone, a strikingly beautiful, American-made coonhound.

- **Area & Date of Origin:** Scotland / United States, 1700-1800s
- **Function:** Scenthound, trail and tree game
- **Height & Weight:** 22-27″ (male); 21-26″ (female); weight in proportion
- **Colors:** Solid red; dark muzzle and small amount of white on brisket and feet okay
- **Coat:** Short, smooth, and coarse enough to provide protection
- **Standards:** Deep broad chest; topline slopes slightly to rear; moderately-broad, flat skull with square muzzle; black nose; dark brown to hazel eyes, round and set well apart; low-set ears; medium-length, saber-like tail with a very slight brush; compact, well-padded feet
- **Life Span:** 10-12 years

■ Appearance and Temperament

The redbone of today is a rich, solid red-colored hound of incomparable beauty and grace. He has a sleek, hard, dense glossy coat that is preferably dark red, with lighter shades of red permissible. No off colors are recognized; however, a small amount of white on the chest and feet is allowed.

Of medium size, this hound depicts grace and should be in symmetry from head to toe. The broad head should blend well with the muzzle without pronounced stop, and the wide-set eyes are preferably dark with a noticeably pleading hound expression that is pleasing to encounter. The body should be in total proportion with good muscles and legs that have slightly angled pasterns and hocks.

The redbone is known for a temperament that is neither too affectionate nor too standoffish. However, he is good in a family environment and is a quick learner.

■ History

By most accounts, the redbone descended from foxhounds of Colonial days and was bred by hunters who desired a hound with the rich red color. Breeding practices included developing a gamey hound that was tree-oriented. In most accounts, the name George Birdsong crops up. From Georgia and a reputable foxhunter and breeder, Birdsong got a pack of hounds from Dr. Thomas Henry in the mid-1800s, from which it is said this breed has its strongest foundation. Then some bloodhound crossing was made.

As the rich red color evolved, the dogs went through a saddleback color phase with red background, a black saddle, and sometimes white points on the chest and feet. In time, the black saddle was bred out of these hounds, with help from other influential breeders of the time such as Brooks Magill and Red Blakesly. Today's dog is solid red with the small amount of permissible white.

This breed was the second to be recognized by the United Kennel Club, way back in 1902. Today it is recognized, as are the other hound breeds, by most North American breed registries.

■ In the Field

The redbone's athletic ability is well celebrated and is perhaps his biggest claim to fame. This hound is adaptable and can handle all types of environmental obstacles while in pursuit of game. In addition, this breed is an extremely competent water dog.

This graceful hound is capable of pushing any type of track to its end; although preferred as a coonhound, the redbone is equally capable of tackling big game. He has a strong innate desire to tree or catch his game. When in pursuit of quarry, they tune out the rest of the world.

The voice of the redbone is almost musical, quite melodious and pleasing to the ear as he opens freely on track and settles to a hard chop on the tree.

■ Trainability

Although the redbone can appear indifferent at times, he is relatively easy to train. Some redbones have been known to have a predisposition to running or treeing off game, perhaps because they are so gamey, and as such must be trained to run the right game desired in these instances.

■ Strengths/Weaknesses

The redbone possesses few faults in health or in temperament. His grace and agility, coupled with endurance and versatility, make him a good choice for the serious hunter.

■ Other Uses

Redbones have enjoyed an upsurge in popularity as pets, but the companion dog owner should keep in mind the strong treeing desire and gaminess of this red hound.

Primarily, this hound is well suited to coonhound and big-game hunting while doubling as a family member. When used for big game, the redbone is usually run in packs, and is popular in Western states.

■ The Show Ring

The red dog is a favorite in the show ring. Depicting grace and beauty, this hound can steal anyone's eye and does its share of winning. Most show-bred redbones can perform well out in the timber, with few exceptions.

RHODESIAN RIDGEBACK

True to its name, this breed has a characteristic line of hair that grows backward on the ridge of its spine. This sight hound enjoys another unique distinction in that it also possesses a keen nose. Rhodesian ridgebacks have been used for virtually all forms of hunting over the years, and may well be the most versatile of all the hound breeds.

- **Area & Date of Origin:** South Africa, 1800s
- **Function:** Sighthound, scenthound, retriever, track and hunt game, lure coursing
- **Height & Weight:** 25-27", 85 lbs (male); 24-26", 70 lbs (female)
- **Colors:** Light wheaten to red wheaten
- **Coat:** Short, glossy, dense; clearly defined ridge is characteristic feature of the breed; it should start with two identical whorls just behind the shoulders and taper to a point between the hip bones
- **Standards:** Strong, muscular, athletic; deep chest; powerful, firm back; flat skull, rather broad between ears; round eyes harmonize with color of dog; high-set ears of medium size taper to a rounded point; ridge on back; tapering tail carried with a slight curve; compact feet
- **Life Span:** 10-13 years
- **Also called:** African lion hound

■ Appearance and Temperament

This well-balanced hound has a slightly sloping top line with symmetry throughout, and has a regal air about him. The ridgeback has a very short, hard coat with a pleasing light wheaten to red wheaten color. His nose should complement coat color, and eye color should match the nose. A black nose should be accompanied with dark brown eyes, while hazel eyes should go the brown or liver nose colors.

The head should have good carriage in proportion to the body, with a somewhat flat skull and fairly pronounced stop. The muzzle is long and appears powerful with the lips close and fitting in line and taper.

Since he displays elegance, grace, and athletic ability, the ridgeback must be well-balanced in form and function. His muscled areas should have clean definition with shoulders blending into body and hindquarters in a pleasing sense. The feet are constructed in such a way as to be extremely durable with very tough pads and hair between the toes.

This dog is fiercely loyal to its family but can be standoffish to strangers. The ridgeback can get along well with dogs and will tolerate other animals as well, especially when properly introduced to them.

■ History

Rhodesian ridgebacks can be traced to the 16th century when Hottentot tribes on the Cape of Good Hope were discovered with dogs that had a ridge on the spine where the hair grew backward. However, no one knows whether these tribes were specifically responsible for this breed.

It is known that people from Denmark and Germany who migrated to South Africa brought several dog breeds with them, including mastiffs, greyhounds, and bloodhounds. A versatile hunting dog was needed in the wild African lands, and through crossbreeding practices between the imported dogs and the Hottentot ridgeback, a new, hardy breed of dog emerged.

Most critics agree that the Hottentot ridgeback had the most influence during selective breeding with other dogs to produce a hound that could flush a bird and retrieve it, catch a stag, bay game, as well as guard family and stock. This dog had to withstand extreme differences in temperature and climate variables and was required to negotiate formidable terrain.

It is told that in 1875, missionary Reverend Charles Helm took two of these dogs with him from South Africa to Rhodesia. There, a celebrated big-game hunter named Cornelius von Rooyen, took these dogs hunting. Upon concluding that they possessed extraordinary hunting traits and qualities, through selective breeding he began cultivating a pack of the dogs for his personal use. They excelled on the fierce African lion. Following extensive breeding in Rhodesia, the breed was named for the country.

In 1922, a standard for the breed was written in Rhodesia that basically holds true to this day. The breed was recognized by the South African Kennel Union in 1924 and admitted by the American Kennel Club in this country in 1955.

■ In the Field

The ridgeback is without question the most versatile hunting dog living today. This dog can be used to hunt virtually every kind of mammal as well as upland birds and waterfowl.

This hound trails silently until it has its quarry within sight. As such, when used for big-game hunting, it is usually teamed with a pack of open trailing hounds. When it bays or trees its quarry, it becomes very vocal, almost ferocious, and absolutely will not back down. The ridgeback is efficient on bear, bobcat, mountain lion, deer, coyote, raccoon, fox, squirrel, and wild boar.

In addition, this dog has such gaminess and nose that it is a good hunting companion for upland birds and waterfowl as well. The ridgeback can flush birds and can retrieve on land or water.

■ Trainability

Because this dog was required to be a strong family member as well as a superb hunting dog, the breed evolved with a tractable, pleasing, intelligent temperament. This hound can be trained to do virtually any task and will attempt it willingly and without further ado.

The Rhodesian ridgeback is an asset to any family and is a pleasure as a companion, working, or hunting dog. He has the rare trait of constantly trying to find ways to please his master and a stubborn streak is almost nonexistent.

■ Strengths/Weaknesses

The aforementioned versatility of this breed remains its strongest asset, along with its superior temperament. In addition, this dog has a coat that sheds very little, and overall the dog is an extremely easy keeper.

However, there are certain health problems to consider. Both hip and elbow dysplasia can pose

problems, and the breed is prone to thyroid conditions and eye abnormalities.

Of most concern is the condition known as the *dermoid sinus*, which is located along the spinal area of the back. It almost never occurs in the ridge of the back. This is a congenital condition that can be palpated on pups. When this condition exists and when it cannot drain, it will form an abscess and swelling that can rupture the skin. This can vary in severity from simply painful to life-threatening. It can be surgically corrected, but responsible breeders have pups with this condition either put to sleep or have the situation corrected and the pup placed in a pet home where it will not be bred.

■ Other Uses

The Rhodesian ridgeback can be successfully used in virtually every performance capacity. These dogs are successful as hunting dogs in pursuit of big and small game and as upland and waterfowl retrieving dogs.

They are used in the popular sport of lure coursing as sight hounds. These hounds have superb tracking ability and can compete successfully in obedience, tracking, and agility.

In addition, this hound is an excellent companion and pet and makes an excellent guard dog.

■ The Show Ring

Because of this breed's incredibly strong hunting qualities, many show animals still retain these skills after generations of strict show breeding. The ridgeback is a popular breed in the ring because of its inherent elegance and grace. However, care should be taken to find a reputable breeder and choose good working stock.

SCOTTISH DEERHOUND

Yes, he looks like an oversized greyhound in a shaggy coat. But in his defense, the Scottish deerhound has an ancient history nearly as celebrated as that of the greyhound, and has many individual qualities as well. A sight hound, he also has a keen sense of smell and is a speed and endurance animal.

- **Area & Date of Origin:** Scotland, middle ages
- **Function:** Sighthound, lure coursing
- **Height & Weight:** 30-32", 85-110 lbs (male); at least 28", 75-95 lbs (female)
- **Colors:** All shades of gray and gray brindle; yellow, red, and fawn are colors of the oldest known strains, and are very rare
- **Coat:** Harsh and crisp, about 3-4" long on body, ideally close lying; hair on head, breast and belly much softer
- **Standards:** Similar to a larger-sized and larger-boned Greyhound; deep chest; well-arched loin drooping to the tail; broad, drooping hindquarters; long head with flat skull, broadest at the ears; good mustache and beard of silky hair; small, folded ears, dark in color; long, tapering tail; compact feet
- **Life Span:** 8-11 years

■ Appearance and Temperament

Overall head and body carriage resembles that of the greyhound. However, the Scottish deerhound has relatively long hair on the head and sports a moustache and beard of soft hair. The coat on the body, neck, and hindquarters should be very coarse, almost wiry and about four inches in length. Stomach and breast hair should be silky and resemble the facial hair.

His head is wide and flat at the rear and continues to taper to the tip of the muzzle, with only slight elevation between skull and muzzle. His nose should be black unless his body is blue, in which case his nose may be blue. Ears should be fairly small and folded back against the head, although during attentive moments they can lift somewhat without becoming erect. In addition, ears should be black or dark in color; also a black muzzle is preferred.

This is a huge dog that reaches sizes much larger than its greyhound cousin in both body and bone mass, with the male attaining weights upward of 110 pounds and a height of 32 or more inches at the shoulder. He is regal, athletic, and powerful in build and stature, with massive, well-defined shoulders blending to a sloping top-line and wide, powerful hindquarters. He has a deep chest and athletic legs and feet. His powerful neck is clothed in a mane that hides much of its obvious strength and grace, and his tail is carried down, with dignity, not high and gay as the tail set of many other hound breeds.

Colors include blue-gray, the prized dark blue-gray, darker and lighter grays, and brindles, with darker shades being preferred in these colors; also yellow, sandy-red or red fawn. Slight amount of white is allowed on the chest and toes.

This immense dog has a graceful disposition with an even-tempered nature. He gets along well with other dogs and children. The Scottish deerhound can be quite affectionate in a reserved, dignified manner.

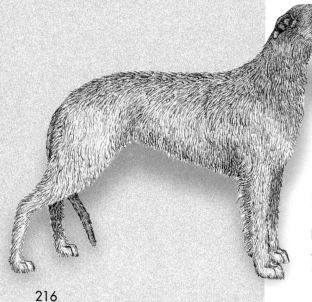

■ History

All accounts agree that over generations of large wolf dogs, wolfhounds, greyhounds, deerhounds, and staghounds various breeds emerged, and the Scottish deerhound has specific history dating back to the 16th and 17th centuries. While the greyhound was used for smaller game and deer, the deerhound evolved specifically to be able to run, catch, and kill the large deer.

At times in history, no one but royalty could own a dog of this breed. In addition, several accounts relate that deerhounds could buy penance for harsh crimes. There are continual references to these huge, gentle dogs throughout literature.

In time, the breed almost became extinct as the greyhound became a dominant breed of choice. Heretofore lies "the rest of the story" regarding the country that preserved the breed and hence added its name. In areas of Scotland, particularly the Highlands, a numerous stag population remained, which required the use of this powerful dog in hunting practices. It remained in those days that royalty owned these docile, powerful hounds in Scotland as well.

The late 1700s proved disastrous to the breed because of the many changes in royalty, nobility, and hierarchy, but concentrated efforts on protecting the breed were resumed by 1825 to save this "Royal Dog of Scotland," and he regained numbers and popularity once again.

This dog appears with royalty in many paintings over the ages; he was a favorite subject in Landseer's paintings. Yes, he's that monstrous, shaggy dog that many folks don't immediately recognize as a breed, yet who has always held such high esteem and prominence in his world.

In the Field

This dog has no peers when it comes to pursuit of fast game. Simply put, he was bred to run the large species of deer, perhaps even overtaking and killing the animal. He has impressive speed and powerful dispatch — which was necessary to handle extremely large deer — and the courage necessary to complete the package. He is fast and demonstrates endurance. With keen scenting ability, he is in rare company as a sight hound, which adds further value to his desirable hunting qualities.

Hunting deer with dogs has been reduced to only a handful of states in this country, and only in certain counties of those. However, this dog has proven extremely proficient on coyotes and is often teamed with his cousin, the greyhound, in these pursuits. In what might be described as "overkill," he also has been used for rabbits.

The Scottish deerhound will work either alone or in a pack, another trait that separates him from some of his cousins.

Trainability

The Scottish deerhound is incredibly docile and gentle. He has superior intelligence and a keen sense of order, and takes well to training of any sort. Perhaps in part because he was primarily in the companionship of his master (as opposed to a kennel life) for so many centuries, this dog has developed a strong character of dignified reserve.

This breed is extremely loyal and devoted to his master. Usually this trait lends to ease in training, because this type of dog harbors a high degree of willingness to please.

Strengths/Weaknesses

The biggest concern for a dog of this size is bloat and torsion. Suitable care should be taken during feed and exercise regimes as preventive maintenance for this life-threatening condition.

In addition, this dog should have supportive sleeping quarters and should not be kept on a hard surface to aid in warding off calluses on elbows and to give joint protection.

Hip dysplasia is a concern as well. Care should be taken to buy from Scottish deerhound stock with OFA or PennHIP certification. Other breed concerns should be derived and briefed to the buyer by a qualified breeder.

This hound's incredibly gentle, tractable nature combined with superb hunting qualities for its purpose remain this hound's strongest suits. In addition, they shed very little.

Other Uses

The Scottish deerhound has been successfully used for tracking and also participates in lure coursing. Of note, the very first National Lure Coursing Champion title was earned in 1994 at the inaugural National Championship in Mount Holly, New Jersey. This title was won by a Scottish deerhound who was only 14 months old.

The Show Ring

The Scottish deerhound exudes such an air of dignified elegance in the show ring that it draws attention, despite its relatively low numbers. This breed glides around the ring with an effortless grace and responds well as a team with its handler.

TREEING WALKER

No other coonhound breed does as much winning in the competition arena as the treeing Walker coonhound. Indeed, it is a fact that more hounds of this breed compete in night hunts than all the other recognized breeds combined. The treeing Walker is widely known and easily recognized throughout the country by a majority of folks, although it is sometimes mistaken for an "overgrown" beagle.

- **Area & Date of Origin:** United States, 1700s
- **Function:** Scenthound, trailing, treeing game
- **Height & Weight:** 22-27" (male); 20-25" (female); weight proportional
- **Colors:** Tri-colored (white, black, tan); white or black may be the predominant color
- **Coat:** Smooth, glossy, hard, close
- **Standards:** Moderately long, muscular back; loins broad and slightly arched; head carried well up; skull broad and full; soft, expressive, dark eyes set well apart; medium-length ears set moderately low, soft and velvety, slight round at tip; tapered tail is strong at root, set high, carried well-up, saber-like, curved up and forward; solid, compact, cat-like feet
- **Life Span:** 11-13 years

■ Appearance and Temperament

The treeing walker is a hound of good size and stature. He is pleasing to look at. Almost always tri-colored in black, white, and tan, he often comes in saddle-back or blanket-back coloration. Predominate white with black or tan spots is allowed. The coat is short, hard, and glossy with a dense undercoat to help protect this hound against the elements. However, the coat should be neither too short nor too thick.

This hound has a pleasing head to behold, with a broad skull that sports a moderate stop; a good muzzle with flews that give a square appearance; and black, well-developed nostrils and a black nose. The eyes are intelligent and dark-colored. His ears should be moderately long and should roll forward somewhat when hanging, with rounded tips.

The strong, powerful body should be in proportion to the head and ears. Movement should be symmetrical, giving the impression of poetry in motion. Above all else, the treeing walker seems to possess "yard dog sense" and is very intelligent. He seems to figure things out. He has an even, agreeable temperament and is good around other dogs and children. However, he can show animosity to other types of pets and animals, such as rabbits, squirrels, and cats.

■ History

This breed of coonhound takes its direct ancestry from the American and English foxhounds of Colonial America, beginning with influence from foxhound packs that belonged to Thomas Walker and George Washington Maupin. Later named for the Walker family of Kentucky — well known for their fox hunting sport, dogs, and breeding — they contributed greatly to the development of the running Walker hound. It is said that Tennessee Lead, a black and tan hound of unknown origin that became a foundation sire for the American foxhound, figures prominently as an outcross in the first treeing Walkers as well, as he put push, drive, and tree desire into the running dogs of the day. Both the Walker clan, including John W.

Walker and George Washington Maupin, figured prominently in the initial development of the treeing Walker hound.

Eventually, the treeing Walker coonhound developed into the superior dog of today. Two men figured prominently in the actual departure from the English coonhound breed and recognition as a separate breed, those being Lester Nance and Raymond Motley. In 1945, the treeing Walker became its own identity.

■ In the Field

Many say that the treeing Walker has it all. Fanciers of other hound breeds may disagree, but it's difficult to argue with the numbers and success that this breed delivers. This tri-colored hound possesses speed, stamina, uncanny gaminess, locating and treeing ability, and a characteristic style that are second to none.

In addition, this hound has a very competitive nature, interesting since this breed began as a pack hound. But over the years it has become increasingly independent and usually requires no help to get his job done; in fact, he often prefers it that way. An amazing degree of consistency in performance wins many supporters.

The desired voice of this hound is a bawl or chop on trail with a good changeover to a resounding chop on the tree. A deep or clear and carrying voice is common. A "yard dog" mouth is frowned upon. Some walkers open freely on trail while others possess the ability to "drift" a track as they bark occasionally, although never in the same place, until they tree their game. Many Walkers also have the scenting ability to tree "lay-up" coon, or raccoons that haven't been down on the ground for some time.

■ Trainability

The tri-colored hound is extremely tractable and friendly and possesses great ability to accept training. As a whole, the breed is not stubborn, although it is focused on game. As such, "trash breaking" procedures are often required.

This dog desires human contact and responds well to attention. He is agreeable and many a treeing Walker hound is even sensitive to the harsh word or strong measure. However, the stubborn hound also exists. It is important with any type of dog training, and particularly with the often-sensitive walker, to read each dog during training and to treat each dog as an individual in method and correction.

■ Strengths/Weaknesses

Some hunters regard the increasing streak of independence in the treeing Walker as an asset while others consider it a fault. Nonetheless, this is becoming a characteristic of the breed as a whole.

The ability of this stylish breed to strike, trail, and tree game

with success and consistency continually puts it at the top of the pecking order for competitive coonhound events. In short, anyone who has a desire to compete with a coonhound has more odds in his favor by choosing a well-bred coonhound by strength in numbers with the availability of a superior gene pool to draw from.

Treeing Walkers have good health with few problems. There are a few that have low thyroid conditions, and some have allergies and other related skin problems.

Although this breed is becoming so independent in the woods, the opposite is true in the kennel or home. This dog requires a lot of attention, possibly a result of his strong, pack-oriented background, and thrives in an environment filled with human support.

■ Other Uses

The treeing Walker adapts well to obedience training and has performed admirably in competitions in registries that accept this breed. Although first and foremost a hunting dog, this dog makes an excellent pet and companion dog, provided he has outlets to his considerable energy and prey drive.

■ The Show Ring

Treeing Walkers have won many of the major shows in this country. Because of the numbers of this breed, some lines have been directed toward primarily show background for several generations. Some of these type Walker hounds still perform well in the field, while others fall somewhat short of the equation. Care should be taken to choose a hunting companion wisely, from good performance hunting stock with good conformation and form.

Cur

CHAPTER 11

THE VERSATILE AND CUR BREEDS

by Vickie Lamb

The Curs

By virtue of their adaptability, a number of versatile dog and cur breeds have carved their way and earned their place with American hunters and in American homes. Some of the breeds worthy of note include the Catahoula leopard dog, the leopard cur, the original mountain cur, the Stephens cur, the blackmouth, the camus curs, the treeing cur, Tennessee treeing brindle, Canadian cur, and a few treeing feist breeds. All of these breeds have characteristics of merit as well as storied histories, but most is probably known about the Catahoula leopard dog and the mountain cur.

The Terriers

With their short stature and fierce demeanor in a fight, terriers were originally developed for hunting furred game, either rooting out from or killing inside the quarry's dens or holes. "Terrier" comes from *terra* — earth dog, a dog that will go down into a burrow or den and fight its quarry on equal terms. There are 26 breeds of terriers recognized by the AKC in the "Terrier" group, but only three have been included in this encyclopedia: the Jack Russell terrier, Airedale terrier, and German jagdterrier. The Jack Russell and German jagdterrier have been gaining popularity among squirrel hunters; the Airedale has become a versatile breed for bird hunters, displaying excellent flushing and retrieving skills, and is also used in the tracking — and sometimes dispatching — of furred game. Admittedly at this time, few Airedales are seen in the field.

The other terrier breeds have fallen out of hunting popularity and are pets or shown in the ring, thus, their exclusion from this book. All make excellent family pets, especially the Jack Russell, which some believe to be one of the most intelligent dogs. These three hunting terriers are dedicated to their task, and their hunting heritage is among the oldest of all canines.

Border Terrier

THE CUR BREEDS

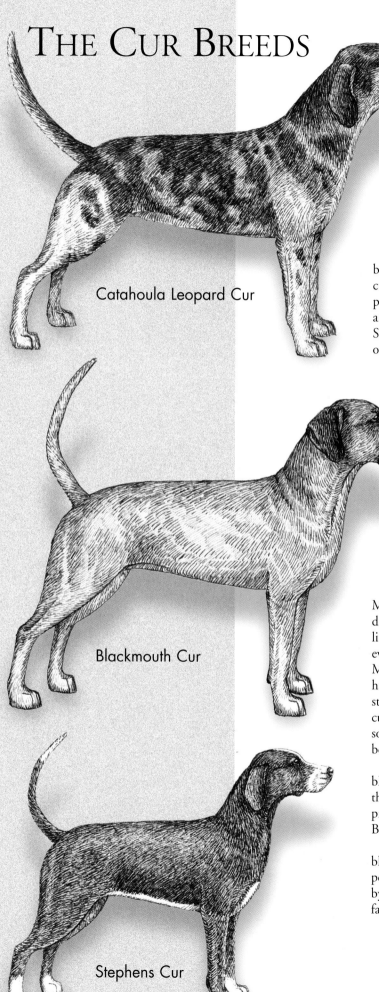

Catahoula Leopard Cur

Blackmouth Cur

Stephens Cur

■ Appearance and Temperament

There is a variety of difference between breeds in appearance, although not that much discrepancy in temperament. Catahoulas are possibly the largest of the breeds and can reach up to 26 inches in height at the shoulder. They can also weigh close to 100 pounds. This breed has several different recognized colors, including blue leopard, red leopard, brindle, and solid colors of black, red, and yellow. There may be tan or white markings that are permitted. The Catahoula is stocky yet athletic, with attitude and purpose.

The mountain cur usually comes in blue, yellow, and brindle colors, some with white markings. The blackmouth cur is usually some shade of yellow, red, or fawn with black points around the muzzle, although black, brown, buckskin, and brindle with small amounts of white are allowed. The Stephens cur is usually black or dark gray with white markings on the feet and chest, and sometimes neck. With the mountain cur and blackmouth cur possibly being the largest of these other included breeds, the others — Stephens cur, camus cur and feist — are all generally at least medium-sized dogs. Some of these breeds are naturally bob-tailed while others have long tails.

Most of these breeds have very strong personalities to match the grit and endurance that they require to do their jobs. While this is true, most of them are also very loyal and surprisingly, not stubborn. The terms "cur" and "feist" should not be taken as any slight to these breeds.

■ History

Mountain cur history reports that the breed descended from dogs brought to America by early settlers, and claim that lineage traces back to Hernando de Soto's dogs. These dogs evolved in the Shenandoah Valley and the Appalachian Mountains and continually moved westward. Today this breed has two recognized lines, those being the original and Kemmer stock mountain curs. Stephens curs descended from mountain curs, but through intensive breeding efforts by Hugh Stephens, soon developed distinctive characteristics of their own and became a separate breed.

Catahoulas may trace descent to mastiff and greyhound blood, again brought to this country by de Soto. Lore states that some of these dogs were crossed with wolf populations to produce wolf hybrids. These dogs were then crossed with Beaucerons brought to this country by French settlers.

In fact, all of these breeds have tracings back to early blood from centuries ago that then evolved with their own peculiarities and talents. However, a main theme was the need by rural America for versatile game dogs that could double as family guard dogs.

In the Field

All of these breeds excel at trailing and treeing game. Some are more adept at baying big game, others do best at squirrel hunting, while a few breeds can seemingly do it all, with considerable skill. This includes big game such as hogs, bear, and mountain lion, as well as raccoons, bobcats, and squirrels.

There are many mouth variations to be found in these breeds. The cur is thought to have a weak, high-pitched mouth with a short, chop bark, and it is true that many of them do. However, some breeds have lines with deep mouths and certain ones have a longer chop, akin to a bawl, on track. Certain of these breeds do not open on track and are said to be "silent," while others can be open trailers. All of them are fairly good tree dogs, and some are extremely hard tree dogs.

Another misconception is that cur breeds are "hot-nosed." While this is sometimes true, many of these breeds have exceptional noses and can work difficult, even cold, tracks with efficiency and accuracy.

Trainability

Without exception, these breeds possess a high degree of intelligence; they demonstrate a high capacity for learning. They can be taught most any task and once something is learned, they do not require constant drilling.

These dogs are somewhat aggressive, however, because of their extremely protective instincts toward home and family, and this must be taken into consideration when any training procedures are done. They have quick response to training methods.

Strengths/Weaknesses

Hardiness has been a necessity throughout the history of these breeds; as such, there are few genetic or health problems to be dealt with. There is an occasional albino that could be deaf, blind, or both. Occasionally, skin allergies seem to cause discomfort, but even this is rare. These breeds are quite healthy.

The assertive nature of these animals should be given consideration by any prospective owners. These dogs need homes and owners who have the time to give them adequate exercise and who can handle their strong personalities.

Other Uses

Probably the Catahoula enjoys the most positive notoriety with regard to additional uses. They have been used successfully as Search and Rescue dogs, and also as drug-detection dogs. In addition, they can be excellent cow dogs and possess good herding instincts.

Since these breeds evolved with heavy accent toward the general-purpose dog, they all tend to be supreme watchdogs and will guard their possessions with a certain degree of fierceness. This personality trait carries over to hunting game, and in certain instances, baying and holding quarry until hunters arrive. The herding instinct appears quite frequently and many dogs are good stock dogs.

Because of their loyalty, they can be excellent companion dogs, but they need lots of exercise, with consideration given to their personalities.

Any of these breeds can excel in the fairly new squirrel dog competitions, and a few have competed successfully in the coonhound competitive events that don't exclude these breeds.

AIREDALE TERRIER

The Airedale terrier is often referred to as the "King of the Terriers," and it is appropriately so if speaking in terms of size and function of the different terriers. Perhaps no other terrier has been used for so many different functions, and it is the largest of the terrier breeds. It fits well its distinction of being a "versatile" dog, able to perform many tasks to serve sportsmen. Though they are far down the list of choices for a hunting companion, they should be given careful consideration due to their versatility.

- **Area & Date of Origin:** England, 1800s
- **Function:** Badger and otter hunting, guardian, police dog
- **Height & Weight:** 23″ (male); female slightly smaller; ~45 lbs
- **Colors:** Tan with black markings on sides and upper parts of the body
- **Coat:** Hard, dense, and wiry, lying straight and close with some hair crinkling or waving
- **Standards:** Short and level back; forelegs perfectly straight; long and flat skull with stop hardly visible; small, dark eyes; black nose; V-shaped ears with fold above the level of the skull; tail set high and carried gaily, of fair length; small, round, compact feet
- **Life Span:** 10-13 years
- **Also called:** Working Terrier, Waterside Terrier, Bingley Terrier

■ Appearance and Temperament

The Airedale terrier is the largest of all the terriers, measuring approximately 23 inches in height to the shoulders. The Airedale is one of the breeds in which there is little difference between the show ring dog and the field dog; it's proponents believe that the form of the dog should follow its function — hunting. In that regard, look for Airedales to be strong, stout dogs with almost an overall square-shaped appearance; overall length of the dog from shoulder to buttocks is about the same as the dog is tall. Their tan fur with dark markings on the side and back is tough and wiry, covering the entire body, legs, and feet, but may be clipped short around the head and face; this tough fur combined with a soft undercoat keeps this hunting dog warm and dry in weather and environmental extremes.

The rest of the appearance is consistent with the other terriers — long and flat skull; short, stiff tail; short triangular ears perky and sitting out from the side of the head — as is the temperament. Airedales are as good-natured as any breed if treated in a kind manner, and they have enjoyed a reputation as being a fun-loving dog, especially with children. But they can be stubborn, and may be inclined to fight it out with other dogs.

President Theodore Roosevelt — who hunted with Airedales — had been known to remark that "Airedales can do anything any other dog can do and then whip him if he has to." While this aggression is not dangerous and at times an asset in the hunting field, it should be considered when deciding on a sporting breed. Most often, though, Airedales are reserved dogs and should not be shy or spooky. Indeed, their inquisitiveness and persistence is what makes them able to be so versatile.

History

Originating from the area of the Aire River in Yorkshire, England, in the mid-1800s as a versatile hunting dog, the Airedale was expected to rid farms of varmints and assist landowners in hunting birds, and small and big game. It also developed a reputation as a "poacher's dog" at a time when an estate's fur and feathers were owned by the lord. Poachers needed a dog that could furtively dart in and out in the kill and retrieve of game from the lord's land.

Airedales were achieved by the blending of otterhound and broken-coated terriers, to name only two of the breeds involved in the recipe that eventually led to the Airedale. At first, however, the dog went by the names of Waterside terrier, then Bingley terrier, and finally the Airedale terrier by 1879.

The Airedale enjoyed a solid reputation in the U.S. — brought here in the late 1800s — and was one of the most popular dog breeds in the 1920s; it was approved for the AKC registry in 1959. It's tough nature and impressive running and swimming abilities prompted its use as a messenger dog during World War I, where it also brought first-aid supplies to wounded soldiers. It also found use as a guard dog and police dog (which it still enjoys overseas).

In the Field

A quote from 1916 by William H. Miller in the book *The American Hunting Dog* says that the Airedale stands on the borderline between bird dog and fur dog. This do-it-all breed has been used for finding, flushing, pointing, and retrieving upland birds and waterfowl; for tracking and killing rodents; and for tracking big game and retrieving small game. It still enjoys extensive use by devotees in all these manners, though not on a widespread basis.

However, those same devotees will be quick to point out that the Airedale does not perform any of its many abilities to the level that specialty breeds do. While it does retrieve waterfowl in all types of conditions, it doesn't do it to the level of a Labrador retriever; though they track fur, a

hound would be a better choice for a dedicated fur hunter. But if your desire is to have one dog that will accompany you in all conditions and be able to perform adequately on any game, then the Airedale may be your breed.

Trainability

It has been stated that an Airedale can be a stubborn dog, often having to be "negotiated" with in order to train reliably. In this regard, many people compare them to the Chesapeake Bay retriever. But just as many people feel that the Airedale, a very loyal dog, will train well under any circumstances. However, it should be generally accepted that a trainer may have to find a way to deal with the "terrier attitude," which is to say a tough, scrappy dog that often has a "my way or the highway" mentality. While this may vary from individual to individual and strain to strain, it is better to go in with a patient attitude in getting the Airedale to perform his many abilities.

Strengths/Weaknesses

As stated before, one of the Airedale's strengths also proves to be one of its weaknesses. While it is a highly versatile dog — able to hunt both the uplands and wetlands in search of birds and fur, battling, pointing, and retrieving all manners of game — it does not specialize in any one manner of hunting to the level that a specific pointing, retrieving, flushing, or hound breed does.

There doesn't appear to be any particular health problems that Airedales experience, other than those injuries or ailments typical to most of the hunting breeds and dogs in general — such as arthritis, canine hip dysplasia, eye problems, and other hereditary abnormalities.

Other Uses

Outside of its extensive hunting uses and show-ring competitiveness, Airedales have also been used as guard and police dogs, employment it still finds in Europe.

The Show Ring

Though most breeds have a distinct difference in appearance between the show ring and field dogs, the Airedale is one breed where the field dogs have been bred to maintain the breed standard. Because the breed was developed as a hunting dog, show-ring Airedales reflect this heritage by staying true in conformation to their hunting brothers.

Though show ring breeding may have depleted some of the hunting stock of Airedales, there are organizations and committees devoted to maintaining the Airedale as a strong versatile hunting dog for the person who wants to do it all.

German Jagdterrier

Yack. Yes, the correct pronunciation of this breed is "yack"-terrier. And supporters of this breed are die-hard believers in this medium-sized dog's versatile contribution to the all-around sport of hunting with dogs. The Jagdterrier is also friendly and devoted, but is best recognized for its feisty hunting personality.

- **Area & Date of Origin:** Germany, 1900s
- **Function:** Den terrier; wild boar, badger, fox, weasel hunting; tree dogs for raccoon and squirrel
- **Height & Weight:** 13-16"; 16-22 lbs
- **Colors:** Black, black and gray, or dark brown with brown, red, yellow or lighter-colored markings on eyebrows, chest, legs, and rear
- **Coat:** Both smooth and harsh coats, but both are thick and abundant
- **Standards:** Squarely-built; deep, narrow chest; straight back; flat skull with slight stop; powerful muzzle with pronounced cheeks; black or brown nose; small, dark, deep-set eyes; v-shaped ears set high; straight, well-muscled forelegs; tail is usually docked, leaving ~5/8 of original length (tail serves as handle for hunters to pull the dog from dens), carried gaily; oval, well-knit feet
- **Life Span:** 12-14 years
- **Also called:** German Hunting Terrier

■ Appearance and Temperament

The lively jagdterrier measures not less than 13 inches and not more than 16 inches at the shoulder, with weights ranging from 16 to 22 pounds. This is a breed standard for which some hunting dogs are slightly under or over specified ranges. An alert demeanor is characteristic for this dog, which has an abundance of energy. Most jagdterriers are black with tan points, although black and gray or dark brown are also fairly common body colors. In the latter cases, point colors can be brown, yellow, red, or other lighter color than the predominant color; small amounts of white on the chest and toes are acceptable. The body and legs should present a square, balanced appearance, with neither a stubby nor leggy appearance preferred.

"Point" colors are found above each eye as well as on the muzzle, chest, legs, and hindquarter area. These colors blend well into a coat that accepts much latitude, being either smooth or rough (harsh). However, this breed must also have coat on its abdomen to help protect the active dog as it burrows into the ground as well as fights through briars and uncompromising weather conditions. The tail is cropped, but is otherwise carried gaily; it can be used as a "handle" when the dog goes to ground.

The chest is narrow to allow ease of fit into ground burrows; the lower jaw is powerful with a chiseled chin.

This breed has an outgoing disposition that is strongly hunt driven. Jagdterriers are very gamey and have the nature to persevere after their quarry until caught or put to ground.

History

This breed is fairly young by hunting breed standards. It originated in Germany shortly after the turn of the 20th century and was developed as a functional hunting breed primarily for boar, weasel, fox, and badger. The German term "jagd" means "to hunt," and terrier, of course, means "go to ground" — *terra* meaning earth — hence the naming of this breed as jagdterrier.

Reportedly, Max Thiel, Sr. came to America in 1951 and imported some of these dogs at that time and later in the year, from which the dogs in this country originated. This breed was not recognized by any major registry until 1993, when the United Kennel Club began registering this dog.

The German Jagdterrier is also known as the Deutscher Terrier, the German hunt terrier, and the German hunting terrier.

In the Field

In this country, the sporty jagdterrier has proven its worthiness on most mammals with a propensity for going to ground, and is used in wooded areas, fields, around hay bales, and under houses and barns. This breed has shown the instincts to bay game such as wild boar, bear, and cougar with its fearless attitude.

Jagdterriers can also be trained to tree squirrels, bobcat, and raccoon, although some, rather than bark, will just whine when they get to the tree. They, unlike most terriers, give voice on trail and are very versatile. Many hunters use this breed to follow blood trails to recover downed and wounded game. This is a popular utilization of many Texas ranches that specialize in exotic game such as antelope.

Trainability

This breed is somewhat willing in that they do like to please their trainers and owners; but because of their extreme game drive, they can be a little difficult to train on certain tasks. However, they are easy starters and most jagdterrier fanciers state that they simply need to expose these dogs to hunting on desired game and they begin learning.

Strengths/Weaknesses

The jagdterrier is surprisingly friendly in contrast to its supreme hunting drive. This little dog is intelligent and clever and quite versatile.

The German jagdterrier is a very hardy breed and has few health problems of concern.

Other Uses

In addition to the above-mentioned uses, this breed is often used with running hounds to bolt game from dens when they go to ground. As such, they have remarkable endurance for their size as well as a smooth running, or galloping, gait.

The German Jagdterriers Club of America was recently formed to test these dogs in a manner similar to the parent breed club, the Deutscher Terrier Club of Germany, in many skills. These include go-to-ground, water, retrieving, gunshyness, tracking, gait, and teeth.

JACK RUSSELL TERRIER

Personality plus. By all accounts, this feisty, sporty dog excels in so many categories and with such an air of individuality that he makes friends while he converts his enemies. The Jack Russell terrier is a multi-talented bundle of energy wrapped up in one tiny package.

- **Area & Date of Origin:** England, 1800s
- **Function:** Earthdog trials
- **Height & Weight:** 12-14", 13-17 lbs
- **Colors:** White, or predominantly white with tan, black, or brown markings
- **Coat:** Can be either smooth or broken; both coarse and weatherproof with short, dense undercoat; the outercoat of the smooth is flat and hard; that of the broken is harsh, straight, tight, and close lying, with no sculpted furnishings
- **Standards:** Small, flexible chest; medium in size and bone; flat and fairly broad skull with well-defined stop; almond-shaped, dark eyes; small V-shaped drop ears carried forward with the tip pointing toward the eye; straight topline with loin slightly arched; tail set high and carried gaily, docked so tip is about level with skull; round, very compact feet
- **Life Span:** 13 -15 years

■ Appearance and Temperament

The Jack Russell is a solid, compact dog with body length balanced to height for a look of symmetry. He should give the look of balanced proportion with emphasis on these categories: skull and face, head and frame, height at shoulder, and length of body. Unlike virtually all other breeds, there is a wide disparity in sizes that are recognized for this dog. Males and females can range between 10 and 15 inches and weigh between 13 and 17 pounds.

The head adds a powerful appearance and type to the rest of the body. A flat, broad skull narrows to the muzzle with a moderate stop, and small ears are carried forward and close to the head. The dark almond-shaped eyes should be rimmed with dark pigment, and should reflect an alert, intelligent expression.

To aid in burrowing into the ground in pursuit of quarry the chest should be narrow and blend with the ribs, shoulders and body. Legs are fairly straight and have good bone density. The whole combination of body parts should contribute to pleasing, coordinated, animated movement.

This little terrier may have either a smooth or broken coat. In either case it is "double-coated" and dense to provide protection from every possible element. The smooth coat is hard and glossy, while the broken coat is wiry but short. It should be noted that abundant coat exists on the abdomen and insides of the legs to aid in protection of this dog.

The Jack Russell should be white or predominantly white with black or tan markings. Tri-color is also acceptable, but brindle is not. "Grizzle," different than brindle, is okay.

The Jack Russell has an almost overbearing cheerful, playful nature around the house and has a tenacious, aggressive attitude toward hunting. He can be contentious with other dogs, and might persecute smaller creatures around the house, from rabbits to mice and cats. Although he accepts children, he should be monitored with infants and preschool age kids — as should any dog — because of his high energy level and hunting instincts, as these traits could generate into rough play. He is cunning, with a keen nature, is affectionate, and protective.

Above all, Jacks are intelligent, regarded by many as the smartest dog alive.

History

This breed was developed by, and takes its name from, the Reverend John Russell (1795-1883) who lived in southern England near Devonshire. This colorful man had an intense passion for fox hunting and rode with foxhounds, reportedly carrying his terriers in saddlebags for use to bolt foxes from their dens. His main drive was to develop a courageous, smart, aggressive, gamey, fearless little dog that would go underground ("go to ground") in burrows after game.

Russell stayed with a strict breeding program of both inbreeding and out-crossing to cultivate the best characteristics and traits for his purposes; other breed fanciers followed his examples while adhering to the desired type. As a result, today's Jack Russell is nearly identical to the dog of mid- and late-1800s, which is to say identical to what the fox terrier would have been had it stayed true to type over the years.

In the Field

Jack Russells are extremely hunt-oriented and gamey, and will pursue their quarry to earth. They have the instinct to take their quarry to ground and will stay for days with their game if they're not recovered, much to the consternation of many a terrier owner. In fact, the "terrier" name comes from *terra*, meaning earth; quite literally, terriers are dogs that go underground.

Certain gear must be transported to any hunt by a JRT owner, with a shovel (the folding military kind usually works well) at the top of the list for use in digging out the terrier. Also of importance is a snack when the dog is going to be working hard in the field for a morning or all day to ward off hypoglycemia.

These dogs are used on many types of game. Having been bred to chase, burrow, and dig out foxes, they are also used with success on woodchuck, badger, raccoon, and opossum. Since this terrier is so hunt-driven, he will pursue just about any creature that he encounters. This includes the skunk. New owners should be aware of this, as well as the fact that the Jack Russell terrier is prone to skunk toxic shock syndrome.

In short, any trip to the field or timber will be a never-ending excursion of excitement with the Jack Russell.

The Jack Russell Terrier Club of America, the registering body, awards three certificates to working JRT's, with the highest esteem attached to The Natural Hunting Certificate Below Ground in the Field, the Sporting Certificate, and the Trial Certificate.

Trainability

Due to its boundless energy and easy boredom threshold, the Jack Russell is not a good candidate for obedience training, but a certain amount of training should be done to deliver some control over this "big" small dog.

The trainer will need to be creative, innovative, and patient yet firm with this terrier. His mind is always wandering after the nearest butterfly or creature.

Strengths/Weaknesses

This breed's strong hunting drive and pleasing, exuberant personality are its best qualities. However, it should be noted that this little dog requires a substantial amount of exercise.

In addition, a number of health and medical concerns affect the Jack Russell. There are eye abnormalities, neurologic diseases, respiratory ailments, and blood and heart diseases. Jack Russells are prone to diabetes, hypothyroidism, cleft lip or palate, dwarfism, and various other diseases.

In 1997, the Jack Russell Terrier Research Foundation was formed to facilitate research in areas affecting this loveable little terrier.

Other Uses

Jack Russell terriers enjoy an enormous popularity as companions, but are first and foremost hunting dogs. This should be considered when evaluating whether this breed would be suitable as a pet in certain environments. Normally, the Jack Russell would not be a good choice for apartment dwellers due to his energy levels and exercise requirements. He will dig and always want to chase or bother something. He needs a lot of attention and loves to play.

This enjoyable breed has made the splash to movies and television. Very few dogs have as much abundant personality as this terrier.

The Show Ring

There has been a tremendous upsurge of show interest in this terrier. While this has contributed to the improvement in conformation, there has been a strong push to maintain this breed's hunting characteristics. The JRTCA helps accomplish this with its three working certificates. It is helpful to the working preservation of this breed that the standard provides for body marks and scars derived from working that should not be penalized.

There's nothing better.

CHAPTER 12

FINAL THOUGHTS

by Bob Wehle

Bob Wehle is the founder of the famed Elhew line of point-ers, considered by many to be the pre-eminent strain of pointers in the world. He has bred, raised, trained, and field trialed these dogs for decades, and is a leader and pioneer in selective breeding and genetics in hunting dogs.

WOULDN'T IT BE FUN TO KNOW just how our dogs see the world, or more importantly, how they see us? Do they perform to please us or because they have been intimidated? This past summer, I taught Hobo to jump a board fence about four feet high. He really enjoyed doing this and would immediately jump up on me for approval, as much as to say, "How did you like that, Boss?" full of joy. This scenario carries over to per-forming on game. When he executes a fine point and watches the bird fly off, he's every bit as happy as I am.

I want all my dogs to be happy. When I go to the kennels in the morning, they go into ecstasy — Hobo whirls around time after time; Snowflake jumps as high as she can on the fence; Snakefoot, he just stands back and kind of half barks and half howls like he's talking. He's the only dog in the kennel allowed to bark. I'm

sure he thinks he's some kind of celebrity. I talk to each one and most mornings give them a treat. It's a happy time for all of us. They think I'm eight feet tall. I just wish I were half as nice a person as they think I am.

When the dogs are this happy and in this mood, it's a great time to start their yard training. Under these circumstances, yard training can be very pleasant as well as rewarding. During this training, it's best to keep talking to them. I usually tell them how beautiful they are. It's not the words, but the tone of your voice. They are so perceptive. They just love to hear your voice.

By the same token, a hoarse voice in an unpleas-ant tone is more hurtful to them than any ill-treat-ment. The important thing is to be sure their tail never stops wagging. If it does stop, you're doing something wrong. It's the sparkle that wins field tri-als. This approach to their development brings out all their great qualities and makes the difference between an ordinary dog and a great dog.

Years back, trainers really cared for their dogs. Earl Crangle, one of the most successful professional trainers of his time, cared for his dogs easily every bit as

much as I. Unhappily, today many trainers treat their charges as commodities to be used solely for financial gain with absolutely no thought to their feelings. To me, this is tragic. The current shortcuts to proper training take so little intelligence. One excellent way to evaluate a training procedure is to ask yourself if you would feel comfortable in using this procedure in front of a group of children. I think, unfortunately, in many cases the answer would be an obvious no.

For over 64 years, I have raised and trained dogs with a reputable degree of success. I have found that training with kindness may take a little longer and try one's patience a bit, but the end result is so much more worth it. A couple weeks ago, a national news magazine posed the question: "Do dogs have feelings?" (I expected some worthwhile information, instead it was very flat.) Surely they have feelings, emotions, and perceptions. They constantly are expressing happiness, affection, fear, intimidation, and even sadness.

Last winter, one of our two house dogs, Bailey, passed away. His brother, Barnum, his best friend and companion for 12 years, showed great emotional stress and to this day, nearly a year later, reacts to the sound of Bailey's name. The bottom line is that they do have feelings and emotions, and are perceptive enough to interpret our moods and attitudes and respond accordingly. They deserve our gentle hands.

To change the subject, I have some observations on the aging process that I find interesting. The pace slows a bit due to the presence of minor physical infirmities. Not much change in the mind, except a slight loss of memory. Probably the most rewarding dividend is the greater appreciation of just being here and enjoying our whole environmental circumstance. My days are more enjoyable than ever.

I'm going to leave you with one last thought and that has to do with our relationship with our dogs. It's incredible how important any expression of affection is to them. Even a pat on the head can be so meaningful. They crave our warmth and approval so much. It also is important to understand their feelings. There's no way they can express their own discomfort. They can't cry out, "I'm cold," "It's too hot," "I'm terribly uncomfortable," "I'm hungry," "I'm thirsty," "The earmites and fleas are driving me crazy." Yet, they still manage to wag their tails and look at us as though we were the most important thing in their lives.

This relationship we have with our dogs has many of the same components as a successful human relationship. There's a mutual respect and admiration, devotion, care, and protection. As a matter of fact, a canine relationship runs the full gamut of emotions experienced by many of us — the warmth and the tenderness, the hurt and the disappointment, and the sorrow of a final departure. These reflections may merely be the manifestation of the aging process, but also may explain why, throughout my life, I have so championed our dogs.

I wish you all great success with your dog training, your campaigning and your breeding of fine hunting dogs — whatever the breed. ■

ABOUT THE AUTHORS

Amy Dahl and her husband, John, have over 30 years of retriever training and breeding experience between them. They have won numerous field trials, five State Gun Dog Championships, handled six dogs to Field Championships, and trained owner-handled dogs to their titles, including two Chesapeakes and two Dual Champions. They are regular and popular contributors to *The Retriever Journal* magazine, and are the authors of *The 10-Minute Retriever: How to Make an Obedient and Enthusiastic Gun Dog in 10 Minutes a Day.*

Tom Davis has been "fooling with dogs" for more than 30 years — and writing about them for nearly as long. The author of seven books, including *Just Goldens* and *Why Dogs Do That: A Collection of Curious Canine Behaviors*, Davis is the Gun Dogs columnist for *Sports Afield* and *Sporting Classics*, as well as Editor-at-Large for *Pointing Dog Journal*. He has also contributed to a number of anthologies of outdoor writing, and his work has won awards from the Council for Wisconsin Writers and the International Regional Magazine Association. Davis lives in Green Bay, Wisconsin, along with wife Joan, stepdaughter Sophia, pointer Traveler, and English setter Ernie (named for Ernie "Let's Play Two" Banks, not Hemingway).

Dave Gowdey is a second generation hobby breeder of German shorthaired pointers who literally grew up around bird dogs. In the early 1960s his uncle, Charles DeMenna, began raising German Shorthairs and using them to hunt desert quail in central Arizona. Dave continues the family tradition, and has spent the last 35 years breeding, raising, training, and hunting his own line of shorthairs. In addition to guiding and hunting his beloved desert quail, Dave has hunted most of the North American gamebirds, as well as gamebirds in Europe and South America. This experience has given him the opportunity to talk to, and learn from, breeders of hunting dogs from all over the world.

Vickie Lamb has campaigned her Labrador retrievers and coonhounds for the past 20 years — earning titles in both fields — and has had the opportunity to work closely with some of the top professionals and amateurs in the country. A lifelong outdoorswoman, she is an avid waterfowler, hunts upland birds and other game, fishes, rides horseback, and hikes. Vickie and her dogs have appeared on ESPN and OLN. As an outdoor columnist, writer, and photographer with more than 250 articles published, her subject matter has covered dogs and dog training, hunting, and people in the sport.

Jason Smith is the editor of *Just Labs* magazine and the managing editor of *The Pointing Dog Journal* and *The Retriever Journal*. He is also the author of *The Golden Retriever: A Comprehensive Guide to Buying, Owning, and Training*, as well as the co-author of three other books on wingshooting. Jason holds both BS and MS degrees in wildlife sciences. He and his wife hunt behind an English setter and Labrador retriever for both upland birds and waterfowl. They live in Michigan with their son.

Steve Smith of Traverse City, Michigan, is the editor of *The Pointing Dog Journal, The Retriever Journal*, and Publications Director of *Just Labs* magazine. He has founded some of America's most popular outdoor and sporting magazines including *Shooting Sportsman* and *Wildfowl*, and was the first editor of *Gun Dog* magazine. He has written 14 books on dogs, wingshooting, upland hunting, and waterfowling, and edited and published more than 100 others. He has been owned by setters, pointers, beagles, and Labs. In his 40-plus year hunting career, he has hunted over practically every breed of pointing dog and retriever. His book *Just Labs* is one of the best-selling breed books of all time.

Robert G. Wehle bred his first litter of pointers in 1936. Today, his Elhew Kennels and the Elhew pointer bloodline are internationally recognized as the standard by which all others are judged — and Bob Wehle himself stands unchallenged as the most respected figure in the world of bird dogs and pointing dog field trials. Many authorities contend that Wehle's first book, *Wing & Shot*, originally published in 1964 and still in print, is the finest work on gun dog training ever written; his latest effort, *Snakefoot: The Making of a Champion*, is an eloquent statement of the desires, delights, and philosophy that continue to drive him. In addition to being an acclaimed author, Wehle is an accomplished sculptor whose dramatic bronzes of sporting dogs earned him election to the prestigious Society of Animal Artists. Perhaps his proudest moment, however, came when the State of Alabama recently dedicated the Robert G. Wehle Nature Center in honor of his lifelong commitment to the preservation of natural resources. Wehle and his wife, Gatra, divide their year between Henderson, NY, and Midway, AL.

Ben O. Williams is a noted photographer, author, bird hunter, and dog breeder. He is the author and photographer of *American Wingshooting* and *Hunting the Quails of North America*. His photography and writing have appeared in many prominent sporting magazines including *Grays' Sporting Journal, Retriever Journal, Pointing Dog Journal* (for which he is a columnist), and *Shooting Sportsman*. He lives along the Yellowstone River outside of Livingston, Montana, with his wife Bobbi, fourteen Brittany spaniels, and two English pointers.

Illustrator Christopher Smith is one of America's most popular dog artists. His work hangs in the Bird Dog Museum in Grand Junction, Tennessee, and is featured in sporting catalogs and galleries across the nation. He has illustrated more than a dozen books and scores of magazine articles. His oil and watercolor commissions are in great demand. He lives in Traverse City, Michigan, with his wife, son, and Labrador retriever.

APPENDIX

Directory of Breed Clubs and Useful and Important Internet Sites

*Please note: Many of the names and postal addresses listed for each club are for their secretaries.
Some of these positions change annually. For the most current information about each of these clubs,
visit their websites or write directly to the AKC or the UKC.*

American Kennel Club
5580 Centerview Dr.
Raleigh, NC 27606
(919) 233-9767
www.akc.org

United Kennel Club, Inc.
100 E. Kilgore Rd.
Kalamazoo, MI 49002-5584
(616) 343-9020
www.ukcdogs.com

Canadian Kennel Club
89 Skyway Ave., Suite 100
Etobicoke, Ontario
M9W 6R4
(800) 250-8040
www.ckc.ca

American Veterinary Medical Association
1931 North Meacham Rd., Suite 100
Schaumburg, IL 60173
www.avma.org

Canine Eye Registration Foundation
(CERF)
1248 Lynn Hall
Purdue University
West Lafayette, IN 47907
(317) 494-8179

Orthopedic Foundation for Animals
(OFA)
2300 E Nifong Boulevard
Columbia, MO 65201-3856
www.offa.org

Synbiotics (PennHIP)
11011 Via Frontera
San Diego, CA 92127
www.vet.upenn.edu/pennhip/

National Gundog Association
www.gundog.org

North American Versatile Hunting Dog
Association
www.navhda.org

■ RETRIEVERS:

Hunting Retriever Club, Inc.
www.hrc-ukc.com

Working Retriever Central
www.working-retriever.com

American Chesapeake Club, Inc.
P.O. Box 58082
Salt Lake City, UT 84158
www.amchessieclub.org

American Water Spaniel Club
Linda Hattrem,
5799 40th St.
Princeton, MN 55371
www.americanwaterspanielclub.org

The Boykin Spaniel Society
P. O. Box 2047
Camden, SC 29020
(803) 425-1032
www.boykinspaniel.org

Curly-Coated Retriever Club of America
www.ccrca.org

Flat-Coated Retriever Socity
of America, Inc.
www.fcrsainc.org

Golden Retriever Club of America
(800) 632-5155
www.grca.org

Irish Water Spaniel Club of America
Rosemary Sexton, Secretary
209 Morton Ave
Elk River, MN 55330
clubs.akc.org/iwsc

Labrador Retriever Club, Inc.
Mr. Christopher G. Wincek, Secretary
secretary@thelabradorclub.com
thelabradorclub.com

Nova Scotia Duck Tolling Retriever
Susan Wright
12 Hales Hollow
Dover, MA 02030
www.nsdtrc-usa.org

Nova Scotia Duck Tolling Retriver
Club of Canada
www.toller.ca

Poodle Club of America, Inc.
www.poodleclubofamerica.org

Versatility in Poodles, Inc.
www.workingpoodle.org

■ SPANIELS

American Spaniel Club, Inc.
www.asc-cockerspaniel.org

Clumber Spaniel Club of America, Inc.
Kimberly Jordan
2901 Shady Ave.
Pittsburgh, PA 15217-2742
www.clumbers.org

English Cocker Spaniel Club
of America, Inc.
Kate D. Romanski, Corresponding
Secretary
P.O. Box 252
Hales Corners, WI 53130
www.ecsca.org

English Springer Spaniel
Field Trial Association, Inc.
Barbara Boettcher
PO Box 1590
Milton, WA 98354
mail@essfta.org
www.essfta.org

Field Spaniel Society of America
Suzanne Fernau
549 Main Rd.
Johns Island, SC 29455
clubs.akc.org/fssa/index.html

Fielddog.com
www.fielddog.com

Sussex Spaniel Club of America
Sylvia Schlueter, Corresponding Secretary
383 Blane Ct.
Dawson, IL 62520-3379

Welsh Springer Spaniel
Club of America, Inc.
www.wssca.com

■ POINTING DOGS

American Brittany Club, Inc.
Mary Jo Trimble, Secretary
10370 Fleming Rd
Carterville, IL 62918
clubs.akc.org/brit

American Pointer Club, Inc.
www.americanpointerclub.org

American Wirehaired Pointing
Griffon Association
www.awpga.com

English Setter Association
of America, Inc.
Dawn S. Ronyak, Secretary
114 S. Burlington Oval Dr.
Chardon, OH 44024
settereng@aol.com
www.esaa.com

French Brittany Gun Dog Association
of America
www.french-brittany.org

German Shorthaired Pointer
Club of America
www.gspca.org

German Wirehaired Pointer
Club of America
Barb Tucker
PO Box 677
Grasslake, MI 49240
www.gwpca.com

Gordon Setter Club of America, Inc.
www.gsca.org

International French Brittany
Club of America
PO BOX 262
Hazen, ND 58545-0262
www.frenchbrittany4u.org

Irish Setter Club of America, Inc.
Jeanette Holmes, Corresponding
Secretary
5389 Harrison Rd.
Paradise, CA 96969
www.irishsetterclub.org

Large Munsterlander Club
of North America
www3.sk.sympatico.ca/munster

Pudelpointer Club of North America
hdhuntclub@aol.com
www.pcna.org

Red and White Setter Club
of America, Inc.
Bob Humphrey, Secretary
(864)287-3203

rednwhitesetters@aol.com
www.redandwhitesetters.org

Small Munsterlander Club
of North America
smallmunsterlander.org

Spinone Club of America
P.O. Box 307
Warsaw, VA 22572
(804) 333-0309
spinone@spinone.com
www.spinone.com

Vizsla Club of America
Kim Himmelfarb, Secretary
16 Deer Run Rd
Collinsville, CT 06022
clubs.akc.org/vizsla

Weimaraner Club of America
Rebecca Weimer, Secretary
324 Sundew Dr.
Belleville, IL 32221
www.geocities.com/~weimclub

■ HOUNDS

www.treehound.com
(lists hound clubs by state)

www.coonhoundcentral.com

American Black & Tan Coonhound
www.abtcc.com

American Bloodhound Club
www.bloodhounds.org

American Blue Gascon Hound
Association
Larry Morgan
68344 Parnell Ln.
Kentwood, LA 70444

American Foxhound Club, Inc.
James M. Rea, Secretary
P.O. Box 2588
Clarkesville, GA 30523

American Plott Association
Brenda Orsbon
7725 Graysport Crossing
Coffeeville, MS 38922

Basset Hound Club of America
www.basset-bhca.org

Dachshund Club of America, Inc.
Andra O'Connell, Secretary
1793 Berme Road
Kerhonkson, NY 12446
www.dachshund-dca.org

English Foxhound Club of America
John D Wickline, Secretary
13311 Williams Dr,
Brandywine, MD 20613-7861

Greyhound Club of America
Beth Anne Gordon, Corresponding
Secretary
P.O. Box 850
LaLuz, NM 88337
www.greyhoundclubofamerica.org

Harrier Club of America
Ellen Parr, Coresponding Secretary
P.O. Box 503
Woodburn, OR 97071
www.oregonsbest.com/~harriers/HCA/

National Beagle Club of America
clubs.akc.org/NBC/index.htm

Professional Kennel Club
P.O. Box 8338
Evansville, IN 47716-8338
(800) 238-5009
www.prohound.com

Rhodesian Ridgeback Club
of the United States, Inc.
Bonnie Louden, Corresponding Secretary
PO Box 37
Columbia, MD 21045-0037
rrcus.org

Scottish Deerhound Club
of America, Inc.
www.deerhound.org

Southeastern Treeing Walker Association
Gene DeMartino
P.O. Box 241
Comfort, NC 28522

■ TERRIERS

Airedale Terrier Club of America
Linda Baake, Secretary
4636 Old Cherry Point Road
New Bern, NC 28560
secretary@airedale.org
www.airedale.org

Jack Russell Terrier
Association of America
P.O. Box 4541
Danbury, CT 06813
www.jrtaa.org

INDEX